RUGBY SCHOOL

H.A. Wise

Tudor House

Rugby School

WHITEHALL—TOWN HALL

WHITEHALL
TOWN HALL

A BRIEF ACCOUNT OF
CENTRAL AND LOCAL GOVERNMENT

by

F. W. G. BENEMY B.Sc.(Econ.)

HEAD OF THE DEPARTMENT OF SOCIAL SCIENCE
AT THE WILLIAM ELLIS SCHOOL LONDON
PART-TIME LECTURER IN POLITICAL ECONOMY
AT THE NORTH-WESTERN POLYTECHNIC LONDON
AND FORMERLY TUTOR DEPARTMENT OF EXTRA-MURAL STUDIES
THE UNIVERSITY OF LONDON

SIXTH EDITION REVISED AND ENLARGED

GEORGE G. HARRAP & CO. LTD
LONDON   TORONTO   WELLINGTON   SYDNEY

First published in Great Britain 1960
by George G. Harrap & Co. Ltd
182 High Holborn, London, W.C.1

Second Edition, revised, 1962
Third Edition, revised, 1963
Fourth Edition, revised, 1964
Fifth Edition, revised, 1965
Sixth Edition, revised and enlarged, 1967

Composed in Times New Roman type and printed by
William Clowes and Sons, Limited, London and Beccles
Made in Great Britain

Preface

The object of this book is to provide all that a boy or a girl at a grammar school requires to know in order to pass the General Certificate of Education examination at Ordinary or Advanced Level in the subject called 'British Constitution.' For the pupil who wishes to read further, with the Scholarship Level in view, a select bibliography is provided.

Both as a student and as a teacher I have found the lack of such a book a great handicap. The fact is that, although so much public money is spent on education, there is still not enough available to provide each pupil with all the necessary books on a particular subject. To have the information he or she requires in one book will, it is hoped, help to overcome this disadvantage.

I have tried to make the book as readable as possible, in the hope that young men and women in the Forces or pursuing adult education in the evenings will find it helpful. If the privilege of voting is to be used sensibly the voter ought to know something about the system of government in which he is participating. If in the future the right to vote is extended to those of eighteen years it will be more than ever important that the British system of government should be studied.

I would like to thank my colleagues who read the manuscript and made many useful suggestions and gave much valuable advice—Mr A. P. Smith, Mr M. Nelkon, and Mr E. Marsh. I also wish to record my gratitude to three ladies—my sister, Miss W. Benemy, Miss Joan Rawlins, and Mrs Dorothy Rice—for having so successfully translated my dreadful scrawl and produced a typescript for me, and to my friend Mr Kenneth Trenholme for helping me with the index. I am also greatly in debt to my wife for patiently enduring the many evenings on which I was unsocial and testy, concentrating on my writing and neglecting my household duties. None of them can, however, be blamed for anything in the book. The faults are entirely to my credit.

F. W. G. B.

Note to the Fifth Edition

As usual many amendments have been made to keep the text up to date. In particular the chapter on Local Government has been virtually rewritten; while in the chapter on the Commonwealth much detail about individual Constitutions has been omitted and the factors which bind the countries of the Commonwealth together have been discussed much more fully. Among other things, there is a note on the new method of the Conservative Party in electing its Leader, and the bibliography has been brought up to date. It has been a great temptation to enlarge the book, but this was resisted because there seems to be some merit in retaining a size and shape with which readers are familiar, and a price which obviously they appreciate. The Constitution is in a continuous state of flux, and one day it may be necessary to rewrite on a large scale. Meanwhile I am much in the debt of those people who write and make suggestions which are usually helpful and which are always carefully considered.

Note to the Sixth Edition

It is most gratifying that yet another edition has been called for, because it provides the opportunity to include as appendices a few notes on matters which often occur in examinations, and upon which some candidates show an alarming ignorance, but which are difficult to fit into the pattern of a text-book because they are purely of an administrative nature, or because they are in a state of flux. As usual, small errors of omission or commission have been corrected. The British Constitution is subject to continuous changes here and there—the introduction of the 'Ombudsman', for example—and no book dealing with it can be completely up to date at any given moment of time. I am always grateful, however, to those readers and teachers who are kind enough to write to me and make useful suggestions.

Contents

Introduction

When I use the phrase "Spirit of the Constitution," I speak of the system of government which has maintained the equilibrium between monarchy and democracy—which has harmonized those apparently conflicting elements—of that system of government which by the constant yet almost unfelt interposition of slight checks, has prevented the necessity of recurring to the use of extreme instruments in the collision of antagonist powers.

SIR ROBERT PEEL, *speaking in the House of Commons on May 27, 1841*

This Constitution of ours, which we have always thought the glory of this country and the wonder of the world.

LORD CURZON, *speaking in the House of Lords on November 30, 1909*

The British Constitution is the system under which Great Britain and a large part of the British Commonwealth are governed. It is a democratic system, which means that there is parliamentary government.

Parliamentary government is government by consent of the people who compose the electorate. It is sometimes called 'popular' government, because if the people dislike the manner in which they have been governed they will return a new Government at the next General Election. A General Election, in normal times, must take place at least every five years. If, on the other hand, the people approve of the conduct of a retiring Government they will re-elect that Government.

There must be a Parliament because a nation of over fifty million people cannot assemble in one place at the same time, and even if they could be so assembled it would be impossible to get any business done by so large a number of people. Too many of them would want to speak; too many of them would have to be silent. It might even be necessary to use force to silence tiresome speakers, which would be fatal to the cause of democratic government. It would be a miracle if so many people could agree on any subject. Therefore a Parliament has evolved, the Members of which are the representatives of the people. The country is divided into a number of constituencies, each returning a representative. The number varies as population shifts.

It has been found from experience that a House of some six hundred Members provides adequate debates, ensuring that important questions are thoroughly discussed before legislation is enacted. But such a House is too large to get business done quickly. Therefore the Commons provides for a Government of about a hundred Members, all of whom, except when there is a coalition, are chosen from one party. From this Government a committee of about twenty Members is selected by the Prime Minister to form what is called the Cabinet. The British parliamentary system is consequently sometimes called a system of Cabinet government. The Cabinet is formed from the party which has a majority in the Commons, or can obtain a majority with the help of other parties. Therefore, looked at from another angle, the parliamentary system is one of party government. Broadly speaking, the system is a two-party one, providing an alternative Government which can, and does, criticize the existing Government, and enabling the people to make a clear choice between two parties. This does not mean, of course, that only two parties are represented in the Commons. At present there are at least three, and there have never been less than that number in the last 200 years.

The British Parliament consists of three parts. They are:

> (*a*) The Crown.
> (*b*) The House of Lords.
> (*c*) The House of Commons.

The first two are traditional parts. The British are great respecters of tradition, and they have accordingly adapted these two old institutions to modern conditions, instead of abolishing them, as some other nations have done, sometimes by violence. To-day the most important working part is the Commons, because the Commons is the only part which has been popularly elected. Both the Crown and the Lords (in the main) are hereditary institutions. In the relatively near future, however, the Lords may well be more largely represented by Life Peers. Since 1958 the practice has been begun of the Prime Minister nominating Lords of Parliament for their natural lives.

The British Constitution is unwritten in the sense that there is no single document (or group of documents) which states in writing what form it will take, and which ranks above the ordinary law of the land. This is in contrast to most Constitutions based on the British model, such as the American and French systems, both of which have written Constitutions. The great advantage that is claimed for the unwritten British Constitution is its flexibility. It has been comparatively easy to change the system, in tune with changing times and ideas, without violence.

The system is unitary, because there is just the one central Government in Westminster, unlike the American system, which is federal, because, apart from the central Government, there are fifty State Governments, each of which has substantial autonomy.

The British Constitution is based on two things:

(a) The conventions of the Constitution.
(b) The Acts of Parliament, upon which a body of judge-made law has been built.

It is a rule of law in which all men are equal before the law. Parliament is sovereign in the sense that only Parliament can make laws on behalf of the people, and only Parliament can unmake those laws.

In Britain we are very near to true democracy, because almost everybody who is over twenty-one years of age has the vote, no one has more than one vote, and great care is taken to ensure that the views of the majority shall prevail, but that the interests of the minority shall never be ignored.

The spirit of the Constitution could thus perhaps be admirably expressed in one word—tolerance. Some cynics have it that tolerance sometimes degenerates into apathy, but one prefers to think that it is a spirit of fair play, patience, and a sense of humour that are characteristics of British public life. For instance, upon the death of Mr Bevan, a stalwart of the Labour Party, the Prime Minister, a Conservative, delivered a moving address in the House of Commons, praising Mr Bevan's qualities as a Parliamentarian and an opponent. The acceptance by a Conservative Government of constant criticism by the trade unions is another example of what is meant by tolerance in this context.

The British Parliament is commonly known as the Mother of Parliaments, because most of the modern systems of parliamentary government have been deliberately modelled on it. The British Empire has been a great and successful experiment in educating new nations or old countries with despotic systems of government in the arts of parliamentary government, and the British Commonwealth is the living proof of the success of this political idea. The British Crown is the symbol of the free association of the independent nations of the Commonwealth.

If the individuals who compose the electorate wish to cast their votes intelligently they ought to know how the system of government in which they are taking part works. It is important that they should be able to appreciate the value of the privilege which they enjoy of being able to speak, think, and meet freely before voting in secret. Every British subject over twenty-one years of age ought, therefore, to know something about the British Constitution. And those under twenty-one ought to be qualifying themselves to exercise this privilege in due course. There is a good deal of support for giving the vote to persons over eighteen years of age. The Labour Party is seriously considering making this extension of the franchise part of its party programme. A proposal was introduced in the House of Commons in 1959, and defeated after a spirited debate. The main arguments in favour of the proposal seem to be that if a young man is fit to fight and die for his country at the age of eighteen, or is able to undertake university work, or has left school, is earning a living, paying taxes, and possibly is married, he is deeply concerned with the way in which the country is governed and is worthy of having the vote. I have discussed this problem with teenagers, who surprisingly considered that their contemporaries were probably too busy enjoying life to be interested in politics.

On the other hand, does a man reach a stage of mature political judgment at eighteen or twenty-one or thirty-one or even forty-one? It depends on the individual, his personality and education, his intelligence and the interest he takes in politics. This will vary from one person to another, and therefore the line has to be drawn somewhere, even if in an apparently arbitrary manner. Perhaps the gratifyingly large amount of time given by television to political affairs will stimulate public interest and produce a better-informed electorate.

BIBLIOGRAPHY

JENNINGS, SIR IVOR: *The British Constitution* (Cambridge University Press; third edition, 1950).

BUTLER, DAVID, and FREEMAN, J.: *British Political Facts, 1900–1960* (Macmillan, 1963).

ROSE, R.: *Studies in British Politics* (Macmillan, 1966).

NICOLSON, SIR HAROLD: *Diaries and Letters, 1930–39* (Collins, 1966).

MACMILLAN, HAROLD: *Winds of Change, 1914–39* (Macmillan, 1966).

WILKINSON, R.: *The Prefects* (Oxford University Press, 1964).

CHAPTER I

The Electorate

Qualifications for voting. Exercise of the franchise. History of suffrage. Reform Acts. Minorities. The party system. The alternative vote. Proportional representation. Voting since the War.

To govern according to the sense and agreeably to the interests of the people is a great and glorious object of government. This object cannot be obtained but through the medium of popular election.

EDMUND BURKE, *speaking in the House of Commons on*
May 8, 1780

I take my stand on the broad principle that the enfranchisement of capable citizens, be they few or be they many—and if they be many so much the better—gives an addition of strength to the country.

W. E. GLADSTONE, *speaking in the House of Commons on*
February 28, 1884

As has been said, every inhabitant of Great Britain who is a British subject and has been resident in Britain for at least one year has the right to vote to return a Member of Parliament, provided that he or she is over twenty-one years of age.

There are, however, a few exceptions. They are:

(*a*) Peers, except peers of Ireland, who may sit in the House of Commons.

(*b*) Persons of unsound mind.

(*c*) Persons who have been found guilty of corrupt and illegal practices in connexion with elections and are debarred for five years.

(*d*) Persons who have been convicted of treason and felony, and are under sentence of more than twelve months.

Peers are not allowed to vote because they are entitled to a seat in the House of Lords and to take part in government there. If the hereditary principle is abolished and the House of Lords becomes either a nominated or an elected Second Chamber, then the right to vote will have to be extended to peers, and they will have to be regarded as eligible to stand for Parliament in the Commons.

With regard to aliens, although the Irish Free State (now the Republic of Ireland) withdrew from the British Commonwealth in 1949, Irish citizens who are resident in Britain are eligible to vote and to hold office under the Crown.

The British Constitution has, therefore, in this respect, come very near to complete democracy, since almost every adult person has the right to vote. It can justifiably be said that Parliament is representative of the whole nation, and that British parliamentary government is genuinely government by consent of the people. It is not perfect democracy, however. Man has not yet succeeded in establishing a perfect system.

One problem is that everybody who has the right to vote does not always exercise that right. At General Elections since 1945 the proportion of the electorate—over 70 per cent.—that has actually voted has been gratifyingly high. What about those who do not vote? Ought they to be made to vote? This question is particularly pertinent at by-elections, where there is often a most disappointing apathy. It is usually difficult to decide whether this apathy is the result of laziness, of a failure to appreciate the importance of the right to vote, of disillusionment with parliamentary government, or whether it is a genuine feeling that none of the candidates is worth a vote. A refusal to vote can, however, serve a useful purpose in that it may indicate that some people are dissatisfied with the Government and wish to record their disapproval without giving their support to the Opposition. This is tantamount to a negative vote, to which the Government is acutely sensitive. The danger of forcing people to vote is that it is interference with the liberty of the individual. If a person were compelled to vote it could well lead in the end to that person being forced to vote as instructed. The better answer is surely for the parties to intensify their efforts to persuade every voter to vote.

The present position has been reached after a period of gradual progress spreading over several centuries. Two hundred years ago only a very small proportion of the population had a vote, and they had to possess a considerable amount of property in order to qualify. The new towns which were springing up as a result of the Industrial Revolution, such as Manchester and Birmingham and Leeds, had no seats in Parliament, whereas obscure villages, even fields, had seats. These constituencies were known as 'Rotten,' or 'Pocket,' Boroughs. They belonged to a few rich members of the nobility, who were able to control the House of Commons by nominating for these boroughs men who could be depended on to vote as their patrons told them. It was one way in which the Crown could manage to influence the Commons, and it was therefore a denial of democratic government. As the people became better educated and more articulate this state of affairs was certain to be changed. The desire for reform was at last realized in 1832, when the first great Reform Bill was passed, to be followed by further Acts in 1867 and 1884, and by the Representation of the People Acts of 1918, 1928, and 1948.

The importance of the Reform Act of 1832 was that it made a fundamental change in the British Constitution. It established a uniformity of the qualifications to vote, and it began to take away some of the power which had hitherto been the monopoly of a few aristocratic landowners. Men who were concerned with industry and trade were now to have an influence in parliamentary affairs. The brazen use of bribery and corruption began to diminish. The Reform Act brought about an enormous change in party organiza-tion. The two great political parties realized that henceforth they must set up a nation-wide organization, with an agent in each con-stituency to nurse it. In 1834 Peel, in the Tamworth Manifesto, set a precedent at a General Election by addressing the electorate, explaining to them what his party proposed to do if returned to power. He realized that future Governments would have to *win* the support of the voters. This precedent has to-day become the con-vention of 'the mandate,' by which a party asks the electorate to approve the legislation it proposes to enact, and agrees that it is not entitled to introduce controversial Bills which have not been put before the voters at an election.

Under the Act of 1832 copyholders with tenements to the value of £10 a year and leaseholders with tenements to the value of £50 a year in the country were enfranchised. So also were owners of tenements to the value of £10 in boroughs. The effects were that the suffrage was increased by 217,000 and the new industrial middle classes now had votes. Seats were redistributed from the small boroughs to the counties and towns. Registration of voters was necessary, and the parties formed registration associations to make sure that all persons who had the right to vote registered and, having done so, were canvassed before an election.

The movement towards true democracy, having begun, could not be stopped, and in 1867 another Reform Bill was passed, increasing the suffrage by a million voters, with the main effect of enfranchis-ing the town artisan. In the country occupiers of houses rated at

£10 a year and in the towns all householders and lodgers paying £10 a year now had a vote.

The Act of 1884 added another million to the electorate, and, generally speaking, gave the vote to the agricultural labourer. All householders in the country and all residents within a radius of seven miles of a town now had a vote. The constituencies were more nearly equalized in size.

So far only men had the vote. It was thought that if women were given the vote they would vote as their husbands or fathers bade. The Suffragettes organized a campaign to win votes for women. They did some spectacular and some foolish things, such as chaining themselves to the railings of No. 10 Downing Street or throwing themselves in front of horses at the Derby. The World War of 1914–18 was the deciding factor. Women played an important part in winning the War, doing great work in the munition factories and driving ambulances, and in 1918 all women over thirty years of age were enfranchised. This Act was to have tremendous social and economic consequences. The suffrage was increased by 12½ million voters, and seats had to be redistributed. No one was to have more than two votes, the second vote being recorded either at one's university or at one's place of business. Logically there was no reason why women of twenty-one could not vote when men of that age could do so. The limitation of the vote to women over thirty was proof of the natural conservatism of the Englishman, who prefers to go forward steadily, observing the results of each step before taking the next one. It was perhaps unexpected, therefore, that, just as Disraeli, a Conservative Prime Minister, had enfranchised the town artisan in 1867, so another Conservative Prime Minister, Baldwin, broke new ground by giving the vote to women under thirty and over twenty-one in 1928, thus increasing the suffrage by another seven million voters.

In 1948, after another World War was over, the Labour Government laid down the principle of "one person one vote." The place-of-business and university votes were abolished. The Conservatives deplored the disappearance of the independent Members, who so often represented the universities, and undertook to restore these seats if returned to office. When they did come back to power in 1951, however, in the face of violent opposition they abandoned the idea—properly so, because it was clear that most of the electorate were in favour of this fundamental principle of "one person one vote." To give a small number of university graduates more than one vote was to create a privileged class. In order to cater for the growth and shifting of population the House of

Commons appointed a Select Committee to meet every third year to consider whether there should be a redistribution of seats.

Despite all the advances that have been made towards genuine popular government, there is still controversy over the fact that minorities are inadequately represented in Parliament. Some minorities, indeed, have no voice there at all. Moreover, most modern Governments have been elected, not by a majority of the electors, but by a minority of them. There has been in consequence much discussion concerning the merits or otherwise of the alternative vote and of proportional representation. This question is constantly discussed, because there are always groups of voters who feel that their views are not adequately represented in Parliament. Under the present system of the single non-transferable vote in a single-member constituency it is objected that a person who belongs to a minority party has a vote that is more or less meaningless, and therefore that the possession of the right to vote is valueless. This is a point of view with which it is not difficult to sympathize.

For instance, say that in a constituency there are three candidates—one Conservative, one Labour, and one Liberal. The first two parties are strongly favoured, and the contest is clearly between them. The Liberal candidate has no real chance of winning. Nevertheless, he takes the field and poses a problem to his supporters. If they vote for him they know they are wasting their votes in the sense that he will not win. If they vote for one of the other candidates they are supporting a party of whose policy they disapprove. If they decide not to vote at all they are deliberately throwing away a precious privilege that has had to be won after a long and hard struggle. No voter in a democracy ought to be put in such a dilemma. The situation is just as bad if there is no Liberal candidate. The voter, to be sure, now has not to worry about voting for a candidate who will not win. He is faced with a straightforward choice between the Labour and Conservative candidates. But if he disagrees strongly with both these parties he might just as well not have the vote. This clearly is wrong. He ought to be able to cast his vote constructively and in accordance with his opinions.

There is another dilemma in which a voter may find himself, but of a very different sort. Suppose that he is a Conservative who believes both in private enterprise and free trade. The Conservative candidate, alas, is an ardent protectionist. The Labour candidate, on the other hand, is a keen free trader, but is also a strong exponent of nationalization of industry. What is the voter to do? Or, to put another possibility, the voter, who has had no say in the choice of the party's candidate, regards the person chosen as a second-rater, whereas the other candidate seems to him to be first-rate. Is the voter to vote for the better candidate or for a party label?

All parties do their best to inform the electorate fully. There is a Conservative Association and a branch of the Labour Party in every constituency. There is a steady flow of literature, of speeches on local occasions, and on the wireless and the television, and of letters and articles both in the national and the local Press. Debates in the House of Commons are addressed not so much to the House itself as to the electorate, to enable the voters to choose between the policies of the parties. The important subjects, or those things which the parties think important, are given ample publicity. There is little excuse, therefore, for any voter who says "I don't know" when he is asked for his opinion on a political problem—political in the sense that it is something which Parliament has to do something about, something which is going to affect him. He ought to have an opinion on it, and he should make it his business to find out something about it.

The Liberals were unable to win more than six seats in the House of Commons in 1959, though they polled more than a million and a half votes in the 217 constituencies which they contested. Is this a good thing or a bad thing? The Liberals naturally say that it is bad, because their supporters ought to have a voice in Parliament proportionate to their numbers, whereas at the moment they can have no real influence on matters. They are not, of course, the only minority party. The Communist Party has no voice at all. Other minorities would undoubtedly spring up if they had a chance to return a representative to Parliament. As, in present circumstances, they see no prospect of doing this, they behave in a characteristically practical manner and compromise by forming 'pressure groups' outside Parliament designed to impress individual Members of Parliament and to persuade them to express the views of these groups in the Commons. As, however, the back-bencher has comparatively few opportunities to speak in the House, and individually has little influence on his party leaders, these minorities are not satisfactorily represented in Parliament, although sometimes a number of back-benchers band together, and can thus exercise considerable influence.

To put right this state of affairs, which is incompatible with true democracy, two remedies are constantly proposed. They are:

        (a) The alternative vote.
        (b) Proportional representation.

The alternative voting system allows the voter to indicate his preference for the candidates in order of merit. Thus in a single-member constituency, if there were three candidates, each from a different party, none of whom obtained a clear majority over the other two together, the candidate at the bottom of the poll would drop out. But those who voted for him would not have wasted their votes. Here is the essence of the idea and its great virtue: no votes are wasted. The voters' second preferences, as indicated on their voting papers, are taken. When this has been done one of the two remaining candidates should obtain a clear majority over the other. It is feasible that there would be a tie. If that highly unlikely event were to happen there would have to be more than one recount, and it is probable that one of the candidates would emerge the winner from these recounts. It is argued that such a winner would truly represent the views of a majority of the electors, whereas under the existing system of the single non-transferable vote that desirable end is often not obtained. For instance, in the Rochdale by-election in 1958, on which the influence of television made a great impact, there were three candidates for the seat. After a fascinating campaign the Labour candidate received 22,100 votes, and the Conservative was at the bottom of the poll with 9800 votes. The Liberal captured the imagination of the voters and polled 17,600 votes. The Labour candidate was returned to Parliament, but he represented a minority of the electors. Suppose there had been an alternative vote? What would have happened? The votes for the Conservative would have been redistributed to the other two candidates according to the voters' second preferences. It might be that some 6000 Conservatives would have given their second preference for the Liberal, because of a greater affinity between these two parties than between the Conservatives and the Labour Party. They both believe in the idea of private enterprise, which is the dominating force in our economy, and economics are of immense importance in politics. Let it be assumed that 500 Conservatives would prefer the Labour to the Liberal candidate, while the remaining 3300 would be 'last-ditchers,' on no account voting Liberal or Labour, and so indicating no second preference. On the second count the Liberal would now win with 23,600 votes, against 22,600 for the Labour candidate—a narrow margin, but, it is argued, a truer reflection of the opinions of the electors.

Under a system of proportional representation there would probably be many parties. There would have to be larger constituencies, each returning, say, three Members; or the whole country could be regarded as one great constituency, in which each party would be represented in proportion to the votes it obtained.

Let us assume that a three-Member constituency is created with 360,000 electors on its register. Each of the two larger political parties puts up three candidates, and the Liberals two. The three Conservative candidates are: Marjoribanks, Tomlinson, and Wainwright. The three Labour candidates are Brown, Smith, and Thomas. The two Liberal candidates are Hathaway and Gladwin.

If you divide 360,000 voters by four it is clear that any candidate who gets 90,001 votes must win one of the three seats. The fourth man cannot get more than 89,997 votes.

In fact, let us suppose that the voting goes as follows:

Marjoribanks (Con.) . . .	100,000
Brown (Lab.)	65,000
Smith (Lab.)	55,000
Hathaway (Lib.)	50,000
Tomlinson (Con.) . . .	35,000
Wainwright (Con.) . . .	25,000
Thomas (Lab.)	20,000
Gladwin (Lib.)	10,000
	360,000

So on the first count the only man who wins a seat is Marjoribanks, and he has 9999 votes to spare. There must be a second count. We can safely assume that 9000 will go to Tomlinson on second preference. He now has 44,000. Wainwright gets 25,000 plus 900, and Hathaway 50,000 plus 99. But even on the second count no one except Marjoribanks wins a seat, so there must be a third count, in which the bottom candidate drops out and his votes are redistributed. This will probably result in Hathaway now having 50,099 plus 10,000. There must then be a fourth count, in which Thomas's votes are redistributed. In consequence Brown will now have 65,000 plus 15,000, and Smith 55,000 plus 5000. A fifth count is necessary, in which Wainwright drops out. Tomlinson will probably get 44,000 plus 24,900, and Hathaway will go up to 60,099 plus 1000. At this point we ought to have a look at the latest position. It is now:

Marjoribanks (Con.) . . .	90,001
Brown (Lab.)	80,000
Tomlinson (Con.) . . .	68,900
Hathaway (Lib.)	61,099
Smith (Lab.)	60,000
	360,000

A sixth count is taken, with Smith dropping out and his votes being redistributed. Brown will undoubtedly get the 10,001 votes he needs to win a seat. In all probability 30,000 of the remainder will go to Hathaway, who will now have 91,099 votes, and 15,000 to Tomlinson, who will have 83,900. The other 4999 votes are of no account, as no further preference is necessary.

As a result of all this laborious recounting each of the three parties wins a seat, and it can fairly be claimed that, as far as possible, a true representation of the voters' views has been obtained. The trouble has been, therefore, worth taking.

Since there appears to be so much to be said in favour of proportional representation and the alternative vote, why has not the House of Commons changed the electoral system? The main argument in favour of proportional representation, as we have seen, is that it enables all minorities to get a voice in Parliament in accordance with their strength. That is very important.

But this advantage is more than outweighed by the disadvantages. The main one is that, instead of two principal parties in Parliament, there would probably be more than three. In consequence, no party would be likely to have a clear majority in the House over the other parties put together. Therefore no party could form a Government until it had secured the support of one or more of the other parties. That support would not be obtained unless each party gave something away. This would usually mean that important but controversial measures would be shelved and only compromise legislation enacted. It would also mean that sooner or later a crisis would arise in which one of the supporting parties would withdraw its support, and the Government would fall. The bargaining which would go on continuously in Parliament would tend to make it a hotbed of intrigue, and it would become increasingly difficult to pass legislation. The constant changes of Government would result in weak, unstable administration. Industrialists at home would not be able to make long-term plans. Foreign nations would be disinclined to enter into negotiations with a Government which was likely to be out of office before those negotiations were complete. The affairs of the country could easily degenerate into political and economic chaos. There could even be a dictatorship set up in desperation.

This is not just theory. It has happened in France since 1945, where (with a system of preferential voting) there were twenty Governments in twelve years, culminating in the upheaval resulting in the rise to power of General de Gaulle without the aid of an election. It seems unlikely, therefore, that proportional representation will ever be introduced into the British Constitution.

The alternative vote is not open to quite such serious objections, but here also an unstable Government could be the result. If the alternative vote were to be introduced and in a House of 650

Members the Liberals obtained 125 seats, the Conservatives had 265, and Labour 240, there could be stalemate. No party would have a clear majority over the other two. Each would have to make a pact with one of the other two in order to form a Government. Sooner or later that pact would be broken because of a serious difference of opinion. The Government of the day would be uneasy and disinclined to take those strong measures that are sometimes necessary, the wisdom of which is not immediately apparent, and which, therefore, are usually unpopular. That "England does not love Coalitions" is historically true. A Coalition is successful only in time of war, and breaks up as soon as the war is over. There would, therefore, be frequent elections in an attempt to break the stalemate. These elections would be unlikely to do that, because our post-war history shows that the political views of the electorate are fairly evenly divided and deeply held. The floating voters are few in number. We had some experience of this state of affairs between the two World Wars, when the Liberal Party was losing ground and Labour was gaining ground, with the Conservatives more or less stable. There were several minority Governments, two or more Coalitions, and a great deal of weakness and vacillation. So, although the alternative vote has much to recommend it, neither of the two main parties at present is likely to introduce it. The existing system, despite its imperfections, does at least provide strong, stable government, and, as has been said, the convention that the majority will allow the minority in Parliament to have its fair say, while that minority will not abuse its privilege and deliberately obstruct and waste time, is by and large scrupulously observed. If this important convention were not honoured, then would be the time to consider some kind of reform of the system. The Speaker's Conference of 1917 did recommend the adoption both of proportional representation and the alternative vote, but Parliament rejected both proposals.

There were seven General Elections between 1945 and 1966. Each time the Government which resulted represented a minority of the electorate. In 1945 Labour polled 48 per cent. of the votes and had 393 seats, with a clear majority of 186 over the Conservatives and Liberals. In 1950 they polled 46 per cent. of the votes and won 315 seats, with a clear majority of only 8. In 1951 the Conservatives polled 48·8 per cent. of the votes, but had a clear majority of 16. In 1955 they polled 49·8 per cent. of the votes and had a clear majority of 59, while in 1959 they polled 49·4 per cent. of the votes and had a clear majority of 100. In 1964 Labour polled 44·2 per cent. and had a clear majority of 5; in 1966 they polled 49 per cent. and had a 99 majority.

It would seem, therefore, that in normal times government is by the party with a majority in the House of Commons, rather than by the party with a majority of the electorate behind it. Nevertheless, the system works reasonably well, because the parties abide by the unwritten rules, the conventions of the Constitution.

It is interesting to compare the situation to-day with that in George III's day when

> Public opinion was something intangible and incalculable; in any case, in more than half of the constituencies it had no importance whatsoever. They were concerned with the hard facts of the electoral system, much of them readily ascertainable and reducible to methodical analysis. What was the state of opinion among the hundred or so patrons of parliamentary boroughs? How many were friendly, how many definitely adverse? Reckoning up in advance what changes they were likely to make in their disposition of the seats which they controlled, how would the balance of parties be affected? Where, in the open constituencies, was there a likelihood of finding wealthy candidates prepared to stand a contest, with or without assistance from the Government?[1]

BIBLIOGRAPHY

JENNINGS, SIR IVOR: *The British Constitution* (Cambridge University Press; third edition, 1950).

NICHOLAS, H. G.: *The British General Election of 1950* (Macmillan, 1951).

BUTLER, D. E.: *The British General Election of 1951* (Macmillan, 1952).

—: *The British General Election of 1955* (Macmillan, 1955).

—: *The Electoral System in Britain, 1918–1951* (Oxford University Press, 1953).

BUTLER, D. E., and ROSE, R.: *The British General Election of 1959* (Macmillan, 1960).

BUTLER, D. E., and KING, A.: *The British General Election of 1964* (Macmillan, 1965).

FINER, S. E.: *Anonymous Empire* (Pall Mall Press, 1958).

BUTLER, D. E., and KING, A.: *The British General Election of 1966* (Macmillan, 1966).

[1] R. Christie in *The End of North's Ministry* (Macmillan, 1958).

CHAPTER II

The Nature of the Constitution

An explanation of the unwritten nature of the Constitution. Conventions. Judge-made law. Statutory Instruments. Some examples of parts of the Constitution which are written. Sovereignty of Parliament.

The Constitution of this country is its glory; but in what a nice adjustment does its excellence consist! Equally free from the distraction of democracy and the tyranny of monarchy, its happiness is to be found in its mixture of parts. It was this mixed government which the prudence of our ancestors devised and which it will be our wisdom to support. They ... extracted a system which has been the envy and admiration of the world. It is this scheme of government which constitutes the pride of Englishmen and which they can never relinquish but with their lives.

WILLIAM PITT, *Prime Minister, speaking in the House of Commons on March* 1, 1784

Constitutions should be short and obscure.

NAPOLEON

The British Constitution is described as being (*a*) unwritten; (*b*) flexible. It thus differs from that of the United States, which is modelled on the British and yet is stated to be (*a*) written; (*b*) rigid.

A written Constitution is one which is set out in one document or a group of documents. The law as written here is held above the ordinary law of the land. The Constitution can be altered or modified only by unusual, special means. For instance, if there were a written Constitution in Britain there would have to be a document which laid it down that the Constitution could not be altered except, say, by a three-quarters majority in both Houses of Parliament, followed by an appeal to the country which confirmed this. It seems unlikely that such a document will ever be written. The British Constitution has evolved gradually over the years, usually without violence, because it is a flexible institution, one which can be adapted to changing circumstances.

This, however, does not mean that it is completely unwritten. It consists partly of a body of constitutional conventions, which are not written down formally in any official document, and partly of a mass of parliamentary statutes, which are in writing, and upon which has been superimposed a judge-made law, also preserved in writing.

CONVENTIONS

A convention is a method of dealing with a constitutional problem which is not written down as a law, but which nevertheless has the force of a law. It starts off as a precedent. A situation confronts Parliament, which decides to deal with it in a certain way that seems best to the majority. A similar situation occurs from time to time. On each occasion fundamentally the original solution is used, until a habit becomes a convention. Once a convention has been established, Parliament is expected to behave in accordance with it. A convention is not to be found in an Act of Parliament. It will probably be written about in biographies or autobiographies of statesmen and in studies of the Constitution by teachers of political science. The sanction lies in the fact that a Government which ignored convention and behaved in an arbitrary manner would incur the displeasure of the electorate, who would show their disapproval at the next election by voting for another Government. That is, of course, the ultimate sanction in any system of popular representative government. The executive has to keep, or to win, the confidence and the trust of the people.

For instance, in 1958 the Prime Minister, Mr Macmillan, informed the House of Commons that the Select Committee of Privy Councillors (all past Cabinet Ministers) whom he had invited to see whether the burden resting on Ministers could be lightened had been unable to find a solution. He hoped, therefore, that Members would not object to their questions being answered from time to time by junior Ministers, who would thus enable their seniors to perform other important work entailing their presence elsewhere. This would not be done out of disrespect for the Commons, but purely to help Ministers to do their work effectively. The Prime Minister expressed the hope that the House would agree to this practice, and that eventually it would become one of the Constitution's conventions.[1]

This draws our attention to one of the most important conventions in the British Constitution—that the Prime Minister shall

---

[1] In 1960 Mr Macmillan, the Prime Minister, agreed, in order to study the convenience of Members, that questions addressed to him should in future start at No. 40 instead of No. 45. This practice will probably become a convention in due course.

always be a member of the House of Commons, and that, as far as possible, the important Cabinet Ministers shall also be members of the Commons. The reasoning behind the convention is that the Commons is the only popularly elected part of Parliament, the only part, therefore, that either speaks for the people or can truly claim to do so. It is only in the Commons that questions can be asked on behalf of the people, so Ministers should be Members of the Commons, entitled to appear there to answer such questions, and to defend and explain their policies in debate. The convention as to the Prime Minister has established itself in the last sixty years, during which only commoners have held the office, and on two occasions when there was a choice between a peer and an M.P. the latter was selected. It is noteworthy that the three key Ministers—the Foreign Secretary, the Chancellor of the Exchequer, and the Home Secretary—are nowadays always M.P.'s, not peers.[1] Mr Churchill in 1951 had in his Cabinet peers who were to co-ordinate the work of several Ministries. He called them Overlords. The idea was hotly criticized by the Opposition, and in a fairly short time all three Overlords resigned. There was an example of the same idea in 1957 in Lord Mills, Minister of Power, a Minister without departmental responsibility.

The basic convention that the majority must always give the minority a fair chance to speak, and that the minority must not abuse that privilege, is seen whenever the House debates. One of the opening two speeches, and one of the closing two speeches, is always made by the Opposition—the minority. Each Government speaker is always 'balanced' by an Opposition speaker. The third party, the Liberal Party, is allowed its fair share of speaking.

Another convention on the same lines is that the Chairman of the Committee on Public Accounts will always be a senior member of the Opposition, who will not hesitate to bring to light any inefficiency on the part of the Government. The Government is saying, in effect, "We have done our job faithfully to the best of our ability. We have no objection to allowing our work to be inspected."

There is a group of conventions relating to the way in which a Government is formed and dismissed:

(a) The sovereign selects the Prime Minister.
(b) The Prime Minister chooses the Cabinet.

[1] An exception to this convention was the appointment in 1960 of the Earl of Home as Foreign Secretary, but opposition to this was considerable. In 1963 Lord Home was appointed Prime Minister on the resignation of Mr Macmillan. He at once disclaimed his titles—possible under the 1963 Act—and stood successfully for the Commons.

(*c*) The composition and size of the Cabinet is decided by the Prime Minister.

(*d*) The Cabinet shall normally consist of members of the party with a majority in the Commons.

(*e*) The fact that the Cabinet exists.[1]

(*f*) The Cabinet assumes collective responsibility.

(*g*) The Prime Minister advises the Crown when to dissolve Parliament.

None of these matters is mentioned in any statute. Nobody is compelled to observe them by law. But unless they are observed the Constitution will not work smoothly.[2]

Then there is the group of conventions relating to the parties:

(*a*) *Hansard* does not recognize the existence of parties.

(*b*) Nevertheless the House sits according to party.

(*c*) The Speaker calls on members of the Government and Opposition sides to speak alternately.

(*d*) The Committees of the House reflect party strength there.

(*e*) The Opposition is allowed to decide which parts of the Estimates shall be discussed and when.

(*f*) The business of the House is settled by the party Whips 'behind the Speaker's Chair.'

(*g*) Every week the Leader of the Opposition asks the Speaker to tell him the Business for the week.

Again, none of these practices is laid down by statute. None of them will be found in the Standing Orders of the House. But they have all evolved in course of time. Experience has shown Members that the system works well if these conventions are observed. It will cease to work if they are ignored.

If these conventions had not been established a set of rules would have had to be written, passed by the House as a statute or statutes, and a written Constitution would have been the result.

We have given the example of the birth of a new convention regarding the answering of questions by Ministers. Here is an example of a suggestion by the Prime Minister which has been rejected—for the time being, anyway. Sir Hartley Shawcross,[3] a distinguished

---

[1] There is no law on the Statute Book which lays down that it should.

[2] The advantage of conventions is illustrated by the following story. A new M.P., on entering the cloakroom in the Commons for the first time, wondered why there were loops of red tape under the hooks for hats. The attendant said that these were to support Members' swords. The M.P. pointed out that Members no longer wore swords. The attendant triumphantly said, "But they do for umbrellas equally well."

[3] Later Lord Shawcross of Friston.

lawyer as well as an M.P. for many years, said in a letter to *The Times* that there ought not to be a Conservative foreign policy and a Labour foreign policy, but a British foreign policy. In other words, in his opinion the nation should present a united front to the world in foreign affairs, lest other nations try to play off one party against the other. For instance, during the Labour Party Conference in 1957 a resolution was passed that if the party returned to office it would grant self-determination to Cyprus. The Conservative Government, which was actually responsible for handling the future of Cyprus, might legitimately have argued that its proposals for a Constitution were rejected because the Cypriots thought that if Labour won the next election Cyprus would get a better offer. It is significant that nine months later, when Parliament debated in June 1958 the Tricondominium which Britain had proposed for Cyprus, the Labour leaders (who had been consulted by the Government) counselled their supporters to exercise restraint in criticism, as the Government's proposals must not be prejudiced.

The Prime Minister had proposed to Mr Gaitskell, Leader of the Opposition, that, in order to avoid unnecessary conflict in the Commons in defence matters and foreign affairs, the Government and the leaders of the Opposition ought to meet regularly, when the Government would give the Opposition secret information on which the Government had acted, but could not quote in defence of its actions. The Government was, therefore, unfairly handicapped in debate, and the picture of a divided House was shown to the world. The Prime Minister contended that the Opposition would, if it knew all the facts, refrain from criticism. Mr Gaitskell, while admitting much of the validity of these arguments, nevertheless felt obliged to decline the invitation, because, in his view, it would tie the Opposition's hands completely. Criticism that it ought to make would be silenced. He thought that the existing position, with its imperfections, was the lesser of two evils.

The Sanctions behind Conventions

These sanctions are best expressed by Vinogradoff[1] as follows:

Constitutional law creates obligations in the same way as private law, but its reactions as to persons possessed of political power are extra-legal; resolutions, active and passive resistance, the pressure of public opinion. The sanction is derived from the threat of these consequences.

The pressure of public opinion expresses itself ultimately in electoral defeat, which no Government will lightly risk.

[1] Sir Paul Vinogradoff.

JUDGE-MADE LAW

Parliament, as a result of Cabinet policy and debate in the House, enacts a substantial amount of legislation in every session. This legislation becomes part of the statute law of the United Kingdom, which, in the course of time, has grown into a formidable mass of documents. These are the laws of the land, which every British subject must observe. Man, being a fallible creature, succeeds, alas, in breaking the law a great deal, or, being an argumentative animal, has a difference of opinion as to what the law is. All these cases eventually come into the law courts, and the judges, with the aid of juries, interpret the laws, pronouncing judgment according to them. In the House of Lords, the Judicial Committee of the Privy Council, and the Courts of Appeal, where there are no juries, the judges not only pronounce judgment but state in writing the reasons why they have come to their conclusions. These lucid and weighty expressions of carefully considered legal opinion are preserved and are referred to in course of time by other judges when they are weighing up the arguments in a case and are making up their minds as to their judgments. The lives of all British citizens are influenced by this body of judge-made law.

STATUTORY INSTRUMENTS

Parliament to-day, administering a complex welfare society, indulging in a considerable amount of economic planning and control, is overworked and cannot find time to enact legislation which would otherwise emanate from it. This legislation has nevertheless to be dealt with, or the intricate business of day-to-day administration in detail would break down. It must go on ceaselessly. So the work is done on behalf of Parliament by the Government departments themselves. This legislation takes the form of Orders-in-Council, Regulations, etc., all of which are for convenience termed Statutory Instruments. The House of Commons confers on Ministers the power to issue these Statutory Instruments, and holds the Ministers responsible if any injustice is done to a member of the public in consequence. Every year several thousands of pages of these Instruments are published, each of which affects some of the people, and some of which affect all of them. In a sense they are minor regulations, but their cumulative effect can be very substantial. For instance, a farmer can be evicted from his farm on the ground that he is inefficient. The rate at which these Instruments are increasing in number and importance will eventually result in the amassing of an enormous amount of written legislation.

The significant place that Statutory Instruments are taking in the Constitution is recognized by students of government, some of whom are alarmed by the danger that the supremacy of Parliament may be threatened and that the rights of the citizen may be imperilled. In consequence there is now a Select Committee of the Commons on Statutory Instruments, whose function is stated at p. 33. In addition, an elaborate system of Tribunals is being devised to enable citizens who feel that their rights have been trespassed upon by Government departments to have any infringement of their rights redressed. These Tribunals are discussed at length in the chapter on the Judicial System.

The question arises whether, even if there were time, Parliament could do the work which is carried out by the Ministers by means of Statutory Instruments. It does, in fact, seem impossible. The Committee on Ministers' Powers (1931) stated quite clearly that the day-to-day administration of the country involved a knowledge of an immense amount of detail, some of it of a highly technical nature, and a knowledge of the problems peculiar to certain places. Parliament could not be expected to possess such knowledge. For instance, suppose that the Ministry of Transport sets up a working party to decide how many lights there should be on a motor-car, where they will be placed, the angle at which the beam will shine on the road, the amount of dazzle that is permissible, and so on. This kind of problem is constantly arising in a community like modern Britain. There must be a regulation to deal with each problem, but Parliament would never have the technical knowledge to deal with such regulations adequately. So there must be delegated legislation in the form of Statutory Instruments published by Government departments, or the conferring of powers upon a body such as the Law Society to administer an important learned profession in close touch with the general public.

Another advantage of the Statutory Instrument is that it can be amended or cancelled and be replaced by a new Instrument far more easily than an Act of Parliament. In a society which is becoming more and more scientific and technical, in which circumstances are changing swiftly, elasticity is essential if day-to-day administration is to adapt itself to new conditions.

In 1920, whereas only eighty-two Acts of Parliament were placed on the Statute Book, nearly a thousand Statutory Instruments were published. The following table shows the great growth in these Instruments:

Year						Total
1906	.	.	.	.	.	986
1914	.	.	.	.	.	1914

Year						Total
1926	.	.	.	.	.	. 1745
1938	.	.	.	.	.	. 1661
1946	.	.	.	.	.	. 2287

The functions of the Standing Committee on Statutory Instruments of the House of Commons are as follows:

(a) To determine whether public money is being raised.

(b) To decide whether the Instrument excludes itself from challenge in the law courts.

(c) To ascertain whether it appears to make unusual use of powers conferred by a statute.

(d) To find out if there has been unjustified delay in placing the Instrument before Parliament.

(e) To consider whether any part of the Instrument requires elucidation.

The Committee must resolve whether to draw the special attention of the House of Commons to the Instrument.

The Written Parts of the Constitution

The House of Commons is its own master and can alone determine how it will carry out the tasks with which the electorate have entrusted it. In consequence, the Commons has drawn up a code of Standing Orders to regulate the detailed procedure of the House.

The bald statement that the British Constitution is unwritten is therefore misleading. It is unwritten only in so far as so much of Parliament's behaviour is governed by conventions which are not to be found in any written law. The important things like the choosing of Cabinet Ministers and the allowing of the Opposition to criticize are governed by unwritten rules—by the spirit, not by the law, of the Constitution. On the other hand, it would be quite impossible to govern a complex society like that of the United Kingdom without having a written set of rules. Otherwise a man could not be assumed reasonably to know the law. Inevitably, therefore, a huge body of written law has accumulated through the centuries in the form of:

(a) Acts of Parliament.

(b) Judgment of the judges in the High Courts.

(c) Statutory Instruments.

(d) Standing Orders of Parliament.

B

Some of the more important statutes are:

(a) The Bill of Rights (1689).
(b) The Act of Settlement (1701).
(c) The Electoral Reform Acts of 1832, 1867, 1884, 1918, 1928, 1948.
(d) The Colonial Laws Validity Act (1865).
(e) The Parliament Acts (1911 and 1949).
(f) The Statute of Westminster (1931).
(g) The Ministers of the Crown Act (1937 and 1965).

THE SOVEREIGNTY OF PARLIAMENT

The Constitution is described as a system of parliamentary government in which Parliament is supreme. Only Parliament can make laws. Only Parliament can unmake those laws. Only Parliament can lay down the procedure whereby the House of Commons will fulfil its functions. Members of Parliament enjoy certain privileges. Only Parliament can tax the people. Only Parliament can spend public money. Although the Fighting Services are still royal and owe allegiance to the sovereign, their existence rests with Parliament.

The supremacy of Parliament has been established to prevent the exercise of arbitrary power by the Crown. If Parliament were truly sovereign there would be nothing to stop the Government from setting up a form of dictatorship. In fact, as we have seen, the sovereignty of Parliament is limited by the necessity to appeal to the electorate every five years. Parliament is able to wield power only by consent of the voters. Those voters have, in theory, selected a small body of able men (and women) to act as their representatives, to specialize in the business of government, but they (the voters) reserve the right to review their appointments periodically, and, if they are displeased with their representatives, to change them. If Parliament tried to challenge the people by perpetuating its life, by ignoring public opinion, violent revolution would probably be the result. The British do not, however, approve of force in this sense. They are practical people who see that the exercise of force by one body of men will inevitably lead to the exercise of force by another later. Constant upheavals of that kind will ruin the country. So affairs are conducted by counting heads, not breaking them.

Whether, in fact, the electorate really chooses its Members of Parliament is, however, debatable. The party system has obtained such a tight grip on the electoral process that, in general, candidates must have the support of a party if they are to have any chance of success. The majority of the electors have no influence in deciding who the candidates will be. They are obliged to choose between the nominees of the parties.

On the other hand, the voters do not as a rule vote for a candidate. They deliberately vote for a party because they agree with the policy of that party. In particular, they vote for the leader of the party, because they think, rightly or wrongly, that he is able to give the nation the wise, decisive leadership it needs. It could be said, therefore, that the leader of the party which wins a majority in the Commons is sovereign, not Parliament as a whole. That leader, however, knows that he can dominate Parliament up to a point, but that if he goes past that point his supporters will rebel and defeat him in a division. He will then have to appeal to the electorate. He knows that his supporters have acted against him partly because of their own consciences, but also because they are sensitive to the views of their constituents. In other words, it is ultimately the opinions of the electorate which count. It is a delicate system of checks and balances in which Parliament is supreme because the people consent to its being so, but where such consent can and will be withdrawn if the privilege of parliamentary sovereignty is abused.

SUMMING-UP

The matter was well expressed by Mr Stanley Baldwin (when Prime Minister), speaking in the House of Commons, thus:

> The historian can tell you probably perfectly clearly what the constitutional practice was at any given period in the past, but it would be very difficult for a living writer to tell you at any given period in his lifetime what the Constitution of the country is in all respects, and for this reason, that at almost any given moment... there may be one practice called constitutional which is falling into desuetude and there may be another practice which is creeping into use but is not yet constitutional.

BIBLIOGRAPHY

AMERY, L. S.: *Thoughts on the Constitution* (Oxford University Press, 1953).

DICEY, A. V.: *Introduction to the Study of the Law of the Constitution* (Macmillan; tenth edition, 1959).

WHEARE, K. C.: *Modern Constitutions* (Oxford University Press, 1951).

GUTTSMAN, W. L.: *The British Political Elite* (MacGibbon and Kee, 1963).

CHAPTER III

The House of Commons

The House itself. The life of a Parliament. The Speaker. The Whips. The business of the House. Back-benchers. Reform of the House. The legislative process. Committees. Privilege. The House and the Government. Who are the Members? The Opposition.

The virtue, spirit and essence of the House of Commons consists in its being the express image of the nation. . . .

EDMUND BURKE

Let us be quite clear about this, that the House of Commons is acknowledged on all hands, with certain reservations in the House of Lords, but without reservation at all in the writings of any high constitutional authority, as the final court in which the will of the nation is declared.

SIR HENRY CAMPBELL-BANNERMAN, *Prime Minister, speaking in the House of Commons on June* 24, 1907

The House of Commons at present consists of 630 Members. This number changes from time to time according to the growth and shifting of population. For instance, before the General Election of 1955 the strength of the Commons was 625. The number is not likely to go beyond 650, or the House would be too large to do business effectively.

These 630 Members represent:

> 511 English constituencies.
> 71 Scottish constituencies.
> 36 Welsh constituencies.
> 12 North of Ireland constituencies.

As we have seen, the House of Commons is the important working part of the Constitution, because it alone can raise money by taxation and authorize that money to be spent. This is natural, because it is the only part of Parliament that has been popularly elected.

The House is rectangular in shape. The Speaker's Chair is at one end, with the Dispatch Boxes and the Mace on a table in front of him. The Members sit on benches arranged in tiers, on each side of the Speaker, facing one another. The Government party sit on the benches on the right of the Speaker and the Opposition on the other side. The members of the Government and the leaders of the Opposition sit on the two opposing front benches. The other Members sit on the benches behind, and are consequently known as 'back-benchers.' There is not enough room to enable all Members to sit in comfort if they are all present. When the House was rebuilt after being destroyed by fire by German bombs a proposal to enlarge it and to convert it into the shape of an amphitheatre, with comfortable modern tip-up seats, was rejected. The House, like the nation, is a great respecter of tradition. The smallness of the Chamber creates an informal atmosphere. Speeches are not public addresses or orations; they are almost conversational in tone, delivered without undue histrionics. Though the House can on occasion be tense, noisy, and bad-tempered, it is generally friendly in mood. Members refer to each other as "my Honourable Friend" if the two Members concerned belong to the same party, or as "the Honourable Member for So-and-so" if they are of different parties. Members with a military background are referred to as "my Honourable and Gallant Friend," while lawyers or members of learned professions are alluded to as "the Honourable and Learned Member for So-and-so."

This recalls the interesting convention that, although the House is based on the party system, party is never mentioned officially. *Hansard* (the official journal of Parliament) merely refers to Mr Bumblepuppy, Member for Slushcombe-on-the-Ooze. It has been suggested that Mr Bumblepuppy's party should be stated after his name, but the proposal was rejected. The House preferred to stick to its traditions. This is a good example of the part played by conventions in an unwritten Constitution.

The life of a Parliament was seven years from 1716 until 1911, when it was reduced to five years. In that year a Parliament Bill was passed which reduced the powers of the House of Lords. The Government felt it right to reduce the life of Parliament, and thus give the electorate an earlier opportunity of pronouncing judgment on the record of the Government.

There are usually five sessions in the life of a Parliament. A session normally starts in November and lasts about eight months. Parliament is opened and closed in each session by the sovereign. The Royal Speech, which begins each session, provides a convenient opportunity for the Government to say what legislation it intends to carry out during the session. There is a brief debate, in which the Prime Minister justifies the legislative programme of his Government and the Opposition points out matters that in its opinion could well have been omitted, and other things that ought to have been included.

The Opening of Parliament is an occasion of splendid pomp and pageantry. The sovereign drives in State to the House of Lords and sits on the Throne. The Gentleman-Usher of the Black Rod (an official of Parliament) is then dispatched to the Commons to summon the Members to appear at the Bar of the House of Lords to hear the Royal Speech. The Commons have shut themselves in by tradition in order to exclude strangers—in particular, the King or Queen. When Black Rod reaches the door of the House it is slammed in his face. On his knocking three times, however, it is opened, and he leads the Members of the Commons to the Lords to hear the Speech from the Throne. The splendour and colour are intended to impress the people, to remind them of the dignity and importance of Parliament, and to stimulate public interest in its working.

THE SPEAKER

The Speaker of the House of Commons takes precedence after the Prime Minister and the Lord President of the Council. He used to be the spokesman of the Commons when they wished to communicate with the sovereign, or when the sovereign wished to communicate with them. He is a Member of the House who has been elected at a General Election. He does not speak in a debate or vote in a division, except in the case of a tie, when he can give a casting vote. He is elected by Members irrespective of party, and by this means a party deliberately deprives itself of a vote, thereby offsetting any advantage it might seem to gain from having one of its Members occupying the Speaker's Chair. He is, of course, expected to be completely impartial in dealing with the affairs of the House. He is paid a salary of £8500 a year, has a house, and gets a pension of £6000 a year and a peerage when he retires. If the Speaker retires or dies his successor is elected by the Commons. In modern times no Speaker has been dismissed.

The Speaker is usually a Member who has had a long experience of the House of Commons, with the result that he has intimate knowledge of the procedure, understands very well the way in which Members' minds work, and has the kind of urbane personality to enable him to deal equably with excited Members. The possession of a sense of humour, as well as a sense of fair play, is a necessary quality in his make-up. He is Chairman of the House of

Commons, and chooses a panel of twelve Members from whom the chairmen of committees are picked.

All disputes are referred to the Speaker for a ruling. He can take disciplinary action against a recalcitrant Member by suspending him and ordering him out of the House. Back-benchers who wish to speak in a debate or ask a question must 'catch his eye.' He decides whether a matter is of urgent public importance and so may be debated at short notice. Ever since the Parliament Act of 1911 he has had the very important task of deciding what is a Money Bill and what is not a Money Bill.

When the House is about to discuss money matters it transforms itself into a Committee of Supply or a Committee of Ways and Means. The Speaker is then asked to withdraw from the Chamber, and his place is taken by the Chairman of the Committee of Ways and Means. This convention goes back to the days when the King used the Speaker to ask the Commons for money and the Speaker was suspected of being a King's man. So when the Commons wished to discuss money they preferred to do so in the absence of the Speaker, in case he carried tales back to the King. This is, of course, no longer true of the Speaker, but the tradition is maintained, and, like so many customs of the British Constitution, it has developed a modern advantage. When the Speaker is in the Chair the House conducts itself formally. No one (except occasionally some one such as the Prime Minister) is allowed to speak more than once. When the Chairman of the Committee of Ways and Means is in the Chair the debate is much more informal. Members can catch the Chairman's eye more than once. This ensures that points are not only made, but answered.

The business of the House—i.e., the subjects, dates, and times of debates—is arranged by the Whips 'behind the Speaker's Chair.' In other words, the business is arranged with the Speaker's knowledge and consent. He knows in advance the order in which Ministers are going to answer questions, and the order in which back-benchers are going to speak in a debate. Indeed, this order is published every day and mentions the M.P., his question, and the Minister who will answer. The Speaker runs the ballot which decides which private Members (or back-benchers) are to be allowed to introduce Private Members' Bills or motions. He has quarters in the House, and begins the day by taking part in a dignified procession to the House, preceded by the Serjeant-at-Arms bearing the Mace, and followed by his Chaplain and his Secretary.

Although he has retained his traditional title, he does not 'speak' in the House. He only answers questions or adjudicates in disputes when they are addressed to him. An example, however, of the performance of his ancient duty was when the Prime Minister requested him to pray the Queen to ask the Judicial Committee of the Privy Council to consider a question of privilege concerning a Member of the Commons.

THE WHIPS

The Whips of the House of Commons are party Members who are charged by their leaders with the following tasks:

(a) Arranging the business of the House in accordance with the wishes of the party leaders.

(b) Advising Members how to vote and what importance the Government attach to a debate or motion.

(c) Keeping their leaders informed of the feelings of back-benchers concerning party policy.

(d) Administering discipline when necessary.

The Whips are usually Members with a talent for organization and man-management who are likely to become leaders of the party later. As far as the Government party is concerned, the Whips are also the Junior Lords of the Treasury, except for the Chief Whip, who is Parliamentary (Patronage) Secretary to the Treasury.[1] As far as the Opposition is concerned, the Whips have no formal appointments.

The term 'Whips' goes back to the days when almost all Members were country gentlemen who rode to hounds and came into the House from riding, and sometimes left the House in order to ride, and who often carried their hunting-whips with them. When they were being called by their leaders to take part in an exciting and important division they were spurred on with the whip and cries of "Tally-ho!" To-day Members are summoned by the more prosaic means of electric bells.

The Whips must be discreet and tactful. Usually the arrangement of the business of the House is a routine matter, but occasionally, parliamentary time being precious, a delicate situation arises which the Whips can cope with only by exercise of diplomacy.

When a Member has been absent from an important debate or has voted contrary to the wishes of the party, or (if he is a Govern-

---

[1] He, among other things, deals with the award of honours, which are made in the name of the sovereign every New Year's Day and on the sovereign's birthday. These awards are in general given for public service of distinction.

ment supporter) has abstained from voting in favour of a Government motion, or been erratic in his attendance in the House, the Whips will take him to task. But they do so tactfully. They must not antagonize Members needlessly. They reason and remonstrate with the Member without threatening him. They want to keep the party together as a team, not disunited by personal faction. When a Member wishes to be absent from the House and informs the Whips they arrange to pair him off against a member of the opposite party who wants to be away at the same time. This is an important duty in a very busy Parliament with a small majority and long hours of work.

When the leaders of the parties leave the business of the House to be arranged by the Whips this is called 'doing it through the usual channels.' The Government and the Opposition Whips meet and agree on dates, times, subjects, and names. After a debate has been arranged and the parties have decided what importance they attach to it the Whips issue notices to Members passing on the information to them. If the debate is so important that the Government would regard defeat as justification for resignation a Three-line Whip is issued. The request to the Member to attend is therefore underlined three times. If the debate is important but not vital the Whip is two-line. If it is merely desirable that Members should be present a One-line Whip is issued. If a party expels a Member or a Member wishes to break with a party he no longer receives the Whip, and is then independent. No Government ever wants to be defeated or to have the House 'counted out.' The Whips must, therefore, make sure that there is a quorum of forty Members in the House, and that sufficient Members are near at hand to avoid defeat in a division.

The leaders and the back-benchers of a party often disagree with one another. If the disagreement is confined to one or two people who are not prepared to be too difficult about it no notice is taken. But when the feeling is both strong and widespread it is the business of the Whips to take note of it and inform their leaders, who will then try to win round the rebellious Members, or even, in an extremity, give way to them. The Whips must, therefore, be in close touch with all the Members of their party in the House, be liked by them, and be taken into their confidence. The Whips must always be accessible to their party Members.

They nominate Members to committees. Members who are interested in certain committees approach the Whips with a view to becoming members. The Whips watch the performance of Members both in committee and in the House in order to discover promising talent that ought one day to be on the front bench.

THE DAILY BUSINESS OF THE HOUSE

The main business of the House is done on the first four days of the week, starting at 2.30 P.M. and ending, normally, at 10.30 P.M. On the fifth day, Friday, business begins at 11 A.M. and ends at 4.30 P.M.[1] The House does not, in ordinary times, meet on Saturdays and Sundays.

The day begins with prayers, because Britain is a Christian country and the sovereign is Defender of the Faith. After prayers the first three-quarters of an hour is given up to Question Time. All Members, except Ministers, the Speaker, and the Leader of the Opposition, are allowed to ask up to two[2] questions a day for oral answer. These questions must be addressed to a Minister, and must be brief and clear. They must be written on a piece of paper, which must be handed to one of the Clerks, who will sometimes reword the question in parliamentary language. They must be relevant to business for which a Minister is responsible. The Member who asks a question is assumed to have satisfied himself that the facts and figures he quotes are accurate. He must not indulge in rumour and hearsay. The Member must say whether he will be content with an answer in writing or wants an oral answer. Ministers come into the House in turn to answer questions (usually there is time for only two Ministers a day to appear), and if, at the end of Question Time, some questions are still unanswered orally the replies are given in writing. If a Member insists on an oral answer he must ask his question again. Some Members particularly want to see the Minister in the House in person, because they hope that the first innocent question will enable them to ask further questions on the grounds that the original answer is not clear. If they can, Members of the Opposition like to score off a Minister, or at least to embarrass him. This sort of duel often ends in the Member giving notice that he will raise the matter again on the Adjournment—*i.e.*, at 10 P.M.—so that the matter can be debated for half an hour. These little scenes can sometimes be lively, and even acrimonious. There are interruptions, and the Speaker has to intervene either to restore order or to point out that a Member is asking supplementary questions which are not permissible and can only be asked separately on another day. There is often heated argument as to what constitutes a proper supplementary question. The point is that the Member asking the question is permitted to ask further

[1] Early in 1967 the practice was introduced of commencement at 10 A.M. on Mondays and Wednesdays.
[2] Three before 1960.

questions designed to produce what is in his opinion a satisfactory answer to his original question if he thinks the Minister is trying to evade the issue. He must not, however, enlarge the scope of the original question. This is where the arguments arise. Some Members are very skilled in staging a short debate on a question.[1]

The questions may be asked for the following reasons:

(a) To publicize a grievance.
(b) To elicit information.
(c) To embarrass a Minister.
(d) To show that Members are active in the House.

All Members have a voluminous correspondence with their constituents and with pressure groups outside the House. They are frequently asked to bring injustices, or alleged injustices, to light. Leaders of parties will, on occasion, arrange for Members to ask questions in order to give a Minister the chance to make public a certain matter. The cruel treatment by the Japanese of British prisoners of war was brought to the attention of the country in this way.

Back-benchers complain that they have little chance to do anything useful in the House. The opportunity to ask questions helps to compensate them. A Member can demonstrate his devotion to his constituents by the zeal with which he asks questions and follows up their complaints. He can also study a particular problem and by regular questions on the subject build up the reputation of being an expert. Finally, he can, by means of a question, draw the attention of the nation to a matter in which a pressure group is interested.

These questions in the House are taken seriously in the Government departments concerned, who quickly make an inquiry and provide the Ministers with answers that they hope will deal with the matters satisfactorily. Sometimes a skeleton is discovered in a Ministry's cupboard as a result of a question. Sometimes a Ministry is genuinely glad to hear about something that it can go into and clear up, and take measures to prevent happening again.

After Question Time is over (about 3.30 P.M.) the main business of the day begins—i.e., the business which the party Whips have agreed shall be dealt with—either the passage of Government legislation or a debate which the leaders of the Opposition have sponsored in order to discuss a matter of urgent public interest or to criticize something the Government has done or failed to do.

---

[1] An M.P. made this amusing comment: "The answer to a question must be brief, accurate, and should not reveal anything that was not already known."

For instance, on May 8, 1958, Mr Alfred Robens (Blyth) begged to move:

> That this House deplores the refusal of the Minister of Labour in pursuance of the economic and industrial policy of Her Majesty's Government to attempt to bring about a settlement of the London bus dispute, which is causing great inconvenience and hardship to the general public.

The Government did not move an amendment to this motion. They merely concentrated on defeating it, and did so by 320 votes to 253.

On January 23, 1958, the Chancellor of the Exchequer, Mr Heathcoat-Amory, moved:

> That this House supports Her Majesty's Government in their resolve to maintain by every effective means the internal and external value of the pound sterling.

The Leader of the Opposition moved an amendment:

> That this House, having regard to the record of the Government, which no longer enjoys the support of the people of Britain, has no confidence in the capacity of Her Majesty's Ministers to pursue policies which will secure expanding production, full employment, and a stable pound.

The motion by the Government was won by 324 to 262.

This kind of business almost always emanates from the Opposition in carrying out its duty of criticizing the Government and impressing on the electorate the public spirit of the Opposition, the zeal with which it looks after the interests of the country, and the desirability of putting it into office. The debates on these motions usually take the same form. A leader of the Opposition, one of the Shadow Cabinet, moves the motion. A Minister responds, sometimes with an amendment to the motion, sometimes by putting forward counter-arguments. Back-benchers who think that they have something worth saying and have been lucky enough to catch the Speaker's eye continue the discussion. Finally, another leader of the Opposition restates the criticisms of the Government and the arguments in favour of the motion. The debate is wound up by another Minister, who tries to demolish the arguments of the Opposition or to justify the amendment. A division follows, and the Government, because of party discipline, will win. The Whips will have made sure that all (or most) of their supporters are there to vote as instructed, whether they have listened to the debate or not.

In fact, many of them have heard little or nothing of the debate. This is why debates in the House to-day are said to be meaningless to the extent that the results are foregone conclusions and that neither eloquent oratory nor cogent argument will sway Members' opinions. It is agreed that the object of such debates is to impress the electorate and to enable the country to choose between the parties at the next General Election.

If the debate has finished by 10 P.M. the Speaker moves the Adjournment of the House. If the debate has not finished by then, either the Whips will agree to continue it on the following day or the Government will move to carry on after the Adjournment if it is anxious to conclude the matter that same day. If the second of these alternatives is adopted the debate will continue into the small hours if necessary, until it has been completed with a division. If, however, the Speaker's motion to adjourn the House is agreed to, half an hour is left in which back-benchers can move motions to discuss questions which they cannot get debated in any other way. A wide variety of subjects is discussed on the Adjournment. Regardless of the state of the discussion, it must come to an end after half an hour, when the House, in theory, wearily goes home for the night, but in practice Ministers go back to their dispatch boxes[1] to get ready for the morrow, and private Members try to catch up with their correspondence. Ministers are known to sit up in bed reading their departmental papers.

In the course of debate Members are expected to behave in accordance with certain well-established conventions. The use of unparliamentary language is forbidden. A Member abusing another Member or accusing another Member of something reflecting on his honour will be required by the Speaker to withdraw his remarks. When the debate is heated there is much noise and confusion, many cheers and counter-cheers; tempers are inflamed, and epithets are hurled across the Chamber in the heat and fury of the moment. Sir Winston Churchill, on one celebrated occasion, to avoid unparliamentary language, used the expression "a terminological inexactitude." This magnificent piece of circumlocution was accepted. More recently Sir Gerald Nabarro was challenged with having said that another Member was a humbug and a hypocrite. He denied this, and said that all he was saying was that the Member concerned was defending a policy that savoured of humbug and hypocrisy. This will probably seem to the ordinary person a splitting of hairs and a wasting of time. Nevertheless, these verbal exchanges do add to the liveliness of a House which can be deadly dull. Nothing derogatory must ever be said about the royal family or the Christian religion.

[1] These are the boxes in which papers of concern to the Minister are placed, and then 'dispatched' to him for his attention.

THE BACK-BENCHER

The daily half-hour's debate on the Adjournment affords back-benchers another opportunity to speak and draw the attention of the electorate (their own constituents in particular) to their zeal and ability. Time is short, and without Government support no one expects to achieve anything in the way of legislation. It is thus an opportunity to ventilate and discuss a multitude of subjects which would otherwise never see the light of day.

Some typical subjects discussed on the Adjournment have been the following:

> Mr Julian Ridsdale (Harwich) raised the question of night work in the baking industry, which was discussed till 10.30 P.M.
>
> Mrs Jean Mann (Coatbridge and Airdrie) raised "with great trepidation" the question of what happened to Dugald Johnstone, a small boy whose bones had been found on a Scottish hillside. This matter was discussed till 11.22 P.M.
>
> Dr J. Dickson-Mabon (Greenock) raised the matter of multiple packs provided by the National Health Service. This debate lasted from 10.11 P.M. to 10.41 P.M., ending by the Under-Secretary of State for Scotland thanking Dr Mabon for raising such an important question and for giving the Government valuable ideas and enabling the Minister to explain the existing position.

Friday is the back-benchers', or private Members', day. It begins early and ends early to enable Members to leave in time to reach their constituencies for the week-end. Owing to the growth of parliamentary business, Members find it increasingly difficult to visit their constituencies, apart from those who sit for London constituencies. Members are most anxious to show their faces in their constituencies regularly, otherwise they will tend to be forgotten by the voters. They may well be regarded as uninterested in the affairs of the people who have returned them to Parliament. Moreover, they want to attend local functions, such as a garden party, which provide them with an excuse to make a speech. It is one of the most important duties of the back-bencher that he should explain the policy of the party to the voters and take back to his leaders the opinion of the voters. The back-bencher cannot be charged with having outlived his usefulness as long as he is able to influence the voters, and is able to influence his party leaders.

As has been said, the back-bencher is a Member with no official party standing. The comment is consequently being made increasingly that he no longer serves any definite purpose, and that, this being the case, the quality of candidates standing for Parliament is falling away, since there is no worthwhile work to be done.

As a result, Parliament is in grave danger of consisting mainly of 'little men.' Lord Shawcross, speaking in 1958, said that no new man of outstanding ability had entered Parliament since 1950. According to Lord Attlee, however, Members are of much the same ability to-day as in the past.

Another suggestion is that 'little men' only are standing because the work of Parliament has increased so enormously. The length of the session has increased from four months to eight months in the year. Attendance in the House nearly every day is more or less compulsory, because the majority which either party can get is comparatively narrow, and the Whips cannot afford to take any chances of defeat in a division. Moreover, the increasing amount of work done in committee means that most Members are in the House all the morning engaged in committee work, and all the afternoon and evening, not to mention part of the night, on the business of the House. The result is that Members are no longer amateur politicians who earn their living in other professions. To-day most of them are professionals, whose principal source of income is their parliamentary pay. There is little or no time for them to do any other work. Therefore they are more or less at the mercy of the Whips. If they do not do as they are told they will not get a party nomination at the next election.

What does the back-bencher do to-day? First, as we have seen, he is a vital link between the House and the elector, between his party and the elector. This is a most important rôle, and it is difficult to see how else it can be played. If the back-bencher does this task well he is a very useful part of the parliamentary machine. Each Member has about 60,000 constituents, and each of these people may have a personal problem. Some of them think that their problems can be solved by the Government; a few, indeed, think they have been created by the Government. So the inevitable tendency is for them to go to their Member and ask for help. They either write to the Member or come to see him. Most Members try to arrange to see their constituents either locally or in a lobby of the House on certain days. Indeed, they are lobbied quite regularly, not merely by constituents, but by pressure groups. For instance, if there is an agricultural question to the fore the National Farmers' Union will lobby all those Members who represent country districts and depend, therefore, on the agricultural vote. The Fighting Services can rely on those Members who are ex-regular officers to represent their interests in the House.

Individual constituents may have complaints to make that a disabled ex-Serviceman has had his pension reduced wrongly; or that a shopkeeper has had his application for a telephone refused, whereas another tradesman who applied after him succeeded with a similar application; or that the Ministry of Agriculture has given notice of eviction to a farmer who is supposed by the Ministry to be running his farm inefficiently, and the farmer does not agree; or that a girl who ought to have been given a grammar-school place has been rejected for unsatisfactory reasons. There is almost no end to the grievances, or supposed grievances, of constituents, most of whom have a firm faith in the ability of a Member to get such grievances redressed. Members are expected to tackle all this work without regard to the politics of the constituent in question.

Back-benchers can open bazaars, write letters to the local Press, take part in local debates, encourage the youth organizations. They can put before the Ministers concerned the interests of local industries. They therefore have very nearly a full-time job on their hands in keeping up good liaison with their constituents. They cannot have very much time for purely parliamentary duties in the House. Indeed, they already complain that they are overworked, and that the work they do is not compatible with their status. With this attitude one disagrees, because the maintenance of good relations with constituents and doing a great deal on their behalf is important and useful work. Not only do the people feel that they are looked after, but there is instilled in them a respect for the usefulness of Parliament. They become aware of the existence of Parliament, and this is important at a time when, some critics allege, the public is losing interest in Parliament because it thinks that the only people who matter in the House are the party leaders. So, on this count alone, the back-bencher does important and useful work.

Secondly, there is the committee work of the House, which is divided into a number of Select and Standing Committees. Every Member is a member of at least one, and probably more than one, committee. One of the most important stages in the passage of a Bill through the House is the Committee Stage. This takes place after the Second Reading, which results in the principles of the Bill being settled. The committee then discusses the Bill in detail (clause by clause if necessary), and puts it into good shape in accordance with the declared wishes of the House. If the Bill is controversial the Opposition uses this stage to oppose it bitterly. For example, several of the Labour Party's nationalization Bills were argued fiercely and at great length by the Conservative Opposition.

All purely Scottish matters are dealt with by the Scottish Committee, rather than by the House as a whole.

There are Select Committees on public accounts and estimates, on the nationalized industries, and, very important indeed, on privileges. From time to time the Prime Minister will appoint a Select Committee to consider some specific question, such as the reform of the House of Lords.

As has been said, these committees work in a more informal manner than the House as a whole. A Member can speak many times as long as he has something useful to say. In a small committee dealing with a matter in which a Member is specially interested that Member is apt to speak independently in accordance with his personal opinions, and not necessarily in accordance with the party line. Whips do their best to secure the compliance of Members with the party line, but they rarely succeed in silencing them. A record is kept officially of the committees' proceedings, and it is possible to know what a Member is doing. We will say a little more about the committee system later on.

On the other hand, a back-bencher (or private Member) has a very poor prospect of getting a Private Members' Bill through Parliament. Two important measures that did go through in modern times were Sir Alan Herbert's Marriage Bill in 1937 and Mr Silverman's Abolition of Capital Punishment Bill. This was for a trial period, from 1965 to 1970. In 1959–60 two Bills were introduced. Mrs M. Thatcher brought in a Bill to ensure the admission of the Press to local-government meetings, and Mr Richard Marsh introduced a Bill for cleaner offices and better conditions for office workers. These—both quite important measures—were enacted. From time to time some small non-controversial Bill on a subject with general appeal, like the protection of wild birds or the prevention of cruelty to animals, will succeed. But normally the obstacles which the private Member faces are too great to be surmounted in the time available to him.

To begin with, there are only ten Fridays in a session on which a private Member can initiate a Bill. And every year about a hundred-odd Bills are put forward to the Speaker. There has to be a ballot for the right to bring in a Bill, so that very few Members can hope to have a chance to get very far with a Bill. For instance, in 1958 as many as 303 Members took part in the ballot, and only forty names were drawn by the Speaker. And only eight of these forty Members would be likely to have a chance of bringing their Bills into the House.

Having secured a place in the draw, a Member must enlist support from both parties, because he must have an attendance of forty in the House, or he will be counted out. He must also be sure of supporters, because there is always some other Member who dislikes either him or his Bill, and will therefore propose an amendment, usually that the Bill be brought up again in six months' time.

If this amendment is carried the Bill is killed. So the Member must be both persistent and popular to overcome all the rebuffs he will meet with and to obtain the support he requires. Unless he happens to be a lawyer himself he will have to go to a firm of legal draftsmen to help him put his Bill into the correct language. If he is popular he might persuade the Treasury Solicitor's department to help him in this connexion. It will cost him a great deal of money if he has to employ legal draftsmen. He is unlikely to get any help from the Government, who might even actively oppose him if they think the Bill will embarrass them. It has, however, been known for the Opposition, who cannot bring in a Bill while in opposition, to appoint one of its supporters to do so as a private Member. In this case he will get plenty of help. On the other hand, he is likely to meet with much opposition as well. If it is an important Bill the Government will either sponsor it officially or ensure its defeat.

POSSIBLE REFORM OF THE COMMONS

Firstly, the question of debate. Most of the speakers in a debate are unlikely to influence the result, and, the leading official party speakers having stated all the important arguments for and against, it is rare that a back-bencher has anything new to say. Indeed, most of the private Members' speeches are mere repetition. It has been suggested, therefore, that these speeches should be reduced in number, and that back-benchers should not speak unless they genuinely feel they have something constructive to contribute. If this proposal were to be adopted a good deal of valuable parliamentary time would be saved, but back-benchers' activities would be curtailed. This reduction in speaking time would have to be compensated somehow, or it would be a very serious disadvantage.

Secondly, the question of correspondence. Members at present have to spend a large sum of money on secretarial assistance and postage, and to be content with uncomfortable quarters in odd corners of the House. This state of affairs is clearly wrong. No great business concern would allow its executives to be hampered by such parsimony. Neither should a great nation do so. Members ought to be housed in a modern building near the Commons, so that they are able to go into the Commons at short notice. They should be provided with first-rate secretarial help, and all their official correspondence should be paid for by the State. This would be of great help to Members, because it would enable them to carry on a certain amount of private work and to be a little more independent of their parliamentary pay.[1]

[1] The new rates of pay (1964), £3250 a year, are designed to ameliorate this position.

Thirdly, the question of voting. Could Members be allowed to vote by proxy? If the speakers are not going to influence them they can say in advance how they intend to vote. If the Whips are informed of such intention they could arrange for the votes to be recorded. This would be a great boon to Members, who would not be obliged to be present in the House so much. They could be away more often, either doing important private business or visiting their constituencies, which they cannot now do. The objection to this idea is that some Members might be tempted to absent themselves often and regard the House of Commons very much as a part-time job. If that happened the reform would defeat its object, because the dignity of Parliament would be seriously damaged. There would have to be rules. Members would have to convince the Whips that their absence was unavoidable and justifiable; leave of absence would be given, say, not more than once a week during the sittings.

Fourthly, the committee system. The House already does much of its work in committee, and the committee system could be extended. The House could be divided into groups of committees, each dealing with a number of related subjects. There could be sub-committees. For instance, the groups could be as follows:

(a)	Foreign affairs.	(g)	Health, pensions, insurance.
(b)	Commonwealth affairs.	(h)	Local government, town-planning.
(c)	Defence.	(i)	Scotland.
(d)	Trade and industry.	(j)	Wales.
(e)	Finance.	(k)	Farming.
(f)	Education.		

Members, according to experience and personal preference, could serve on committees long enough to become specialists. As they already serve on unofficial committees within their parties, this proposal is not breaking entirely fresh ground. On the contrary, it is making better use of energy that is already being generated.

Instead of the Committee Stage coming after the Second Reading of a Bill, it could precede it. In other words, the Committee Stage could be used to discuss the Bill thoroughly. The Minister would defend it and explain it, accompanied by his experts. The Opposition could criticize it and propose amendments. Witnesses could be called, consisting both of experts and of interested parties, who would be cross-examined by the committee. Eventually a Bill that had been put into good shape would be submitted for the consideration of the whole House. This is the procedure adopted both in France and in the United States. It seems logical, and it would save parliamentary time, because several committees would be at work on several Bills at the same time. *Hansard* could report all committees fully, and the proceedings would be public. The national Press and B.B.C. would be encouraged to cover committees fully.

The objection to the proposal seems to be that it is against the tradition of the House, and that it might detract from its dignity. We must be careful before meddling with a well-tried tradition, but no tradition should be sacrosanct for ever. We must move with the times. As for the dignity of the House, its committees are miniature Houses of Commons, and, in any event, the work of the committees would require the approval of the House as a whole before the Bills would go further. The House would still be able to assert itself at the Second Reading.

Finally, there could be some revision of the financial procedure of the House, which we shall discuss later. The effect of this revision would be a saving of Members' time.

The essence of the problem of reform of the Commons is to save Members' time. The less time they spend in Parliament and the more time they spend in maintaining first-hand experience of the economic affairs of the nation and of international relations the better equipped they will be to govern the country.

THE PASSAGE OF A BILL THROUGH THE HOUSE OF COMMONS

In a complex society like modern Britain a Government which takes an ever-increasing part in our economic and social affairs has so much legislation to enact that inevitably it must deny private Members anything but the smallest proportion of parliamentary time. Therefore, as we have seen, public Bills—*i.e.*, Bills which the Government sponsors—constitute almost all those with which Parliament deals. Public Bills may be divided into two classes—Money Bills and Non-money Bills.

Money Bills must be certified as such by the Speaker. A Money Bill, briefly, is one which seeks to raise money from the public by means of taxation, or which seeks to spend money which has been raised by taxation.

Non-money Bills of a non-controversial nature can be initiated in the House of Lords on behalf of the Government and come to the House of Commons in the form of polished Bills which the House of Commons can accept with the minimum of discussion. In other words, the House of Lords is helping to save parliamentary time because two Bills are being dealt with at the same time, one in the House of Commons, the other in the House of Lords.

A public Bill starts life in a Government department, which appoints a Departmental Committee to make exhaustive inquiries spread over many months. A mass of evidence is taken from all the experts and interested parties, until the Minister is satisfied that he has considered all points of view and that the final Bill, which his civil servants draft, is the best that could possibly be constructed. This concern is of vital importance, because any Bill is bound to affect all or most of the people.

For instance, if it is an Education Bill the Ministry will have interviewed university teachers, school teachers, clergymen, doctors, associations of parents, local-government authorities—everybody, in short, with an interest in and a knowledge of the subject. The Minister then puts his Bill before the Cabinet, and, presuming that the Cabinet accepts it, he is ready to introduce it into the House.

This is done by means of the purely formal First Reading, which is tantamount to notice being given that the Bill is proposed. Copies of the Bill are then 'laid on the table,' so that all Members get a copy and are able to study the Bill. They have about three weeks in which to do so before the very important Second Reading stage is reached.

At this stage the Minister introduces his Bill, defending it and explaining it. An Opposition leader criticizes. Speeches from back-benchers follow. Then another Opposition leader criticizes it all over again. Finally, the Minister's deputy restates all the arguments for the Bill. There is then a division, and if the Government supporters vote as requested by the Whips the Bill passes and is referred to a committee. What happens at the Committee Stage has already been described.

The committee reports back to the House. If it is not a very controversial measure this stage is short. If it is controversial the Opposition will take the chance to dissect the Bill again and bring to the attention of the electorate its imperfections and their alternative proposals.

The Bill then goes through its Third Reading, before being passed on to the Lords. At this stage only verbal alterations can be made.

The objects of such a lengthy process, when one takes into account the work of the House of Lords on the Bill, are:

(a) To ensure that legislation is not rushed through without adequate consideration.

(b) To ensure that all arguments for and against are considered in order to produce a well-designed Bill of sound principle.

(c) To give the electorate every opportunity to be informed about the Bill and decide between the parties.

Because parliamentary time is so limited the Government must have ways and means of preventing obstruction by the Opposition.

This was a particularly important matter at the end of the last and the beginning of the present century, when the Irish Nationalists habitually delayed Bills. There are now three devices by which Bills can be given a comparatively speedy passage. They are:

> (a) The Guillotine.
> (b) The Closure.
> (c) The Kangaroo.

These devices can be used to control committees as well as the House as a whole.

The Guillotine is an arrangement by which a definite time is fixed for the discussion of each stage of a Bill. When that time is up no further discussion is allowed.

The Closure is a device for ending a debate or a speech by a Member moving that "the question be now put." This motion is usually moved by a member of the Government party, because the Government is anxious to get on with the business of Parliament. If the Speaker considers that the right of a minority to have its say has been infringed he can refuse the motion.

The Kangaroo is a device which enables the Government to pass from one stage of a Bill to another without consideration of the clauses in between. In other words, certain amendments only are chosen to be debated, and those passed over are not debated.

A private Bill (which must not be confused with a Private Member's Bill) is promoted by a local-government authority, or a public corporation, or a corporate body of that kind. The Home Office (or whichever Ministry the promoting body is directly connected with) sponsors the Bill in the House. When the railway system was being built up many such Bills were promoted to acquire compulsory purchases of land. Local-government authorities promote this kind of Bill nowadays in order to preserve the rural amenities of a district, or a Fighting Service or the Atomic Authority may wish to buy land. These Bills are necessary because, under a rule of law, a citizen cannot have property or amenities taken away from him without compensation being paid by Parliament.

Private Members' Bills have already been discussed.

THE COMMITTEE SYSTEM

We have already discussed the work of some of the committees and the possibility of increasing the system to give back-benchers more constructive work. The House can make itself a committee (the Committee of the Whole House), when the Speaker leaves the

Chair. The parliamentary method seems to be the committee method.

This happens, among other occasions, when the House is dealing with finance. The Speaker leaves the Chair, which is taken by the Chairman of Ways and Means (who is the Deputy Speaker). He sits, however, in the Clerk's Chair. In his absence the Chair is taken by his Deputy, or by one of the temporary chairmen.

Select Committees

These may be permanent or sessional, with usually not more than fifteen Members. First, there is the Committee of Selection, which chooses standing committees. Then there is the Committee of Privileges, to which are referred all questions of parliamentary privilege. The Committee on Statutory Instruments has become of great importance because of the huge number of these Orders put out by Government departments which affect the lives of the people, and over which the House has little control. The committee examines all Statutory Instruments, and will report any cases of misuse of powers. The Committee on Standing Orders is concerned with the way in which the business of the House is conducted.

A Committee on Nationalized Industries has been formed to inquire into each of these public corporations at a time, and report to the House as to whether it is giving the public the service for which it was formed. Public Accounts and Estimates committees have been mentioned. Finally, the Government will appoint a Select Committee to consider a specific subject, if and when necessary. Select Committees are chosen by the Chief Whips in consultation with the Leader of the House.

Standing Committees

There are six of these. One is the Scottish Committee,[1] on which all Scottish Members serve, plus a few 'experts' to make the committee a reflection of party strength in the House. This committee deals with money as far as Scotland is concerned. The other five committees deal with Bills as they are appointed to do by the Speaker. They consist of a nucleus of twenty members, to whom can be added a further twenty-five. The parties are represented according to their strength in the House. The Chairmen are nominated by the Speaker from a small panel of about twelve. A Chairman is appointed for one Bill at a time.

The committees on opposed and unopposed private Bills consist of four and five Members respectively. Their names indicate their

[1] There is now a Welsh Committee to deal with purely Welsh affairs.

rôle. Joint Committees of the Commons and Lords are set up to consider a particular problem which affects both Houses. For instance, if the House of Lords is reformed and the hereditary principle is retained it is suggested that a Joint Committee should elect those hereditary peers who sit in the reformed House.

PRIVILEGES OF THE HOUSE OF COMMONS

The privileges of the House of Commons are of the utmost importance, because they are linked with the principle that Parliament is sovereign in Britain. The monarchy is constitutional, which means that it must do what Parliament says. This position has been arrived at only after a long, and sometimes bloody, struggle, and it is one which Parliament is never likely to surrender. In order to encourage Members of Parliament to speak in the House of Commons without fear or favour, and with the public interest only in mind, they must be given certain privileges. There can be no argument about this, but the question does arise whether Members are at times inclined to go too far and arrogate to themselves privileges that tend to make them a small group of men who are above the ordinary law of the land. The danger is that a small, privileged class tends to become dictatorial and autocratic. This would not be accepted by the British people without serious opposition.

The main privileges of Members of Parliament are as follows:

(a) Immunity from prosecution in the courts for anything said or written in the business of the House.
(b) Immunity from arrest while in the precincts of the House.
(c) Access to the Crown for the purpose of tendering advice.
(d) Respect must be shown for the dignity of Parliament.
(e) Parliament must be the judge in its affairs.

At the opening of every new Parliament the Speaker attends in the Lords for the royal approval of his election, and he claims "the ancient and undoubted rights and privileges of the Commons."

The first of the privileges is important, because Members, like judges, are obliged in the public interest to bring to light matters or to make comments for which they could be sued, since they might not have legal proof to support their statements. They get letters from constituents complaining about matters which, if the occasion was not privileged, might well result in damage to a constituent. It seems to be a question of common sense, of a sense of responsibility, on the part of Members of Parliament. Mr Speaker Peel said that "it has been the practice of the House to restrain privilege under great limitations and conditions."

A case of the use of privilege occurred when the question of a Bank Rate leak was being discussed. Government spokesmen said that the Opposition speaker who had been mentioning the name of the Deputy Chairman of the Conservative Party (who was not a Member of Parliament) was abusing the privilege of the House in that he was attacking some one who was unable to defend himself, and that if the same remarks were made outside Parliament the Member in question would have to pay damages. The Member did not, however, apologize, and there the matter rested. Whether he was wise in taking up that attitude is arguable. It is vitally important that Members exercise great restraint in using privilege, lest they abuse it.

Immunity from arrest is no longer of serious importance, because Members can be arrested out of the House if they commit an offence.

Though Members have a right of access to the Crown, it is a right that is seldom, if ever, exercised to-day. If the Crown is to remain aloof from party controversy the sovereign cannot keep in touch with individual Members of Parliament. The only Minister with whom the sovereign has regular contact is the Prime Minister.

THE HOUSE OF COMMONS AND THE GOVERNMENT

The Constitution assumes that it is the House of Commons which controls the Government. In other words, it is assumed that there is always a body of Members in the House whose judgment is independently exercised, and who would, therefore, in a moment of crisis, bring about the defeat of the Government if they felt this was in the public interest. In fact, it is the Government who are in control of the situation. This problem is discussed at length in Chapter IV.

WHO ARE THE MEMBERS?

Both main parties have branches in every constituency. These branches have a selection committee which chooses the candidate who will stand for election on behalf of the party. Sometimes this committee finds its own candidate, but more often the headquarters of the party puts forward for acceptance by the local committee two or three candidates. If the latter want the support of the party officially they will fall in with the wishes of the headquarters.

The qualities which are looked for in candidates are these:

(a) Integrity of character.
(b) Ability to get on with other people.

(c) Ability to speak well.

(d) Proof of sincere conviction of the rightness of the party's policy.

(e) Knowledge of some important subject, such as industry or banking, or trade unionism.

At one time the Conservatives expected a candidate to contribute towards his election expenses and to his local party funds. No doubt this is still a very acceptable qualification, but the party pays expenses and is more interested in the quality of the candidate.

The Labour Party is closely connected both with the trade union and the Co-operative movements. The former reserves the right to nominate about one-third of the party's candidates, and at present there are 132 trade union Members.

Some Notes on the Composition of the House of Commons[1]

(a) *Age*

	Conservative 1959	Conservative 1966	Labour 1959	Labour 1966
20's	10	4	—	11
30's . . .	62	48	18	83
40's . . .	137	92	57	90
50's	119	82	103	111
60's, etc. . . .	37	27	80	68
	365	253	258	363

Members are, therefore, on the whole middle-aged.

(b) *Sex*. 11 Conservative and 13 Labour women M.P.'s were elected in 1959, 7 and 19 respectively in 1966.

(c) *Local-government Experience*. 122 Conservative and 130 Labour M.P.'s had such experience.

(d) *Education*

	Conservative 1959	Conservative 1966	Labour 1959	Labour 1966
Elementary . . .	6	2	92	80
Secondary . . .	52	18	60	93
Secondary and university .	44	29	59	124
Public school and university	174	141	42	62
Public school only . .	89	63	5	4
	365	253	258	363

[1] The 1959 figures are reproduced from *The British General Election of 1959*, by D. E. Butler and Richard Rose, by kind permission of the authors and Messrs. Macmillan. The 1966 figures are from *"The Times" Guide to the House of Commons*, 1966.

In 1959, of 263 Conservative M.P.'s who had been to a public school, 73 had been to Eton.

(*e*) *Professions*

	Conservative 1959	Conservative 1966	Labour 1959	Labour 1966
Lawyers . . .	86	70	37	54
Armed Services . .	37	19	3	3
Teachers . . .	5	4	36	72
Others . . .	39	24	22	27
	167	117	98	156

(*f*) *Business*

	Conservative 1959	Conservative 1966	Labour 1959	Labour 1966
Directors or managers .	88	57	6	17
Commerce . . .	22	16	8	13
Small business . . .	3	2	12	2
	113	75	26	32

(*g*) *Miscellaneous*

	Conservative 1959	Conservative 1966	Labour 1959	Labour 1966
Private means . . .	4	5	—	—
Journalists . . .	26	17	25	29
Farmers	38	27	3	2
Others	16	10	16	35
	84	59	44	66

(*h*) *Workers*

	Conservative 1959	Conservative 1966	Labour 1959	Labour 1966
(*Manual mainly*) . .	1	2	90	109

It will be seen, therefore, that Parliament is still mainly a masculine profession. A woman M.P. seldom attains Cabinet rank. Only one Conservative woman M.P. has become a Minister, but several Labour women M.P.'s have reached that eminence. On the whole, the Labour Party appears to attract and to favour the woman M.P. more than the Conservative Party.[1]

It has been said that, no matter what the subject, Parliament will always contain an expert on it. This is probably too sweeping an assertion, but the House of Commons does seem well qualified to deal with its primary task of legislating, thanks to the presence in the House usually of approximately a hundred lawyers. Education,

[1] There were six women in the Labour Government in 1966.

defence, local government, and industry (from both sides) are adequately catered for. It is also clear that, the Commons being in essence a middle-aged assembly, the average Member is likely to be a person of experience.

The broad conclusion can be drawn that the House of Commons is a fair sample of the people of Britain, reasonably well educated, not only in the academic sense, but also in the hard facts of life. It is still an assembly to which most people are proud to belong.

THE OPPOSITION

The Opposition in the Commons has been mentioned elsewhere, but it is worth while to state the functions of the Opposition specifically. They are:

(a) To direct a stream of constructive criticism at the Government, drawing the attention of the country to the weaknesses and omissions in the Government's policy, and suggesting alternative measures.

(b) To keep the Government on the alert and prevent it from becoming complacent, and therefore inefficient.

(c) To provide an alternative Government to the Government of the day which the electors can choose if they wish.

BIBLIOGRAPHY

CHESTER, D. N., and BOWRING, N.: *Questions in Parliament* (Clarendon Press, 1962).

HANSON, A. H., and WISEMAN, H. V.: *Parliament at Work* (Stevens, 1962).

TAYLOR, ERIC: *The House of Commons at Work* (Penguin Books, 1951).

JENNINGS, SIR IVOR: *Parliament* (Cambridge University Press; second edition, 1957).

MORRISON, LORD: *Government and Parliament* (Oxford University Press; second edition, 1959).

LAUNDY, PHILIP: *The Office of the Speaker* (Cassell, 1964).

RICHARDS, PETER: *Honourable Members* (Faber, 1964).

The Times: "The House of Commons, 1964."

CRICK, B.: *The Reform of Parliament* (Weidenfeld and Nicolson, 1964).

The Times: "The House of Commons, 1966."

CHAPTER IV

The Government

The need for a Cabinet. The way in which it works. Who is the Prime Minister and how is he chosen? The forming of the Cabinet. Relationship between the Prime Minister and M.P.'s. Dispensation of patronage. The Prime Minister and his party. The Prime Minister and the electorate. The Prime Minister and the Civil Service. The Prime Minister and the Crown. The Prime Minister and the Dominions. The burden on Cabinet Ministers. Do Ministers change posts too often? The Cabinet and the House of Commons.

"As far as I can see there is no great difficulty in government. A man must learn to have words at command when he is on his legs in the House of Commons. He must keep his temper; and he must be very patient. As far as I have seen Cabinet Ministers, they are not more clever than other people."

LADY LAURA STANDISH, *in "Phineas Finn," by Anthony Trollope*

The House of Commons provides a body of Members to form the Government of the day to carry on the day-to-day administration of the country. The Government is usually about a hundred strong. It consists of:

(*a*) The Prime Minister.
(*b*) The other Cabinet Ministers.
(*c*) Non-Cabinet Ministers.
(*d*) The Parliamentary Secretaries.
(*e*) The Whips.

THE CABINET

This body of a hundred is, however, too big to form a committee that can decide policy quickly and secretly, so from the Government is formed a smaller committee, called the Cabinet. The British parliamentary system is, therefore, as we have seen, one of Cabinet **government**.

A form of Cabinet government existed in George I's reign (and even before). He was more interested in Hanover than in England. He spoke English with reluctance, and found it difficult to maintain normal relations with Parliament; he was often in Germany and entrusted the affairs of government to Sir Robert Walpole, who carried them on with the help of a small group of Whigs whose political ideas were in harmony with his own.

The modern Cabinet began to take a more definite shape after the Reform Act of 1832. In 1834 Peel became Prime Minister, and he managed the country with a Cabinet of fourteen. He is supposed to have been acquainted with all the Government business of the day. The amount of such business was, however, small by comparison with that of to-day.

Disraeli, when Prime Minister in 1874, had a Cabinet of twelve. The offices filled were those of:

(a) First Lord of the Treasury (Prime Minister).
(b) Lord Chancellor.
(c) Lord President of the Council.
(d) Lord Privy Seal.
(e) Chancellor of the Exchequer.
(f) Home Secretary.
(g) Foreign Secretary.
(h) Colonial Secretary.
(i) Secretary of State for War.
(j) Secretary of State for India.
(k) First Lord of the Admiralty.
(l) Postmaster-General.

As Government business grew, so did the Cabinet grow, until in the early years of the twentieth century it consisted of twenty-two to twenty-four members. This number tended to be too large, because the Cabinet threatened to develop into a debating society, and it was difficult to find so many men who were not only of first-rate ability, but who thought on the same lines.

In the World War of 1914–18 Lloyd George, when Prime Minister, worked with a War Cabinet of five, but the circumstances were exceptional. Sir Winston Churchill, in the Second World War, had an inner War Cabinet of eight and a larger Cabinet of eighteen to twenty. He was emulating Lloyd George's method. Lloyd George's and Churchill's War Cabinets concentrated on the prosecution of the War, while the larger, outer Cabinets dealt with the ordinary affairs of the nation. Although in 1965 Mr Wilson had a Cabinet of twenty-three, the modern Cabinet tends to be from seventeen to twenty strong, and this appears to be the ideal number. It may seem odd that the Cabinet should have diminished in size, whereas the growth of Government business and of the Ministries has been enormous. Logically, the Cabinet should have grown as well.

The explanation of this paradox is that secrecy, collective responsibility, speedy dispatch of work, have all become more and more important, and they can best be achieved by a comparatively small Cabinet. Experience shows that a large committee tends to waste time in talk, because each member considers it to be his duty to speak on every subject. It becomes increasingly difficult to obtain agreement on policy. In consequence the progress of business is delayed. If there are serious differences of opinion Ministers' resignations are frequent, and Ministers who have resigned are apt to reveal Cabinet secrets.

The main principles on which the modern Cabinet works are therefore:

(a) The Prime Minister is the chairman and leader.
(b) The Cabinet must be large enough to tackle the work, but small enough to get that work done rapidly.
(c) Proceedings must be secret.
(d) There must be collective responsibility.
(e) Cabinet Ministers must, as far as possible, belong to the House of Commons—the Prime Minister in particular.
(f) The Cabinet is formed from Members of the party which has a majority in the House of Commons.
(g) The Prime Minister chooses and dismisses Cabinet Ministers.

The Cabinet has three principal functions. They are:

(a) To formulate the legislation which is placed before Parliament for approval.
(b) To control the executive on behalf of Parliament.
(c) To co-ordinate the work of the Government departments on behalf of Parliament.

This was the view of the Haldane Committee (1918), which was set up to examine the way in which the Cabinet system worked.

The Way in which the Cabinet works

Ever since 1916, when Lloyd George (then Prime Minister) converted the Secretariat of the Imperial Defence Committee into the Cabinet Secretariat, there has been a Cabinet Office. This office is in charge of all Cabinet papers. It prepares the agenda for Cabinet meetings and circulates the minutes of these meetings. It has a statistical section, which compiles the information upon which the Cabinet bases its policy. One of the Joint Permanent Secretaries to the Treasury was head of the Cabinet Office as well until 1962, when the offices were separated.

The Cabinet in normal times meets once a week. The meetings last about two hours. There is a great deal to be done at these meetings, so Ministers are expected to read in advance the papers circulated to them, and thus to cut down discussion to the minimum. Lloyd George once said that Ministers who speak for more than five minutes are a bore. The Ministers who are not actually in the Cabinet, but whose departments are under discussion, are called to attend the meeting while their business is being dealt with. They withdraw immediately afterwards.

The Prime Minister approves the agenda and determines the order in which the business is put down. He decides when a matter has been adequately discussed, and he then takes the sense of the meeting and summarizes the action which is to be carried out. There is never a vote. If the Cabinet is strongly divided the matter is usually referred to a committee of the Cabinet to produce a solution which the whole Cabinet can accept. The object is to keep the Cabinet united. The Secretariat takes the minutes and writes up the discussion fully, but never ascribes the arguments put forward to any Minister by name. This practice is designed to encourage free expression of opinion within the Cabinet, and at the same time to preserve secrecy. All Ministers receive the minutes, to make sure that if a Minister is required to take action he knows what that action must be, and he cannot evade his responsibility by saying that he was not aware of the decision of the Cabinet. It is the duty of the Secretariat to follow up the minutes and ensure that action is taken without delay. This has not always been the case. Before 1916 there were instances of Ministers who disagreed with a certain policy 'forgetting' to carry it out, and excusing themselves on the ground that they were not aware that the Cabinet had come to any decision. This sort of unbusinesslike behaviour was intolerable to a man like Lloyd George, and he reformed this method, or lack of method.

The proceedings in Cabinet are secret, and students of the Constitution are obliged to rely on the books which Ministers write or which are written about Ministers or monarchs long after the events described have taken place.

Foreign affairs are always taken first at Cabinet meetings, not only because they are of great importance, but because in these days of rapid communications they must be dealt with expeditiously. It is necessary as a rule for action to be taken and instructions to be given to Ambassadors before the Cabinet can be called. The Prime Minister and the Foreign Secretary must thus work very closely together. The Prime Minister receives copies of all Foreign Office papers at the same time as the Foreign Secretary. If possible, they consult each other. Except for matters of the greatest importance, however, the Foreign Secretary acts on his own initiative, and for this reason the Prime Minister must have complete confidence in his ability and discretion. In the case of affairs of great importance the Prime Minister must be consulted before action is taken. If possible, the Cabinet is told before action is taken, but as a rule the discussion of foreign affairs in Cabinet meetings is a recital by the Foreign Secretary of what has already been done by him in the name of the Cabinet. This practice sometimes imposes a strain on collective responsibility, but there is no alternative course. When the Foreign Secretary is away the Prime Minister acts for him. But it does not necessarily follow that when the Prime Minister is away the Foreign Secretary is his deputy. That task is usually assigned to the senior Cabinet Minister.

The Basic Principles of Cabinet Government

It used to be the case that the Prime Minister was *primus inter pares*—first among equals. This was the only way in which collective responsibility could be achieved. To-day, however, the facts that the Prime Minister chooses and dismisses the members of the Cabinet, that he is leader of his party, and that he is closely associated by the electorate with the success or failure of the Government have made him essentially the head of the Cabinet. The composition of the Cabinet must inevitably depend on his personal ideas. He will naturally gather round him not merely able men, but men whom he likes and who agree with his views.

The size of the Cabinet will depend partly on the circumstances of the moment, partly on the ideas of the Prime Minister. For instance, at one time the Ministers for the Army, Navy, and Air Force were all in the Cabinet. To-day they are omitted in order to reduce its size, but the Minister of Defence, a new office, is in the Cabinet to co-ordinate the needs of the three Fighting Services. As India is now independent, there is no longer a Secretary of State for India. He used to be one of the more senior and important Ministers. In 1959, in view of the importance of scientific developments, a Minister for Science and Technology was appointed.

Proceedings must be secret, for obvious reasons. To begin with, honest, frank opinions are vital if the Government is to succeed in formulating a wise policy that is generally accepted. This condition

C

cannot be combined with collective responsibility unless proceedings are secret. Moreover, much of the information on which the Cabinet works, particularly in foreign affairs, cannot be revealed for reasons of security. Nor can the intentions of the Cabinet be disclosed in anticipation of legislation, or there would be financial speculation of a disastrous nature.

The Cabinet must work as a team, otherwise legislation and administration cannot follow a consistent pattern. If a Minister disagrees with a proposal he is entitled to say what he thinks in private. Having done that, he must either accept the view of the majority of his colleagues or resign if he feels so strongly that he cannot accept the policy. Even if he resigns neither he nor the Prime Minister gives the impression of deep cleavage, if that can be avoided, because it is important not to make the country suspect that Government policy is sufficiently unsound for an able Minister to reject it. The country must have confidence in the Government's wisdom and capacity. Important examples of the working of this doctrine were the resignation of Mr Eden from Mr Chamberlain's Government in 1938 because he was unable to accept the Prime Minister's ideas on foreign policy; that of Mr Bevan from Mr Attlee's Government in 1951 because he could not accept the rearmament policy of the Government; and in 1958 that of Mr Thorneycroft, who wished to impose a rigid monetary control to cure inflation, but could not persuade the Cabinet to accept his views entirely. There are probably frequent differences of opinion, but they are not fundamental, so they are not made public and no resignations are involved. However, in 1966 Mr Frank Cousins disagreed with the Government's policy on wages, as well as their policy on Vietnam. He subsequently announced that he was unhappy in the House of Commons and intended to return to his trade-union work and give up his membership of Parliament.

As we have seen, the convention has generally been accepted that Cabinet Ministers ought to be Members of the House of Commons, so that they can attend in the Commons to answer questions, to defend their policies, to explain their estimates, to take responsibility for their departments. This convention applies particularly to the Prime Minister. For over fifty years all Prime Ministers have been commoners. The Ministers of the Crown Act, 1937, did, however, visualize three Ministers in the Lords, and it is usual nowadays to give these posts to Ministers without departmental responsibility.

Since the Cabinet cannot legislate satisfactorily unless it can rely on sufficient support in the Commons, it follows that the Cabinet must be formed from the party which has a majority in the

Commons. As long as party discipline is strict the Cabinet is assured that all its proposals will go through Parliament successfully, except for the occasional measure which is clearly unacceptable even to the Government's supporters, in which case a wise Prime Minister will shelve it. The Shop Hours Bill of 1957 is a case in point. It was dropped.

THE PRIME MINISTER

The head of the Cabinet is the Prime Minister. He is probably the most powerful man in the country, for four reasons:

(a) He chooses and dismisses the members of the Cabinet.
(b) He advises the Crown when to dissolve Parliament, and the Crown customarily accepts that advice.
(c) He is leader of the party which for the time being has a majority in the House of Commons.
(d) He dispenses patronage.

Furthermore, the Cabinet exercises great power over the House of Commons because:

(a) Almost all legislation must be sponsored by the Cabinet.
(b) The tightness of party discipline ensures that this legislation is passed by the House of Commons.
(c) The timetable and business of Parliament is controlled by the Whips, who in turn are controlled by the Cabinet.
(d) The information which is at the disposal of the Cabinet is far greater and more up-to-date than that available to any individual Member, or even to the official party in opposition.

Moreover, apart from the reasons already mentioned, the Prime Minister has considerable power over the Cabinet, which has developed since 1916 through changes in Cabinet procedure. These developments are:

(a) His control over the agenda of Cabinet meetings.
(b) His control over the actual meetings.
(c) His control over the Civil Service.
(d) His control over foreign affairs.

To sum up, the Prime Minister is:

(a) Head of the Cabinet.
(b) The sovereign's Chief Minister.
(c) Leader of the party with a majority in the Commons.
(d) First Lord of the Treasury.
(e) A member of the House of Commons.

By Royal Prerogative the Prime Minister is chosen by the sovereign, on whose behalf the Government is conducted. The sovereign opens Parliament and makes a speech saying what the Government intends to do in the session just opened. In practice, these powers of the sovereign are legal fictions. As a constitutional monarch, the King or Queen is in the hands of the House of Commons. If he or she behaved in an autocratic manner and flouted the wishes of the Commons as expressed by the leader of the party with a majority, this would be done only at grave peril. Unless there were an overwhelming mass of opinion in the country, dissatisfied and disillusioned with the two great parties, desirous of breaking up political stagnation and stimulating new ideas, willing, therefore, to support the sovereign in imposing his or her will upon the Commons, any true exercise of such prerogative by the sovereign would probably result either in a change in the succession to the throne enacted by Parliament or in the abolition of the monarchy.

The choice of a Prime Minister arises either after a General Election, when a new Government must be formed, or if, during the life of a Parliament, the Government of the day is defeated and resigns because the Prime Minister is no longer able to command a majority in the Commons, or because the Prime Minister desires to resign for personal reasons, such as illness. The sovereign must, by convention, invite the leader of the party with a majority in the Commons to form a Government. As a rule there can be no doubt who this is. For instance, in 1945 Mr Attlee was the acknowledged leader of the Labour Party, and in 1951, when the Conservatives won the election, Sir Winston Churchill was the undisputed leader of his party. King George VI had no problem. There have, however, been occasions when an apparent choice has been made.

In 1923 King George V was faced with a choice between Lord Curzon and Mr Baldwin. He chose the latter. The convention was thus established that the Prime Minister should be in the House of Commons, and it was re-established in 1940, when King George VI chose Mr Churchill, instead of Lord Halifax. The nation was at war, and, as usual in such circumstances, the Government was a Coalition. The Labour Opposition made it plain that they would not serve under a Member of the Lords, and that they would serve only under Mr Churchill. Lord Halifax gives an account of the matter in his autobiography, *Fulness of Days*. He records there that he considered that the appointment should be given to Mr Churchill because he (Lord Halifax) could not have a point of vital contact with Parliament in the House of Commons. The King's choice was, therefore, no choice at all. No other man was likely to command the support of the House of Commons.

In 1957 Sir Anthony Eden resigned because of ill-health. He himself had succeeded Sir Winston Churchill in 1955, when the latter resigned because he felt that he was no longer able at his age to bear the immense burden of his office. The Queen had no problem in choosing Sir Anthony. He was clearly leader of the Conservative Party. When he resigned, however, she was in a predicament, because there were two candidates. Most people presumed that Mr Butler would be chosen. The Queen was made aware, however, that Mr Butler might not be able to command a majority in the Commons. She consulted the elder statesmen of the Conservative Party, who must have advised her to choose Mr Macmillan. The Conservative Party a few days later vindicated her judgment by formally electing Mr Macmillan its leader. In a sense the Queen exercised a choice. In fact, however, she knew from the advice given her that only one man was acceptable to the Conservative Party as a whole, and she chose that man.

Perhaps the nearest approach to a choice was made in 1931, when King George V asked Mr Ramsay MacDonald to form a National Government at a moment of grave crisis. Britain, like the rest of the world, was in the throes of a disastrous economic slump. The nation was in danger of becoming bankrupt. The Labour Government of the day was in a minority opposed to the combined Conservative and Liberal Parties. There seemed to be an irreconcilable difference of economic doctrine between it and its opponents. So Mr MacDonald went to the King and offered to resign. The King, feeling that at such a moment of national crisis, the country ought not to be plunged into the turmoil of a General Election or involved in party conflict, advised Mr MacDonald to wait until he had discussed the situation with the leaders of the other two parties, Mr Baldwin and Sir Herbert Samuel. He consulted these two gentlemen, and they both agreed that a National Government, a coalition of all three parties, should be formed as a short-term measure to deal with the crisis, and they pledged their parties to support such a Government. They both undertook to serve under Mr MacDonald, and the King invited him to form a national administration, which he agreed to do. In due course his Labour colleagues charged him with betrayal of his party. They accused him of not having confidence in them and not trying to obtain their approval. They also charged him with having involved the King in party controversy. This, however, was purely a domestic party dispute. The facts seem to be that the King behaved correctly: he merely gave his Prime Minister advice. He encouraged him to stay at his post. He never at any time refused to accede to the Prime Minister's wishes. Not until Sir Harold

Nicolson's book of the life of the King, in writing which he had access to the King's private papers, did a full and accurate account of the negotiations appear, showing that the King behaved in a constitutional manner. So that although in a sense the King did exercise a choice on this famous occasion, in fact he was governed by the opinions of the three party leaders. If they had not agreed to unite in a Coalition he would have been obliged to choose the acknowledged leader of one of the parties. If all three leaders had refused to form a Government and advised a dissolution and General Election the King would have had to dissolve Parliament.

In 1942, when the Prime Minister, Mr Churchill, was obliged to travel and expose himself to grave dangers, the King asked him to nominate his successor. In this way, in the unfortunate event of the Prime Minister's death, the King would be saved from becoming embroiled in party controversy. Mr Churchill recommended Mr Eden. In 1943, when Mr Eden also was forced to undertake dangerous journeys, the King asked the Prime Minister to nominate a successor to Mr Eden. Mr Churchill replied in writing, submitting the name of Sir John Anderson, an independent M.P., more likely than any other Member of the House of Commons to command the support of the House as leader of a Coalition Government.

The conclusions to be drawn, therefore, are that by convention:

(a) The sovereign chooses the Prime Minister formally; in fact, the choice must fall on the leader of the party which, for the time being, commands a majority in the House of Commons.

(b) If in any doubt the sovereign must take advice and, above all, avoid becoming involved in party controversy.

(c) The Prime Minister must be a member of the House of Commons, where he can answer in the popularly elected assembly for the policy of his Government.

The Choice of Cabinet Ministers by the Prime Minister

Once he has accepted office the Prime Minister's first task is to form a Government, choosing his Ministers on these principles:

(a) They must be from his party.
(b) They must be willing to carry out his general policy.
(c) Three of them must be in the House of Lords.
(d) They must be likely to work well as a team.

He will probably appoint the most important Ministers first—say, the Foreign Secretary, the Chancellor of the Exchequer, the Home Secretary, and the Lord Chancellor. He will probably discuss the composition of the Cabinet with them, though he will in the end make his own decisions. He asks the potential Ministers to come and see him, tells them the broad line of policy he intends to follow, offers them a Ministry, and, if they are willing to serve, there is usually an exchange of letters. If one of the people he wants is unable to accept his general policy, then this is the time for that candidate for office to say no, because once he is in the Cabinet he must carry out the doctrine of collective responsibility.

There are only two statutory references specifically to the Prime Minister: one is in the Act which accepts Chequers as his country residence, the other in the Ministers of the Crown Acts, 1937 and 1965, which lay down how many Ministers receive Cabinet Ministers' salaries, which Ministers shall be eligible for these salaries, and stipulate that three Ministers at least shall be in the House of Lords. As we have seen, however, the Prime Minister is not bound to have a Cabinet of a certain fixed size. He decides the size of his Cabinet according to his own views and in accordance with the experience of his recent predecessors. For example, in 1967 the Cabinet was as follows:

(a) Prime Minister.
(b) Deputy Prime Minister and Foreign Secretary.
(c) Secretary of State for Economic Affairs.
(d) Chancellor of the Exchequer.
(e) Lord President of the Council and Leader of the House of Commons.
(f) Lord Chancellor.
(g) Secretary of State for Defence.
(h) Home Secretary.
(i) Commonwealth Secretary.
(j) Secretary of State for Scotland.
(k) Secretary of State for Education and Science.
(l) Secretary of State for Wales.
(m) Lord Privy Seal and Leader of the House of Lords.
(n) President of the Board of Trade.
(o) Minister of Labour.
(p) Minister of Housing and Local Government.
(q) Minister of Agriculture, Fisheries, and Food.
(r) Minister of Transport.
(s) Minister of Power.
(t) Minister of Technology.
(u) Minister without Portfolio.

The Prime Minister keeps the size of his Cabinet to the minimum because, as has been said, the fewer Ministers there are, the more likely is he to get complete agreement among them on policy.

As Ministers are usually men of personality and ideas, they may have differing views on many problems. It is generally possible to reconcile these differences; but if the number of Ministers is large there are much more likely to be irreconcilable differences between them, and also incompatibilities of temperament.

The Prime Minister, having kept his Cabinet to the minimum size, must arrange for the administration of the country to be carried on satisfactorily. He does this by the following means:

(a) Appointing Cabinet committees to consider matters on which the Cabinet as a whole needs advice and to recommend a policy. If three or four committees are at work at the same time a great deal of Cabinet time is saved.

(b) Having two or three Ministers-without-Portfolio, who have no departmental responsibilities and can therefore concentrate on the completion of committee work.

(c) Nominating Junior Ministers, who are not in the Cabinet, to serve on Cabinet committees, thus giving them valuable experience and training them for future promotion.

(d) Circulating papers giving as much information as possible concerning matters on the agenda of Cabinet meetings, so that Ministers will consider these matters in advance, talk them over informally, perhaps, and be able to give their opinions at the meetings without wasting time on discussion and the asking of questions.

When the Prime Minister decides that he wishes to dismiss a Minister, or if a Minister wishes to resign, there is usually a polite exchange of letters, which are almost always published. A Minister who refuses to resign after it has been made clear to him discreetly that he is wanted to do so would be dismissed, but as a rule he takes the chance given to him to resign gracefully. The resigning Minister is thus spared as much embarrassment as possible.

THE PRIME MINISTER AND M.P.'s

To-day Members are reluctant to hazard their seats by exposing themselves to the ordeal of a General Election, and they are anxious, if they can, to have a 'safe' seat. In consequence, the Prime Minister, when threatened with a revolt, will generally compel submission by talking of a dissolution of Parliament. This course means an election, and at such an election a candidate who is not supported officially by a party would be most unlikely to win. A candidate who has displeased the Prime Minister will not be supported. In fact, he will probably be opposed by an 'official' candidate, and will most certainly not be proposed for a 'safe' seat. M.P.'s are therefore only too willing to do what the Prime Minister asks, except in some unusual emergency.

THE DISPENSATION OF PATRONAGE

The Honours Lists are the military and civil awards approved by the Queen at New Year and on her official birthday, and on other special occasions. In making the awards, the Queen is guided by the Prime Minister, and it is perhaps only natural that those who accept and carry out his policy are rewarded by an honour. Politics, however, play only a small part in the dispensation of patronage, and many people are honoured for their services to science, the arts, sport, etc. Mr Wilson has departed a little from the usual and has honoured men for services to industry and export, to local government, to trade unions, to public corporations, and to education. The Prime Minister also advises the Queen on the giving away of important appointments, such as the Governorships of Colonies or the Chairmanships of Royal Commissions. There are many able men who seek these appointments for a variety of reasons.

THE PRIME MINISTER AND HIS PARTY

The Prime Minister is always leader of his party. There are some interesting points in this connexion, points of difference between the parties.

The Labour Party in Parliament—*i.e.*, all those Members of the Lords and the Commons who take the Labour Party Whip—meet together at the start of each parliamentary session and elect a leader of the Parliamentary Labour Party. According to them, this is a democratic way of conducting things, because the leader must submit himself to re-election each year, he must hazard opposition, he must keep the support of his colleagues, he cannot afford to be a despot. Moreover, the sovereign is left in no doubt as to who the leader is, and will not be embarrassed when having to invite the leader of the party to become Prime Minister: it is quite clear on whom the choice must fall.

The Conservatives, on the other hand, do not ask their leader to stand for re-election annually. Once the leader has been elected, he remains leader until he dies or retires. No doubt the party would remove him if he proved to be absolutely incompetent and was threatening to ruin it. Moreover, the leader is not elected by Members of Parliament only, but by prospective candidates and representatives of the party unions throughout the country. This means the assembling of some 1500 people representing the whole national party, which the Conservatives claim to be a more democratic way of doing things than the Labour method. Normally the Conservatives have an acknowledged leader; there is no need to elect one. If the sovereign had to choose a Prime Minister there would be no doubt whom to invite. But if this leader resigns from office during the life of a Parliament there must be no Prime Minister until a new leader is chosen, as the sovereign must choose the person who will probably be leader, and he is subsequently elected. In 1957 the Labour Opposition claimed that the Conservatives had involved the Queen in a party dispute by forcing her to choose between Mr Butler and Mr Macmillan. The resignation of Sir Anthony Eden had left the party for the time being without a leader. The Conservatives affirmed that the Queen was advised quite clearly what to do. The Parliamentary Labour Party thereupon held a special meeting, at which it passed a resolution that if its leader were ever in the future to die or resign during the life of a Parliament, it would at once elect his successor in order not to embarrass the Crown in any way.

THE PRIME MINISTER AND THE ELECTORATE

The Prime Minister in the eyes of the public is the Government. Nowadays he is able to impress his personality upon the electorate through the media of the radio and television. It is no longer necessary for him to tour the country, as Mr Gladstone once did. He can speak to the whole nation on one evening on the television screen. This, of course, is a two-edged weapon. The Prime Minister can destroy his popularity completely if he fails to make a good screen impression. A quiet, confidential manner with no irritating, distracting mannerisms, a pleasant voice with no oratorical tricks, a reasonably engaging appearance, the ability to state his case simply and clearly, will establish him as a man of common sense and integrity. The mass of the people tend to vote for a person and a leader, rather than for an ideology, or a party, or a group of candidates, or even a programme. They may not accept a platform loaded with flattery and fair promises. Sir Winston Churchill's reputation as a great Englishman capable of piloting his country through the perils of a possible nuclear war, and of throwing off the shackles of the economic controls imposed by the Labour Party, probably won the 1951 election for the Conservatives. Sir Anthony Eden's reputation as an expert on foreign affairs, a man of peace, but also a man of courage, who would not be afraid to stand up for his opinions in the public interest, probably won the 1955 election. In the 1959 General Election the electors were probably much influenced by Mr Macmillan's efforts to ensure world peace and his ability to represent Britain at a possible Summit Conference.

The idea of 'Summit' meetings between heads of Governments only has become a crucial point in foreign affairs. If international disputes can be settled only by a meeting between the Prime Ministers of Britain and Russia, and the Presidents of the United States and France, then the person who is to be Prime Minister must clearly have a decisive influence on the result of an election.

THE PRIME MINISTER AND THE CIVIL SERVICE

Since the inception of the Cabinet Secretariat its head (who is also the head of the Civil Service) and the Prime Minister keep in very close touch. Promotions to the senior posts in the Civil Service are settled in consultation with the Prime Minister, and only with his consent. As the Administrative grade of the Service is its dominating part, its brain, its thinking and directing centre, the Prime Minister has thus a great influence over it. Senior civil servants will not lightly damage their prospects by opposing him unnecessarily.

THE PRIME MINISTER AND THE CROWN

The Prime Minister is the sovereign's chief Privy Councillor. It is his duty to see that the sovereign is kept fully informed of affairs and receives all the relevant papers. He used, at one time, to write regularly once a week to inform the sovereign of what had happened during the week. During the War Mr Churchill lunched with the King once a week and told him personally what was happening, and no doubt heard the King's views. No letters were written, except on special occasions. The regular luncheon has become a convention. The sovereign thus has a frequent opportunity to ask the Prime Minister questions, to express opinions, and to take a discreet part in affairs. This intimate contact with the Crown helps to build up the Prime Minister as the most powerful man in the land. More is said about this in Chapter VII on the Crown.

THE PRIME MINISTER AND THE DOMINIONS

Now that the British Commonwealth consists of an ever-increasing number of self-governing Dominions the relations between the Prime Minister and his opposite numbers have grown greatly in importance. They are in constant touch with one another, and meet at regular intervals. With his advantages of representing the Mother Parliament, he has the moral leadership of this group of leaders. If he uses his opportunities he can establish himself as a truly great man, an architect of Commonwealth unity. He can equally be a disintegrating force.

THE BURDEN ON CABINET MINISTERS

In our modern society, living in a troubled world, oppressed by the fear of atomic war, existing in a state of cold war, worried by economic ills, the burden resting on Cabinet Ministers is extremely heavy. In the case of the Prime Minister and the Foreign Secretary this burden is almost intolerable.

Sir Anthony Eden, a sick man, it is true, was obliged to resign from office because of the immense strain which the 'Suez Incident' had imposed upon him. Ernest Bevin found the burden of the Foreign Office a heavy one, and he, alas, died in office, refusing to spare himself. In a debate in 1958 on the circumstances in which the U.S.A. had sent troops into Lebanon, and Great Britain troops into Jordan, the Prime Minister, Mr Macmillan, told the House that he had never in his life had to make so difficult a decision. He knew that, in trying to keep the peace of the world, he had to be bold, but that the risk he had to take was that he would provoke a disastrous war. For two days he had been making up his mind to take action which might precipitate Britain into a nuclear war, whereas, if he did nothing, murderous anarchy might spread throughout the Middle East, and the Western democracies would be in grave danger of having their vital supplies of petrol cut off. In the course of the debate Emanuel Shinwell, a senior member of the Opposition, said that he appreciated the great responsibility resting on the Prime Minister, and would therefore do nothing to embarrass him. Not only do Ministers work a very long day, but the work has such fateful consequences for so many people that they must be under an almost unbearable strain.

We are indebted to Lord Morrison of Lambeth for an account of his day as a Minister. The Minister usually arrives at his office at about 10 A.M., reads his official papers, and then has his daily meeting with his Junior Minister and senior civil servants, at which all those present give the latest information at their disposal, and the Minister lays down his policy, answers questions, gives directions. After lunch he has to be in the House of Commons quite frequently in order to answer questions, though this is a task that he will in future hand over to his junior more and more. After Question Time there may be a debate in which he has to speak and to vote, a committee which he has to attend, a public meeting at which he is expected to speak (and is naturally assumed to be speaking for the Government); in the evening there may be a dinner at which he is the principal speaker. All through these activities he is haunted by the spectre of a harassed messenger hunting him with urgent dispatches. At the end of the day he will be presented with several boxes of official papers that have come up during the day, which he takes home with him. And, if Lord Morrison's account is characteristic, he sits up in bed and works at those persistent papers, which have an apparent tendency to grow. Eventually Nature must be obeyed, and he allows himself to snatch a few hours of sleep. In the morning the round begins again. Nor can he obtain much relief during a parliamentary recess or at week-ends. As a Minister, he must ensure that the day-to-day administration of the country goes on efficiently, that his constituency is nursed, that the party flag is kept flying at public meetings, that the many people who wish to see him are interviewed and sent away happy, if possible. There are conferences overseas to attend, such as a U.N.O. meeting in New York or an economic conference in Ottawa, a European congress at Strasbourg, a S.E.A.T.O. meeting in Colombo. At the best he manages to get a few weeks' genuine holiday, though even then his telephone number must be known at the Ministry, in case they wish to get in touch with him in a hurry. After all, history tells us that foreign affairs have a habit of erupting unpleasantly at week-ends. Foreigners persist in ignoring the admirable English Sunday!

Lord Strang has spoken of the qualities that he thinks a Foreign Secretary must have to be able to bear his heavy burden. Judging by him and other authorities, these qualities are:

(a) The strength and constitution of a horse.
(b) The strength of mind not to worry.
(c) The capacity to work twenty hours a day.
(d) The ability to eat or drink at all hours of the day.
(e) The habit of snatching a few moments' sleep whenever possible, relaxing completely.
(f) A sense of humour capable of sustaining daily rebuffs and criticism.
(g) Almost unlimited patience.
(h) The phenomenal memory of the elephant.

In short, he must be a very remarkable man. Lord Strang has given us a vivid picture of Ernest Bevin at work, showing us how this remarkable man, self-made, comparatively uneducated, was never-theless one of the greatest of British Foreign Secretaries. Mr Bevin was never too busy to see his subordinates and help them, if he could. He had a clear policy. He was willing to listen to the other side of the case. He trusted his subordinates. He backed them up loyally. Therefore they backed him up in turn. Mr Bevin was, of course, an exceptional man, but Prime Ministers are looking for exceptional men to put into the Cabinet, and in a nation of fifty-one million people with a political genius they ought to be able to find them.

Do Cabinet Ministers change their Jobs too frequently?

Right up to the comparatively recent past Cabinet Ministers have been specialists, whether in office or in opposition. Sir Anthony Eden, for instance, concentrated on foreign affairs for almost the whole of his career. He was a great and acknowledged expert on the subject. Lord Morrison of Lambeth specialized in home affairs and local government. Going much farther back, Lord Palmerston was a great Foreign Secretary who spent a large part of his career at the Foreign Office. A more recent instance is that of Lord Monckton's long and successful tenure of the Ministry of Labour.

In view of the massively onerous duties that fall on a Cabinet Minister, he cannot be expected to carry them out unless he knows a great deal about them. During his political career, on the way up to office from being a humble back-bencher, he will inevitably have acquired a wide general knowledge of political affairs. He will also have shown a preference for one kind of work. He will have a talent for this office rather than that one. According to the theory of the division of labour, specialization is the main reason for efficiency. A Member with ambitions to be a Minister must make up his mind which office he will aim at, and pursue that end resolutely. Other-wise he might possibly be at the mercy of his permanent Civil Service advisers. The object of the Alternative Government with its Shadow Cabinet, the members of which concentrate on different subjects, is to reap the fruits of specialization.

It has been suggested that Ministers have been in the habit of changing jobs too frequently. If that charge were true Cabinet government would deteriorate. Perhaps too much is made of the many reshuffles of the Conservative Governments since 1951. These have been due to the resignations of Sir Winston Churchill and Sir Anthony Eden during the lifetime of a Parliament. There have been disagreements on policy which have resulted in resigna-tions, such as that of Mr Thorneycroft. There have been profound differences of opinion on defence policy, which is scarcely surprising in a nuclear age, when the swift march of science renders modern weapons obsolete overnight and entails the recasting of strategy completely at short intervals. Ministers are found wanting at certain jobs; they can do others better. However carefully a Prime Minister picks his Cabinet Ministers, he is still human, and so are they. He is bound to make some mistakes of selection. The task facing a Minister in a complex society is a most difficult one, and from time to time a Minister finds his work too much for him. There is nothing to be gained by clinging obstinately to the same team of Ministers despite changing circumstances. The Prime Minister must watch the situation vigilantly and use his discrimination when to make a change. He must not, however, make changes unnecessarily. He must encourage potential Ministers to specialize. He must build up a team. But he must also be ready to alter the composition of that team from time to time.

THE RELATIONSHIP BETWEEN THE CABINET AND THE HOUSE OF COMMONS

As we have seen, in theory the Commons is master of the Cabinet. In practice the Cabinet dominates the Commons. In a democratic system, in which the view of the majority must prevail, the Commons, with some five hundred Members not in the Government, ought to be master of a Cabinet of twenty and a Government of about a hundred. The Cabinet must command the support of a majority in the Commons, otherwise it will be defeated in debate, and if that defeat is sustained in a matter of first-class importance the Government will have to resign. Unless another Government can be formed from the existing House, and it can count on the support of a majority of that House, there will have to be a dissolution of Parliament and a General Election. If there were many such defeats the country would be constantly plunged into the uncertainty and expense of elections, and there would be no continuity or stability of government. Such a state of affairs would be disastrous: the prestige of the nation would be seriously damaged.

In the planned Welfare State the Government has an enormous amount of work to do. It must have a policy, which must express itself in a legislative programme. That programme must be carefully co-ordinated. Each Bill must be related to the others. Moreover, the policy cannot be expected to exercise a decisive influence in a day. It must be given time in which to take effect. The five years' period for which a Government is elected is a convenient one in which a constructive programme of legislation can be enacted and its influence felt decisively. The electorate can decide whether the Government has or has not been successful, and whether an alternative Government ought or ought not to be put into office.

Parliament is said to be overworked. There is very little time into which to crowd all that has to be done. There are about 144 days in a session, in which all the business of Parliament must be done. About forty days are usually taken up with the discussion of the Budget, the Estimates, and the Finance Bills. Up to eight days are generally devoted to debating the Royal Speech. Time has to be allotted to passing the annual Bills, such as the Consolidated Fund Bill, concerning which there is no dispute. The Opposition must be given the opportunity to raise and discuss matters of urgent public importance. In the end the Government is left with about forty days in which to enact its legislative programme. With time so short and so much work to be done, the Government must be sure of its majority in order to be certain that it will succeed in passing all its legislation. The Government—*i.e.*, the Cabinet—is therefore obliged to sponsor almost all the legislation which the House of Commons considers. Private Members' Bills are relegated to ten Fridays in a session, and even then, in an emergency, the Government may decide to use some of this precious time. Moreover, the Government decides what is to be discussed by Parliament, on what days such discussion will take place, and how long each discussion will last. It is true that by convention the Opposition is allowed to choose what parts of the Estimates it will criticize in detail. It is also true that if the Opposition wishes to debate a matter of urgent public interest, and to introduce a motion criticizing the policy of the Government, the latter will, by convention, always find time to meet the Opposition. Nevertheless, the Government is ultimately master of the timetable of the House of Commons.

The basis of the Government's control of the Commons is party discipline. The Prime Minister, as leader of his party, commands the strictest loyalty from his supporters. Members are nevertheless not the absolute slaves of the party. For example, the Conservatives have formed the 1922 Committee, to which only back-benchers belong when the party is in office. This forms unofficial committees to work on the matters which are occupying the attention of the country. It meets once a week, and a Minister is usually invited to attend each meeting in order to answer questions, justify the policy of the Government, and be told clearly what the attitude of the party is. These meetings are held in private. Rumours of what takes place circulate in the Press, but in general dissension in the party is concealed. If the opinions of the back-benchers are held strongly enough by a large number of them the Government will take serious notice of this attitude. It will reconsider its policy, will probably modify it, and may even drop a Bill entirely. It knows that Members are usually influenced by their constituents and by pressure groups outside Parliament. It will not recklessly lose votes in order to carry out a policy at all costs.

The Labour Party in Parliament meets at the beginning of each session to elect a committee, whether it is in opposition or not. It meets regularly in private, and its back-benchers express their opinions forcibly. Indeed, the party has a clause to the effect that Members must be allowed to vote in accordance with conscience. In general, the relations between the leaders and the rest of the party are the same as in the Conservative Party.

If the Government has a substantial majority the recalcitrance of a few supporters will not be taken too seriously. The obstinacy will be ascribed to conscience, and the rebellious ones will be forgiven. It is only when the majority is in danger that the Government must enforce party discipline strictly. It is hard to see a situation arising, however, in which the Cabinet will need to be so stern. The days when there was a large moderate body of opinion in the Commons, floating precariously between the Whigs and the Tories, are gone for ever. The Conservative and Labour Parties are much more deeply divided doctrinally. The economy of the country could not survive frequent and violent fluctuations of policy. Neither party can afford to give way an inch to the other. Rebellious Government supporters may, therefore, grumble and criticize in private, but at a pinch they will vote for the Government as the lesser of two evils. The ultimate disaster would be to let in the Opposition. There is to-day consequently no 'floating vote' in the Commons.

As we have seen, however, Members are moved to express strong feelings to the Government by pressure from their constituents or by a pressure group. For instance, a Conservative sitting for a Lancashire constituency will strongly criticize the Government's policy regarding cotton if that policy is likely to result in a contraction of the industry and unemployment among its workers. He will be subjected to a formidable barrage of propaganda from his constituents, and he knows that he will probably lose their votes if he fails to support their interests. On the other hand, he may honestly think that the Government is right, in which case he will go down to the constituency, meet as many people as he can there, and explain to them that what is happening is inevitable, and that some change in the pattern of industry must take place, that the Government will do its best to compensate businessmen and enable them to start in some other industry, that wage-earners will be looked after while they are seeking new jobs.

This, of course, brings up the classic dilemma of the Member. Is he the representative of the voters or merely their delegate? If he is the latter he must vote as the local party committee tells him. If he is the former he will vote as his conscience and judgment prompt him. It is a dilemma very hard to resolve. There seems to be no doubt that if a constituency elects a man to represent it in Parliament the voters, in theory at all events, should regard the Member as an able, experienced man of affairs, the best man for the job, a man who can be trusted to adopt a sensible, patriotic attitude to the affairs of the nation. In short, they should give him their confidence. But nowadays it is probable that the voters do not see an election in that way. People to-day vote for a general policy. They are not looking for an independent Member.

To sum up, it seems clear that the electors vote not for an individual candidate, but for a party, and in particular for a party leader. The Cabinet containing that leader will inevitably, therefore, dominate the Commons. But if the Cabinet pushes its views too far, regardless of public opinion, then the rank and file of the party, with their seats in jeopardy, will rebel, and the electorate will take their revenge at the next General Election. That is the ultimate sanction against excessive Cabinet dictatorship.[1]

BIBLIOGRAPHY

JENNINGS, SIR IVOR: *Cabinet Government* (C.U.P.; third edition, 1959).
CARTER, B. E.: *The Office of Prime Minister* (Faber, 1956).
MACKINTOSH, JOHN P.: *The British Cabinet* (Stevens, 1962).
DAALDER, H.: *Cabinet Reform in Britain, 1914–63* (O.U.P., 1964).

[1] Mr Wilson in 1964 introduced several new ideas which can only be noted here because they may not become 'permanent' conventions. He appointed a First Secretary of State and Minister for Economic Affairs, and thus split up the handling of the economy between the Minister and the Chancellor of the Exchequer. He appointed a Minister of Technology, choosing Mr Frank Cousins, who was not at the time a Member of Parliament. He also started to create an intelligence branch, as it were, to help the Cabinet, who were not Civil Servants, by appointing Mr Balogh of Oxford and Mr Kaldor of Cambridge special economic advisers to the Government. He is obviously impressed by the importance of television as an influence upon public opinion. He has continued to make experiments. He has made important changes in the Ministry of Defence. He has published a list of Ministers in order of importance. When Mr Brown was at the Department of Economic Affairs he was First Secretary and Deputy Prime Minister. In August 1966 he became Foreign Secretary, but remained Mr Wilson's Deputy. Mr Wilson has said on television that the Cabinet is the power-house in the system, and the Commons can never recapture its control over the Government. Mr Wilson also thinks that a Prime Minister must keep his Cabinet together as a team. So the process of evolution continues.

CHAPTER V

The Party System

The rise of political parties. The Conservative Party. The Labour Party. Difference between the parties. The need for a party system. The significance of pressure groups. Education of the electorate.

We maintain that party is public opinion embodied, whether it represents the opinion of a majority or a minority; it at all events represents the opinion of a great section of the community. In this country, where the nation is divided into parties and where great results are brought about by public discussion . . . we arrive in times of change at the solution of controversies the most difficult. However fierce the controversial strife, however violent the agitation of the nation, still you will always find that when a question is settled by the legitimate influence of 'party,' which is in fact national organization, the nation is content and satisfied with the decision: and you seldom see a question so settled reopened.

DISRAELI, *speaking in the House of Commons on February* 20, 1846

British parliamentary government is based to-day on a two-party system. It is this two-party system which gives us the strong, stable, central Government which is its outstanding characteristic.[1]

There have usually been two major parties in the House of Commons. There were the Cavaliers and Roundheads, then the Whigs and the Tories, followed by the Liberals and the Conservatives. Between the two World Wars the Liberals began to lose and the Labour Party to gain ground. While this shift of power was going on there were three important parties in Parliament, and some consequent instability. After 1945 the Liberals lost further ground, and the contemporary party scene is still dominated by the Conservatives and the Labour Party.

Before 1832 Parliament was an assembly of country gentlemen, men of independent means and minds. They were not disposed to be slaves of the party Whip, or to be the servants of their

---

[1] That is to say that there should be two major parties which dominate the House of Commons. There may be, and usually are, other and smaller parties represented in Parliament.

constituents. They were not divided by any deep cleavage of economic or political ideas, and could be swayed by eloquent oratory or cogent argument in debate. The electorate was small. The need for party organization was comparatively small.

After 1832 the position changed radically. The Reform Act of that year, followed by a series of further reforms, vastly increased the electorate, and it became clear that if the parties were to win future elections they must nurse every constituency. In 1830 an M.P. represented about 350 voters; to-day he represents roughly 60,000. Registration associations were formed all over the country, and these had, as we have seen, two things in view:

(a) To ensure that all persons entitled to vote were on the electoral roll.

(b) To ensure that all voters on the roll were persuaded to vote.

In 1867 the National Union of Conservative Associations was formed, followed by the National Liberal Federation in Birmingham in 1877. Each of these central bodies was designed to organize its party branches in the constituencies. By now a third very important object had been added: to educate the electorate.

In 1924 and 1929 there was a Labour Government, but neither introduced Socialistic legislation, because both were minority Governments and neither had a long life. In 1945, however, the Labour Party came into its own, when a nation, tired by a long and destructive war, expressed a desire for a new order by returning it with a large majority. An immense programme of Socialistic legislation followed, and an entirely new situation had been created. The 1964 Labour Government promised some fundamental legislation.

The two main parties to-day are divided by a deep economic ideological gap. The Conservatives believe in private enterprise and the minimum of planning; Labour, on the other hand, favours public enterprise and the maximum of planning. The result of an election has suddenly become a matter of vital importance to businessmen. Trade and industry would be reduced to chaos if they were nationalized and denationalized by alternative Governments. The electorate has split up into two political camps of nearly equal strength. The need for strict party discipline and efficient organization has thus become imperative.

To-day the two parties are hard at work all the year round keeping their organizations ready for an election. Each party has a headquarters at Westminster; each has a branch in every constituency; each has a Member or prospective Member in nearly every constituency. Members are constantly arguing on the radio or on the television, 'putting across the party line'; they write in the national newspapers; their leaders make party broadcasts regularly; there is a flood of party literature. The electorate is thus subjected to an intensive and continuous political attack.

The idea of party discipline is not new. In 1872 the Earl of Shrewsbury said: "The duty of a soldier is obedience, and discipline is the great characteristic of the Conservative Union." In 1878 Disraeli said that "in the conduct of public affairs there is nothing more precious than discipline, and it is a great mistake to suppose that discipline is incompatible with the deepest convictions and even the most passionate sentiments." This conception of discipline has grown until to-day, as we have seen, M.P.'s are expected to vote exactly as their Whips tell them.

THE CONSERVATIVE PARTY

At the head of the party is the leader. The party has three parts:
- (a) The Conservative M.P.'s in Parliament.
- (b) The National Union of Conservative and Unionist Associations.
- (c) The party organization and Central Office.

In each constituency there is an association and an agent, who works directly under the Central Office.

The party holds an Annual Conference, generally in the early autumn, before the new parliamentary session begins. Usually about 3000 delegates assemble. The occasion is used to demonstrate the solidarity of the party and enthusiasm for the leader. Many resolutions are put forward, some of which may be critical of the party leadership. The leaders of the party in Parliament reply, and the leader himself attends at the end of the meeting, usually to receive a great ovation. Occasionally attempts have been made to unseat him. These have all been failures. If a leader is to be defeated it will be by the 1922 Committee. The Conference does not attempt to lay down a legislative programme. That task is left to the leader. Each constituency association has equal representation (seven) and equal voting rights.

The tasks of the National Union are:
- (a) To promote the formation and development of a Conservative Association in every constituency, and to foster thought and effort in furtherance of the principles and aims of the party.
- (b) To form a centre of united action and to act as a link between the leader and all organizations of the party.
- (c) To maintain close relationship with the Conservative Central Office.

The functions of the National Union are primarily deliberative and advisory.

The Central Council meets once a year. It consists of the leader, the Chairman, all Conservative M.P.'s and peers taking the party Whip, all prospective Conservative candidates, and representatives of the National Union and the constituency associations. It is this Council which elects the leader when one has to be elected.

The constituency association's tasks are:

(a) To provide an efficient organization in the constituency.
(b) To spread the knowledge of Conservative principles and policy.
(c) To secure the return of a Conservative M.P.
(d) To secure the election to local-government authorities of candidates approved by the association.
(e) To watch the revision of the electoral register.
(f) To keep in touch with neighbouring associations.
(g) To co-operate with party headquarters.
(h) To raise adequate funds.

The party has about 3,000,000 members. The association committee consists entirely of amateurs, and it relies on amateurs to do its work. Women members are particularly active in this way. There is one professional—the agent. His job is:

(a) To see that the Member is well known.
(b) To keep him informed of all political activities in the constituency.
(c) To arrange for him to attend all important local meetings.
(d) To see that his speeches and activities are reported in the local Press.
(e) To inform him of local matters requiring his attention.
(f) To arrange for him to meet electors who wish to see him.
(g) To relieve him of as much routine work as possible, so that he can spend his scanty time locally to the best advantage.

At one time the candidate was expected to find funds for the party. To-day the party finds funds for the M.P. This makes it difficult for the Member to carry out Burke's dictum:

> Your representative owes you not his industry only but his judgment; and he betrays instead of serving you if he sacrifices it to your opinion.... Authoritative instructions which the Member is bound to obey blindly and implicitly, though contrary to the clearest convictions of his judgment and conscience, are utterly unknown to the laws of the land, and against the tenor of our constitution.

Sir Winston Churchill in 1945 spoke of the importance of the local workers as follows:

> The prime thing I have to say is that party organization must begin from the bottom. In every ward, in every village, in every street, we must have a stalwart band of men and women who are convinced and active workers for our party, and who know what to say and how to bring their influence to bear upon all the issues. Once you have ardent partisans in any locality, it will be easy to build up a structure which will give these leading men and women an even more effective share in inspiring the policy of the party and help them to make a lively and vigorous contribution to the guidance which they will receive from the summit of the party.

The leader has enormous power in the party for the following reasons:

- (*a*) Once he has been elected he is not required to submit himself periodically for re-election.
- (*b*) He is not asked to submit a report.
- (*c*) He chooses his own Ministerial colleagues.
- (*d*) He has the sole responsibility for formulating the policy and the electoral programme of the party.
- (*e*) The resolutions of the Annual Party Conference are conveyed to him, but are not binding on him.
- (*f*) The party Central Office is his personal machine, because he appoints all its principal officers.

Nevertheless, it is leadership by consent. We know this from the fate of Neville and Austen Chamberlain and of Arthur Balfour, who were all driven from the leadership.

THE LABOUR PARTY

The Labour Party also has at its head a leader. He is not, however, necessarily the leader of the Labour Party as a whole, but the leader of the Parliamentary Labour Party only—*i.e.*, of all those M.P.'s and peers currently taking the party Whips.

The Conservative leader is given advice and opinions from the party, but he is not bound to act on what is put before him. On the other hand, the leader of the Labour Party in Parliament is obliged to act in accordance with the policy agreed on at the Annual Party Conference, which is held, generally, just before the new session of Parliament begins. As has been said, the Labour Party claims that its method is the more democratic one.

The Labour Party Conference is usually attended by about 1000 people. According to the official party publication, *The Rise of the Labour Party*:

> The final word rests with the annual Party Conference, and between conferences the National Executive Committee is the administrative authority. The Parliamentary Party carries through its duties within the framework of policy laid down by the annual Party Conference, to which it reports each year. The Parliamentary Party has no power to issue orders to the National Executive, or the Executive to the Parliamentary Party. Both are responsible only to the Party Conference.

The leader of the Parliamentary Labour Party must therefore attend the Conference and report to it. The Conservative leader is not bound to attend his Conference, and rarely does so. He goes to the Mass Rally immediately after the Conference is over in order to give an excuse for the party to show its solidarity and enthusiasm. It would be a mistake to interpret the above passage too literally, however. The Parliamentary Labour Party leader and his front-benchers, who are all experienced parliamentarians, well-known public figures, experts in the arts of debate and persuasion, do not accept the views of the Conference passively. They argue, and more often than not they win.

The Conference is made up as follows:

(*a*) Each trade union may send one delegate for every 5000 members.

(*b*) Constituency parties may send one delegate for every 5000 members.

(*c*) If there are at least 2500 women members an additional woman delegate may be sent.

(*d*) Each Central Labour Party or Federation may send one delegate.

(*e*) About 200 *ex officio* members drawn from:

    (i) The National Executive Committee.

    (ii) The Parliamentary Labour Party.

    (iii) Prospective candidates whom the National Executive Committee have adopted.

    (iv) The Secretary of the Labour Party.

    (v) The Chairman and one delegate of the Labour League of Youth.

The local agents may attend as a courtesy.

As at the Conservative Conference, many resolutions are submitted on a variety of subjects. There is much discussion. The leaders of the Parliamentary Labour Party and the Trade Union

Congress make the important speeches, and a general policy is agreed on for the Parliamentary Labour Party to follow.

The National Executive Committee consists of:

(a) The leader of the Parliamentary Labour Party.
(b) The deputy leader of the Parliamentary Labour Party.
(c) The Treasurer of the party (who is elected at the Conference).
(d) Twelve members of the trade unions.
(e) One member of the Socialist societies.
(f) Seven members of the constituency parties.
(g) Five women members, who may be nominated by any affiliated body and are elected by the Conference.

There are thus twenty-eight members, to whom one can add the Party Secretary, who now attends meetings, but is not allowed a vote.

DIFFERENCE BETWEEN THE PARTIES

The main difference between the members of the two parties is an economic one. The Conservatives are recruited mainly from the upper class and the wealthier middle class. The Labour Party depends mainly on the trade unions for its membership. The division, however, is far from clear-cut. There are many members of the middle class whom one would normally expect to be Conservative who are, in fact, Labour. To-day the Labour Party has its Lord Attlee (educated at Haileybury and Oxford). It has had its Sir Stafford Cripps (educated at Winchester and London) and its Mr Gaitskell (educated at Winchester and Oxford). The Conservatives, on the other hand, do get the support at elections of a large number of trade unionists—it is hard to say how many. The skilled craftsman is usually a conservative type of fellow, who respects the old, familiar ways of doing things, and who likes to be sure that a change is an improvement before he will support it.

Is a party system necessary? The answer is emphatically yes. If there were no parties the electorate would in the end be organized into one party, as in Germany and Italy before 1939, or in Russia to-day. This one party sooner or later becomes autocratic, permitting no opposition. Its leaders are ruthless, and eventually a dictator arises. On the other hand, as we have seen, if there are too many parties a weak, constantly changing Government is the result.

The British two-party system thus works well. It has the three advantages we have already noted:

(a) It provides a strong and stable Government.
(b) It provides an Opposition.
(c) It provides an alternative Government.

A party which takes office for five years with a substantial majority in the Commons and a well-disciplined band of supporters can undertake to carry out a legislative programme. Its policy will be consistent. It will be resolute because it has reliable support.

The idea of proportional representation, as we have seen, has one outstanding merit: it enables the views of minorities to be heard in Parliament. In a democracy the right to speak is a right of such importance that the problem of these minorities is one that cannot be ignored.

In a complex economic society like that of Britain there are bound to be many organized minorities. As long as they can make their views heard in Parliament through the parties they are content. Men have always been inclined to form societies. In Britain there are over 8000 Friendly Societies registered. Some of these societies form political pressure groups, which have become an important feature of a modern parliamentary system. They exert legitimate pressure upon Members of Parliament. Legislation is rarely introduced by the Government until after the Minister concerned has, through his departmental officials, consulted as far as possible all the interested groups and experts in the country, heard their views, considered their advice, and framed the Bill in the light of that knowledge. As long as the pressure groups can be assured of having their interests taken into account, as long as they can, either as a body or as individuals, have access to Members of Parliament, they will not feel any desire to form parties. Therefore the two great parties consist of groups within the parties, the members of these groups being drawn together by their common special interest.

Each of these groups has some particular interest, common to its members, which it wishes to promote. Each of these groups will look for, and will sooner or later find, at least one Member in sympathy with its ideas. That Member will take every opportunity of promoting the interest of the group in the Commons. He will be provided by the group with facts and figures to do so.

For instance, the National Union of Farmers is a very influential body. In the country districts the farmers are naturally interested in M.P.'s who will support a constructive agricultural policy. From the farmers' point of view that means a policy of subsidization, of tariffs against imports of food from overseas, of effective marketing arrangements. For strategic reasons in an age in which war is always a serious possibility a prosperous British agriculture is important. To the Conservative Party, which, by tradition, nearly always holds the country seats, the farmers' votes are essential. To the Labour Party, which must capture a few of the Conservative strongholds in order to win a majority in the House of Commons, the farmers' votes are almost as desirable.

The National Union of Teachers is another influential group, with a membership of over 200,000. Its views on education, and presumably on teachers, are always, therefore, heard respectfully by Governments.

The National and Local Government Officers Association, a very numerous body of people, waged a nation-wide campaign lasting many years to obtain compulsory superannuation for all its members. It tried to persuade candidates to say whether they would support a superannuation scheme if they were elected. In the end it made its presence felt to such an extent that the Government of the day asked it to end its campaign on condition that the Government passed a Bill acceptable to it, which was done in 1937. The Civil Service Association, another very large body, has conducted an equally vigorous campaign to get equal pay for men and women for equal work.

The trade unions are probably the biggest and most powerful pressure group. If they wish they can obtain economic and political ends by industrial means. They have said that they will work with the Government of the day regardless of party. They have certainly shown praiseworthy restraint at moments of crisis. Because of a sense of responsibility, and perhaps fear of the monster which they have created, they have not so far abused their enormous potential power. But every year, before the Budget, they call on the Chancellor of the Exchequer to acquaint him with their ideas on the economic position. When the bus strike of 1958 threatened to become a general strike they asked for an interview with the Prime Minister to see whether the policy of the Government could be brought into line with their own. They prevented a general strike because they knew this would be looked upon as an attempt by them to browbeat the elected Government of the people. They were granted a long interview by the Prime Minister to discuss British policy on Quemoy.

As has been said, there is an intimate association between the trade unions and the Labour Party. Their political aims are in close harmony. The trade unions put up some hundred and fifty candidates at General Elections, and a hundred or so are elected. These M.P.'s are professedly in Parliament to further the interests of the trade union movement. They meet regularly. So far, since 1906, they have all without exception been members of the Labour Party. Nevertheless, the Conservatives must live on good terms with the unions or they cannot hope to win future elections. It is known that a proportion of trade unionists vote Conservative.

There are, of course, a great many other pressure groups, such as the Lord's Day Observance Society, the Federation of Employers, and the Federation of British Industries. Few of them try to get individual M.P.'s into Parliament, but they most certainly keep in touch with M.P.'s who are in sympathy with their views, and it would seem that they are satisfied with this way of voicing their opinions in Parliament. This list of pressure groups is not, of course, comprehensive. It is intended to give the reader a fair impression of the significance of the pressure groups in contemporary party politics.

It is possible for Members on both sides of the House to come together on some special problem in which they are interested. For example, the question of parliamentary privilege. For some time certain Members have been very touchy about privilege. They have been inclined to regard any criticism of them individually as a criticism of Parliament amounting to a breach of privilege. Other Members deplore this sensitivity, because it could lead the House into arrogating to itself privileges that were unwarranted, privileges that would tend to make Members superior to other people. Consider the Strauss case, which will probably become a classic constitutional text-book case. Lord Morrison of Lambeth, on the Labour side, found himself in agreement with Sir Reginald Manningham-Buller, on the Conservative side. They found themselves in opposition to Mr R. A. Butler (Conservative Leader of the House) and Mr Hugh Gaitskell (the Leader of the Labour Party). The matter was debated. The House divided. The Whips were off. It was a free vote. Another occasion was the celebrated debate on the Prayer Book. A third example was the Bill for the Abolition of the Death Penalty, in which the sponsor, a Labour M.P., was supported by several Conservative Members.

EDUCATING THE ELECTORATE

Both parties spend much time and money on educating the electorate. In consequence it seems, as we have seen, that the voters tend to identify the party with its leader. It is worth considering, therefore, briefly the way in which leaders have imposed themselves, or been imposed, on the public mind.

Stanley Baldwin, the simple, honest Englishman, with his pipe and his bowler hat, his pigs and his love of cricket, was built up into the Englishman whom the country could trust. Neville Chamberlain, with his rolled umbrella, his prim appearance, his business as usual, his peace-at-almost-any-price policy, was seen by the electorate as the shrewd businessman who could keep Britain at peace, who would enable our economy to flourish by keeping us out of foreign entanglements.[1]

BIBLIOGRAPHY

MACKENZIE, R. T.: *British Political Parties* (Heinemann, new edition, 1963).

BULMER-THOMAS, IVOR: *The Party System in Great Britain* (Phœnix House, 1953).

JENNINGS, SIR IVOR: *Party Politics*, Volumes I, II, and III (Cambridge University Press, 1960–61).

BULMER-THOMAS, IVOR: *The Growth of the British Party System*, Volumes I and II (John Baker, 1965).

[1] The sudden illness of Mr Macmillan in 1963 precipitated a crisis in the Conservative Party, who after some mysterious exercises behind the scenes accepted Lord Home as Leader. He later renounced his peerage and was elected to the House of Commons as Sir Alec Douglas-Home after a very convenient by-election. In 1965, after much private discussion and public speculation, the Party decided to adopt a new method of choosing the Leader. This will be by means of a ballot run by the Chairman of the 1922 Committee in which Conservative members of the House of Commons will vote. To win the First Ballot a candidate must get an overall majority plus 15 per cent. more of the votes cast for any of his rivals. If a Second Ballot is necessary there will be new nominations, and an overall majority will be enough. In the event of a Third Ballot there will be a Preferential vote to ensure that one candidate will get a decisive majority. The new Leader must then go before a Party Meeting of M.P.'s, candidates, peers, and non-parliamentary members of the National Union Executive. The Conservatives will thus in the future spare themselves the pangs of 1963, and the Leader will have emerged democratically.

In January 1967 Mr Grimond resigned the leadership of the Liberal Party, and immediately afterwards the handful of Liberal M.P.'s met and elected Mr Jeremy Thorpe as his successor. The party still appeals to a large proportion of the electorate: it polled 11 per cent. of the votes cast in the General Election of 1964, but lost nearly a third of this support in 1966. It is too soon to say anything positive about the future of the Liberals as the Third Party in what is at present a Two-Party System.

CHAPTER VI

The House of Lords

The origin of the House. The Parliament Act, 1911. Reform of the House. Present powers of the House. Composition of the House. Present work of the House. The future of the House. Summing-up.

I think ... an institution of antiquity should require, if not reconstruction, if not new machinery, at least a slight readjustment and some repair.

I believe that an institution of this antiquity, however efficient and however popular it may be, cannot exist without some small occasional modification.

THE EARL OF ROSEBERY, *speaking in the House of Lords on June* 20, 1884

A Second Chamber ought to possess, if possible, the largest measure of moral authority. By moral authority I mean ... the influence exerted on the mind of the nation which comes from the intellectual authority of the persons who compose the Chamber, from their record in public life and from the respect which their characters and their experience inspire.

LORD BRYCE, *speaking in the House of Lords on March* 21, 1921

As we have seen, the British system of government is a bicameral, or two-chamber, one, the two chambers being the House of Commons, which is the first, or lower, House, and the House of Lords, which is the second, or upper, House.

The origin of the House of Lords goes back to the days when the Norman Kings met the great men of the realm each year in order to discuss the government of the country and how to raise money. Until the Reform Act of 1832 most of the members of the House of Lords were wealthy and aristocratic landowners. They knew one another well, and had common interests. Their sons and heirs were in the House of Commons, learning the arts of government. They were all well known to the sovereign, who had their support.

Through them the sovereign was sometimes able to influence the House of Commons. After the passing of the Reform Bill, and as a consequence of the Industrial Revolution, the political preserves of the landowners were invaded by the rich industrialists, who were being ennobled as a reward for their generous contributions to party funds. The House of Lords nevertheless remained staunchly conservative in character, an inevitable characteristic of an assembly the members of which were men of property, men who wished to preserve that property and pass it on to their heirs.

The history of the House of Lords is one of stern struggle between Lords and Commons until 1911, when a Liberal Government passed the Parliament Bill, which deprived the Lords of most of its power. Since 1911 there has been promised reform which somehow or other has never taken place, until in 1958 the Conservative Government of Mr Macmillan introduced three relatively mild reforms.

The Liberal Government introduced the Parliament Bill of 1911 because it found the existence of a permanent Conservative majority in the House of Lords intolerable, and because it considered that a hereditary assembly was not entitled to thwart the wishes of the elected representatives of the people. The Liberals' Budget of 1909 was rejected by the House of Lords by 350 votes to 75. Even after the passing of the Parliament Bill the House of Lords in 1912 rejected the Liberals' Government of Ireland Bill by 362 votes to 69.

The rejection of the Budget in 1909 was followed by the dissolution of Parliament. In the General Election the Liberals proclaimed their intention of reforming the House of Lords, and they asked the electorate for a mandate to carry out this reform. They were returned to office, and proceeded to initiate the Parliament Bill. The Prime Minister saw King George V and obtained a promise from the King that he would, if necessary, create enough peers to overcome the Conservative majority in the House of Lords and to carry through the Parliament Bill. The King consented to this extreme measure reluctantly, because he did not wish to make honours cheap. He asked the Conservative leaders in the House of Lords to come to see him. He pointed out to them the disastrous consequences to the Lords if they persisted in their opposition. He entreated them to give way in the national interest. His efforts were successful in that many members of the Lords abstained from voting against the Bill, which became law in 1911.

POWERS OF THE HOUSE OF LORDS AFTER THE PARLIAMENT ACT, 1911

The Preamble to the Act said:

Whereas it is intended to substitute for the House of Lords as it at present exists a Second Chamber constituted on a popular instead of hereditary basis, but such substitution cannot immediately be brought into operation.

This intention half a century later has still to be carried out. Nevertheless, the Act did substantially reduce the powers of the House of Lords. It provided that:

If a Money Bill, having been passed by the House of Commons and sent up to the House of Lords at least one month before the end of the session, is not passed by the House of Lords without amendment within one month after it is so sent up to that House, the Bill shall, unless the House of Commons direct to the contrary, be presented to His Majesty and become an Act of Parliament notwithstanding that the House of Lords have not consented to the Bill.

This meant that the House of Lords no longer had any power to interfere with the policy of the Government as far as finance was concerned. The Speaker of the House was in future to certify whether a Bill was a Money Bill or not. Such a Bill was defined in the Act as follows:

A Money Bill means a Public Bill which in the opinion of the Speaker of the House of Commons contains any provisions dealing with all or any of the following subjects, namely, the imposition, repeal, remission, alteration or regulation of taxation; the imposition for the payment of debt or other financial purposes of charges on the Consolidated Fund, or on money provided by Parliament, or the variation on appeal of any such charges; supply; the appropriation, receipt, custody, issue or credit of accounts of public money; the raising or guarantee of any losses on the repayment thereof; or subordinate matters incidental to those subjects or any of them.

The Act also severely curtailed the power of the House of Lords to delay legislation not primarily concerned with finance. It laid down:

If any Public Bill (not a Money Bill) is passed by the House of Commons in three successive sessions and is sent up to the House of Lords in each of those sessions, that Bill on rejection by the House of Lords a third time be presented to His Majesty and become an Act of Parliament provided that two years have elapsed between the date of the Second Reading in the first of these sessions of the Bill in the House of Commons and the date on which it passes the House of Commons in the third of these sessions.

This meant that the House of Lords could no longer delay a Non-money Bill for more than two years.

THE REFORM OF THE HOUSE OF LORDS

In accordance with the declared intention of the Parliament Act, 1911, a conference consisting of thirty Members of all parties from both Houses, with Lord Bryce as Chairman, met in 1917, and reported in the following year. The conference considered five possible methods of constituting the House of Lords, the hereditary principle having been abolished. They were:

(a) Nomination through the Crown on the advice of the Prime Minister.

(b) Direct election by large constituencies using proportional representation. This was unpopular because it might have produced a rival to the House of Commons.

(c) Election by local authorities grouped together in large areas for electoral purposes. This also was unpopular on the ground that local authorities should not be confused with national politics.

(d) Selection by a Standing Joint Committee of both Houses. This was rejected too.

(e) Election by the House of Commons using proportional representation, the country being divided into thirteen geographical areas for electoral purposes, so as to weaken the influence of party Whips.

The conference recommended a Second Chamber elected for twelve years, with one-third of the members coming up for election every four years. This gave two advantages:

(a) That a Second Chamber, while not suddenly changing as a whole under a momentary popular impulse, shall be kept in constant touch with public opinion.

(b) That it will always contain a number of members who have legislative experience and a mastery of public affairs by a service of some length in the House.

The conference had in mind a House of 327 members, 246 elected in the above manner and 81 elected from among existing peers by a Joint Committee of both Houses.

Nothing came of the Bryce conference. In 1948 the Labour Government of the day, like their Liberal predecessors in 1909, was finding the Conservative majority in the Lords an intolerable handicap. In addition, most Labour M.P.'s wished to abolish the

D

hereditary principle. So a conference of party leaders took place which reached a large measure of agreement. The meeting was prepared to consider the following reforms:

(a) The Second Chamber must be complementary, and not a rival, to the House of Commons.

(b) The revised composition of the Lords would ensure that there was no permanent majority for any party.

(c) The hereditary principle would no longer entitle anyone to membership of the reformed House.

(d) Members would be called Lords of Parliament.

(e) Women would be eligible for membership.

(f) Allowances would be paid to cover expenses of attending the House.

(g) Peers who were not Lords of Parliament could stand for election to the Commons and vote at a General Election.

(h) Members who failed to carry out their duties could be disqualified.

Once again the meeting failed to produce a reformed House, because the Labour Party and the Conservatives disagreed on the delaying power for Non-money Bills. The former wished to reduce the period of delay to one year, and the Conservatives would not agree. Instead, the Parliament Bill, 1949, was eventually passed. It was substantially the same as the Act of 1911, with one important exception: the delaying period *was* reduced to one year in practice.

In 1958 the Conservative Government of Mr Macmillan introduced three reforms. A Bill was enacted whereby members of the Lords were paid expenses, women could be elected to the House, and life peers, called Lords of Parliament, would be created. As a result the new Lords of Parliament, four of whom were women, took their seats. The Government was unwilling for the time being to abolish the hereditary principle, and proposed that all existing peers should be written to and asked if they intended to attend the House regularly, or if they wished to be regarded as purely passive members. It was expected that the majority of the eight hundred peers would prefer to stay away. They have rarely attended recently, and are popularly known as "the backwoodsmen." They have no special aptitude or liking for politics.

THE PRESENT POWERS OF THE HOUSE OF LORDS

The Bryce conference made a classic statement of the functions of the Lords. They are:

(a) The examination and revision of Bills brought from the Commons.

(b) The initiation of non-controversial Bills at the request of the Commons, which will have an easier passage there because they have already been fully discussed and put into good shape by the Lords.

(c) The delaying of a Bill long enough to enable the electorate to express an opinion on it adequately—a most important function when the Bill is one on which the people are evenly divided.

(d) Full and free discussion of large and important questions the Commons has no time to consider adequately.

These are still the functions of the House, apart from its work as a court of law. It could also be said that the Lords provides a refuge for senior members of the Commons who no longer wish to bear the strain and stress of an election, but of whose wisdom and experience the country ought not to be deprived. They themselves would be rewarded for distinguished service with a peerage.

The important things to remember are that the House cannot delay or discuss a Money Bill at all, it can delay a Non-money Bill for only one year, and it is the Supreme Court of Appeal in the Commonwealth.

COMPOSITION OF THE HOUSE OF LORDS

In 1966 there were:

> 853 hereditary peers of the United Kingdom.
> 16 Scottish peers.
> 127 Life Peers and Peeresses.
> 14 Law Lords.
> 26 Lords Spiritual.

The Law Lords and the Lords Spiritual do not make any claim to belong to a party. Of the others, approximately 400 were Conservatives, 50 Liberals, and 50 Labour in 1959.[1]

The following members of the Lords are the Lords Spiritual: The Archbishops of Canterbury and York; the Bishops of London, Durham, and Winchester; and the twenty-one senior English Bishops. The Law Lords are: The Lord Chancellor; the Lord Chief Justice; the Lords of Appeal in Ordinary (nine in number); and any ex-Law Lords.

Half the peerages in 1955 dated from 1906. The usual road to the Lords is through the Commons—i.e., a senior member of

[1] These figures have been taken from *Dod's Parliamentary Companion*.

the Commons is rewarded with a peerage. According to Sir Ivor Jennings, of the 137 peers created between 1922 and 1936, 74 came from the Commons, and between 1937 and 1956, 81 of 188 were from the Commons. Of the others, the choice of the Prime Minister has fallen on distinguished lawyers; scientists (for example, the late Lord Cherwell); doctors (for example, Lord Moran); diplomats (for example, former Ambassadors); retired civil servants; generals, admirals, and air-marshals (for example, Field-Marshal Montgomery). There have been about ten peers created annually, and, generally, they have been men of outstanding ability and character, leaders of their professions, and there has been little criticism of the appointments. Few, if any, of the awards have been political in the sense that they have been purely party promotions. The days when honours were sold for the benefit of party funds are now gone. The House of Lords is no longer an assembly of only aristocrats.

The Scottish peers meet at the beginning of each new Parliament and elect sixteen of their number to sit in the Lords for the duration of the Parliament. In 1957 there were 77 peers with Scottish titles, 44 of whom had English titles as well, and so were in any event entitled to a seat in the House. Since the Act of Union in 1707 there have been no new Scottish peers. Similarly, the Irish peers used to meet to elect 28 of their number, but to-day, there is no Irish peer in the House. An Irish peer can decide to stand for the House of Commons if he prefers to do so. Lord Winterton exercised this preference. When a bishop who has a seat in the House of Lords dies his place there is not taken by his diocesan successor. It is filled by the next senior bishop not in the Lords. The Law Lords are appointed by the Lord Chancellor in consultation with the Prime Minister.

THE PRESENT WORK OF THE HOUSE OF LORDS

The Leader of the House, by convention, is the Lord Chancellor. The proceedings of the House are run on more or less the same lines as in the Commons, except that they are less formal. The Royal Speech is always made in the Lords. Bills go through the same stages in the Lords as in the Commons. The assent of the Lords is necessary before a Bill can become an Act of Parliament. As we have seen, the Lords can, and does, initiate non-controversial Bills at the request of the Commons. For instance, in 1958 the Lords introduced the Kent County Council Bill. The work of the Lords as the Supreme Court of Appeal and as the Judicial Committee of the Privy Council is described in Chapter VIII.

In recent years the attendance in the House has usually been about forty, and about eighty peers have been in the habit of attending regularly to the work of the House. The quorum is three, compared with forty in the Commons. The difference is startling, and indicates why there is so much criticism of a House that seems unappreciative of its great privileges. The small size of the House numerically, when it is debating, results in shorter, more informal debates than those in the Commons. The speakers address their remarks to the whole Chamber, and not to 'the Chair.' Debates are seldom carried to a division. Usually a peer will raise a subject and make a speech about it. He will, by convention, 'move for papers.'[1] The debate follows. Then, as a rule, the request for papers will, by leave, be withdrawn. The point is that the matter has been discussed and the speaker is satisfied. It may well be asked what purpose is served by debates of this kind. They enable a question of importance to some section of the public to be brought to the attention of the Government, such as the rate of pension paid to retired officers. The standard of debate is usually high, because the speakers are well qualified to talk about the topics they choose to raise. Party discipline is not as strong as in the Commons because if the Government is defeated in the Lords this is not taken as a reason for resignation. The defeat may be irritating to the Government, and it may warn the Government that its attitude needs reconsideration. This position is typified by Augustine Birrell's classic comment that the Lords "represents nobody but itself, and has the full confidence of its constituents."

By convention the Law Lords do not vote in a division in which there is a party conflict, because it is important that a judge cannot be accused of prejudice in hearing a case in court. They will, however, speak on matters on which they may be justifiably regarded as experts, such as the abolition of the death penalty. Also by convention, when the House is sitting as a law-court only the Law Lords sit. If a person were impeached by the Commons the case would be tried by the Lords, but there has been no instance of impeachment since 1806. By convention, too, the bishops do not attend the House except on occasions when the matter under discussion is one on which their opinions are welcome and proper, such as the revision of the Prayer Book or the complicity of Archbishop Makarios in terrorism in Cyprus. Another convention is that a retiring Prime Minister shall be made an earl. Mr Asquith, Mr Lloyd George, Mr Baldwin, Mr Attlee, and Sir Anthony Eden all accepted earldoms. This is not only a mark of gratitude for their

---

[1] A conventional phrase which, if it means anything at all, is a request for the relevant documents to be made available to the House.

great services to the nation, but it enables these wise and experienced men to continue to give their services to the country. Sir Winston Churchill was one who broke this convention, it is said because he did not wish to prejudice his descendants' chances of entering the House of Commons.

The Future of the House of Lords

The future of the House is interesting because there is every indication that the Conservative Party really does wish to reform it. It has already introduced three reforms. As we have seen, it is the intention to write to all peers to inquire whether they wish to attend the House regularly or not. It is presumed that only about 100 to 150 peers will wish to take part in parliamentary proceedings. That would enable the Government of the day to nominate, or in some way secure approval by the Commons to add, about another 150 life peers, to bring the House to a strength of 300. The Labour Party is not in agreement with this proposal, however, because it strongly disapproves of the hereditary principle. Many Labour Members would like to abolish altogether the Second Chamber, which they regard as a rival to the Commons. By convention it has been the practice for the parties in the Commons not to tamper with the constitution of the Lords unless they are all in agreement. This convention may, perhaps, be broken in the near future.

The question thus arises as to whether a Second Chamber is necessary. In New Zealand it was abolished in 1951. On the other hand, the new Constitution in India deliberately included a Second Chamber. When the two parties in the Commons are deeply divided on economic policy there is always the possibility of hasty, controversial legislation. In that case the Second Chamber can serve a useful purpose by delaying such legislation until the electorate has had an adequate opportunity to consider the matter and make its opinion known. The Abbé Sieyès said that when the Upper House disagrees with the Lower it is obnoxious, and when it is in agreement it is superfluous. Sir Winston Churchill, however, whose views must always be treated with great respect, has wondered whether a Third Chamber might be useful in discussing economic affairs. About half the time of the busy Commons is spent in talking about trade and industry, finance and labour relations with management. The Government of the day takes an ever-increasing part in managing the national economy. The House of Commons is not merely busy; it may well lack the specialized knowledge required to debate economics. Why not, rather than have a Third Chamber, nominate to the Lords experts on economics, such as industrialists, trade-union leaders, university professors, to the number of, say, thirty? They would be well qualified to give the Commons valuable advice. They could be purely an advisory, rather than a legislative, body.

SUMMING-UP

To sum up, the House of Lords serves a useful purpose in helping an overburdened Commons.[1] That being so, the retention of the Upper House is worth while, and therefore its constructive reform is also worth while.[2]

BIBLIOGRAPHY

BAILEY, SYDNEY D. (ed.): *The Future of the House of Lords* (Hansard Society, 1954).

BROMHEAD, P. A.: *The House of Lords and Contemporary Politics, 1911–1957* (Routledge, 1958).

[1] In 1965 the Lords twice rejected Government proposals in one week. On one occasion it amended the suggestions of the Lord Chancellor to nominate Commissioners to deal with law reform for an indefinite period, and on the other occasion opposed a proposal to carry out retrospective legislation concerning war damages claimed by the Burmah Oil Company.

[2] Mr Wedgwood Benn when he inherited his father's title began a spirited campaign that ended with the Act of 1963 by which hereditary peers could renounce their titles for their natural lives and seek election to the House of Commons. Mr Benn stood for Bristol South East, was elected, but was refused permission to take his seat in the Commons so long as he was Lord Stansgate. He thus enlisted popular support as the underdog, and eventually a Conservative Government was responsible for the legislation which made him plain Mr Benn again. This Act also enabled Sir Alec Douglas-Home and Mr Quintin Hogg to return to the Commons and to seem to establish beyond argument that any future Prime Minister must be a member of the House of Commons where he can be responsible to the electorate. In the meantime Mr Wilson's policy has been to recommend the creation of Life Peers only, with the result that there are now well over a hundred of them in the House as a consequence of the Peerage Act, 1958, and the balance of power within the House is slowly changing. The Conservatives are still in the majority, but not overwhelmingly so. It will be time at the end of the 1966 Parliament to reconsider the position.

CHAPTER VII

The Crown

A constitutional monarchy. Functions of the Crown. Opening and closing of Parliament. Dissolution and summoning of Parliament. The choice of Prime Minister. The Crown above party. The fountain of justice and honour. Head of the Commonwealth. Encouraging, warning, and advising. Pomp and circumstance.

All the people took notice of it, and it pleased them: as whatsoever the King did pleased all the people.

2 SAMUEL iii, 36

In my judgment it is the duty of statesmen and responsible politicians in this country, as long as possible, to keep the name of the sovereign and the Prerogative of the Crown outside the domain of party politics.

H. H. ASQUITH (AFTERWARDS LORD OXFORD AND ASQUITH),
when Prime Minister, speaking on February 21, 1910

The British monarchy is constitutional. That means:

(a) The Queen's succession is settled by Parliament. Every time a member of the royal family is born or dies a change, if necessary, is made in the line of succession to the throne. The Queen is not in a position to choose her own successor.

(b) The Queen must be a Protestant, because that is the established British religion. She is Defender of the Faith. If she decided on conviction to become a Roman Catholic, for instance, she would have to abdicate.

(c) The Queen must do what Parliament advises. She has various prerogatives in theory, powers of enormous importance, but in practice she is obliged to take the advice of the Prime Minister. For instance, when Edward VIII wished to make a marriage which the Prime Minister regarded as unsuitable the King had to abdicate.

(d) The Queen must not be involved in political controversy. If she were she would immediately be accused of taking sides. If the side she chose happened to lose it would probably mean the end of the monarchy.

(e) The Queen's income is paid to her out of the Consolidated Fund, which has to be approved each year by Parliament. It is unconventional to criticize the Queen in the Commons, so that the allowances are not discussed. If, however, the Queen were to offend Parliament it would not be too difficult to imagine her allowances being reduced or cut off entirely.

The main functions of the Crown to-day are:

(a) To open and close Parliament.
(b) To dissolve and summon Parliament.
(c) To choose the Prime Minister.
(d) To be the Fountain of Justice.
(e) To be the Fountain of Honour.
(f) To be head of the Commonwealth.
(g) To encourage, warn, and advise the Prime Minister.
(h) To be the formal, ceremonial part of the constitutional machine.
(i) To recommend spending of public money to Parliament. Before a Minister can ask Parliament to approve the spending of money he must formally submit the matter to the Crown and present it to the Commons in the form of a recommendation from the Crown.

THE OPENING AND CLOSING OF PARLIAMENT

This prerogative could be of immense importance if the Queen were genuinely able to exercise it. In fact, the date on which Parliament opens and closes is fixed by Parliament itself. The Queen is merely required to attend the Opening Ceremony and to make the occasion one of great pomp and pageantry. She drives in the State Coach from Buckingham Palace to Westminster. The route is lined by the Guards, and she is escorted by the Household Cavalry. She is received on arrival by a guard of honour of the Fighting Services. Great crowds of people assemble to watch. It makes a colourful interlude in their lives. It stirs up emotion in them, and they feel a loyalty to the Queen. They feel a respect for the British system of government, which normally, perhaps, they do not think about at all. The Queen has accomplished something useful, because she has drawn the people's attention to Parliament.

As part of the Opening Ceremony she sits on the throne in the House of Lords, which is always crowded on this occasion. The Commons come to the Bar of the House in order to hear the Queen's Speech. That speech has, however, been written for the Queen by the Cabinet, and it contains a list of the legislation which the Government proposes to initiate during the forthcoming session. That it is the Queen's Speech is a legal fiction, one of those historic romantic conventions in which the Constitution abounds.

The Dissolution and Summoning of Parliament

In theory, the decision to dissolve Parliament is made by the Queen. In practice, she does so on the advice and at the request of the Prime Minister. Mr Wheeler-Bennett's book on King George VI, published in 1958, gives us two examples of this royal prerogative being exercised in the accepted constitutional and conventional manner.

In 1945, the war with Germany having ended, but not that with Japan, the Labour and Liberal Parties wished to hold a General Election. Mr Churchill, the Prime Minister of the Coalition Government, decided to defer to this point of view, and on May 23, 1945, he had an audience with the King, following a letter in which he explained the position. The King made a note that when he saw the Prime Minister at twelve noon he was unable to accept Mr Churchill's resignation, because he needed time for reflection. At 4 P.M. he again saw Mr Churchill, and on this occasion he accepted the Prime Minister's resignation, asked him to form a new Government from the Conservative Party (which had a majority in the House of Commons) in order that the administration of the country could be carried on, and then agreed to Mr Churchill's request for a dissolution of Parliament.

In 1951 King George VI again found himself in a difficult position. As a result of the General Election of 1950 the Labour Party was returned to power, but with a majority of only 8 over the Conservatives and Liberals. Because of the smallness of this majority a defeat for the Government was a distinct possibility, but the Conservative Party, the only alternative Government, would have had an even more precarious existence. The King therefore caused discreet inquiries to be made by his private secretary as to the constitutional position. He was informed that if the Government suffered an early defeat the King could refuse a dissolution until financial legislation had been enacted in order to pay for the administration of the country. Happily, the House of Commons behaved with traditional good sense, and the Labour Government lasted for nineteen months. Eventually, however, the situation became intolerable. Mr Attlee wrote to the King that "it was not pleasant to have Members coming from hospital at the risk of their lives to prevent a defeat in the House." This uncertainty was a cause of worry to the King, who raised the question with the Prime Minister, pointing out that the political instability would make it impossible for the King to carry out his planned visit to Australia and New Zealand. Mr Attlee, in reply, wrote to the King:

> I have been giving much anxious thought to the question of a General Election. Among the factors to which I have given particular attention was the need for avoiding any political crisis while your Majesty was out of the country. I have come to the conclusion that the right course would be to have a dissolution of Parliament in the first week of October.

A few days later the Prime Minister formally made his submission for the dissolution of Parliament, and the King approved.

This prerogative has probably been retained in case a Prime Minister, desirous of securing party advantage, should advise a dissolution for tactical reasons. In such a case the Crown could refuse to grant a dissolution, and would ask some one else to form a Government, provided that that other person had a chance of commanding a majority in the Commons. Mr Asquith said in 1923 that:

> It is not a mere feudal survival but it is part of our constitutional system, for which there is no counterpart in any other country. It does not mean that the Crown should act arbitrarily and without the advice of responsible Ministers, but it does mean that the Crown is not bound to take the advice of a particular Minister to put its subjects to the turmoil and tumult of a series of General Elections so long as it can find other Ministers who are prepared to give it a trial.

Before a General Election the Queen signs a proclamation summoning the new Parliament.[1] Presumably if she refused to do this the new Parliament could not legally assemble. On the other hand, there would then be no parliamentary government. The Queen would have to govern the country with the aid of the House of Lords. Clearly the country would never tolerate such behaviour unless it had lost confidence completely in the House of Commons and wished to try some new system. In fact, Parliament would probably assemble in any case, and would pass the necessary legislation embodying its existence and would go on to remove the Crown. It is, however, almost inconceivable that this state of affairs would ever arise.

[1] The same proclamation dissolves the old Parliament.

THE CHOICE OF PRIME MINISTER

In theory, the Queen has the right to choose the Prime Minister. This problem is discussed at length in Chapter IV.

THE CROWN IS ABOVE PARTY

The doctrine that the Crown can do no wrong is laid down in order to keep the Crown out of party strife. It is assumed (as the Earl of Shelburne said in 1779) that the King can do nothing without consultation and advice. Lord Erskine averred in 1807 that

> No act of State or Government can be the King's: he cannot act but by advice: and he who holds office sanctions what is done from whatever source it may proceed.

This point of view has led to the doctrine of Ministerial responsibility, whereby Ministers are held responsible by Parliament for the actions of their departments. It is customary for a Minister to accept responsibility for the acts of his civil servants. Sir Thomas Dugdale, Minister of Agriculture in Sir Winston Churchill's Government, resigned his office because of the findings of a Court of Inquiry that three of his civil servants had acted improperly in the Crichel Down affair. (This case is discussed further in Chapter VIII, in connexion with tribunals.)

THE FOUNTAIN OF JUSTICE

The courts are by tradition, and also by design, the Queen's courts, to keep them independent of Parliament. The judges are Her Majesty's judges, and the counsel the Queen's counsel. The power to reprieve a murderer or to pardon belongs to the Queen. Petitions are addressed to her. All these powers, however, are theoretical. The Lord Chancellor appoints judges and counsel. The former can be dismissed on an address to the Queen by both Houses of Parliament. The Home Secretary makes the necessary inquiries and advises the Queen in questions of pardon.

THE FOUNTAIN OF HONOUR

Here the Queen does have a real power to appoint distinguished persons to certain great honours like the Order of the Garter and the Victorian Order; but all the other honours bestowed on New Year's Day and the Queen's official birthday are recommended to her by the Prime Minister, the Fighting Services, and the Colonial

Office. The honours are given in her name, and she could presumably object to certain names, but as far as is known this has not happened, and it will probably never happen. This power to create peers is, however, a weapon of enormous importance. If the Prime Minister requests the Crown to create peers to give himself a majority in the House of Lords the Crown must acquiesce. As we have seen, the Reform Act, 1832, and the Parliament Act, 1911, were both carried through on the threat that peers would be created to pass these Bills in the Lords. It is most improbable that the power will ever be needed again.

HEAD OF THE COMMONWEALTH

This is undoubtedly important, though its precise practical importance is difficult to determine. The Commonwealth is a free association of peoples. The Queen has become not just Queen of England, but Queen of Canada, Queen of Australia, and so on. When she was in Canada in 1957, and again in 1959, she called herself Queen of Canada. She opened Parliament, and made the Queen's Speech in the traditional manner. When she visited the U.S.A. she said, "I come as Queen of Canada," and took with her the Prime Minister of Canada as adviser. The same sort of thing happened when she visited Australia. If all this means anything it means that the peoples of the Commonwealth want some one to be the outward and visible symbol of their free association, the personification of the ideals for which the Commonwealth stands, and the recipient of the affection which a family feels for its head. The Queen fulfils these wishes admirably. This function of the Crown is discussed more fully in Chapter XIV.

ENCOURAGING, WARNING, AND ADVISING

Bagehot, writing in 1867 in a celebrated and classic study of the Crown with Queen Victoria in mind, said even then that the Queen's function was simply to warn, encourage, and advise. She probably still does that, though, as we have seen, there is no law which compels the Prime Minister to consult her. Nevertheless, the convention is that he should do so. The Prime Minister has an audience with the Queen once a week as far as possible, and informs her of the general situation, and no doubt hears the Queen's views in response. The Queen also receives copies of all official documents, so that she is as well informed as any Cabinet Minister on public business. She also is in personal contact with all the Prime Ministers of the Dominions, and is therefore even better informed than some Cabinet Ministers on Commonwealth affairs.

If a monarch stays on the throne for a long period he or she acquires through personal experience a vast store of knowledge, and also develops a soundness of judgment in constitutional matters, born out of this long experience. The monarch therefore possesses an enormous moral advantage in dealings with the Prime Minister, tempered only by the fact that contacts with 'the outside world' are of necessity limited and tend to give a relatively narrow angle on affairs.

If the Queen uses her position with discretion she will find that the Prime Minister, if he is a wise man (and he ought to be a wise man if he is Prime Minister), will wish to consult her and give himself the benefit of her experience and her sound judgment. He is not obliged to accept her advice, but he ought to hear it and consider it. He is, as we have seen, not bound to consult her, but he ought to do so. It is common sense that since the Prime Minister and the Queen must work together they should work as a team as much as possible. The Prime Minister does not therefore treat the Queen as a public meeting. Queen Victoria complained that this was Gladstone's attitude towards her. Nor does he wish to flatter her fulsomely. He must establish the normal relationship of partners in the business of government.

There is now available ample evidence to show that behind the scenes King George V exercised great influence for good—for example, in the part he played in the Irish Question. He counselled against impulsive action. He advised that every effort should be made to find a satisfactory solution to this extremely difficult question. He even summoned a meeting at the palace on the theory that men round a table behave much more reasonably than in any other form of negotiation. He did the same sort of thing over the reform of the House of Lords. He saw the Conservative leaders of the Lords in private, warned them of the grave dangers if they persisted in their opposition to the Government, and ultimately he won them over to a sensible acceptance of the facts of the situation.

There is further evidence of the influence which the Crown exercises behind the scenes, thanks to the biography of King George VI mentioned above. The Labour Party had won the General Election of 1945, and Mr Attlee was forming his Cabinet. The King asked him whom he would make Foreign Secretary, and the Prime Minister suggested Dr Hugh Dalton. The King disagreed, and expressed the hope that Mr Ernest Bevin would be appointed. The Prime Minister, having taken this advice into consideration, appointed Mr Bevin. There is, however, no evidence that Mr Attlee's decision was forced upon him by the King, who had merely exercised his constitutional right to give advice.

In 1944, when the British and Americans were about to invade Normandy, the Prime Minister, Mr Churchill, wished to accompany the invading forces, travelling in a warship. The King (who also would have liked to be present on this momentous day) realized that the presence of the sovereign and the Prime Minister would be unfair to the commanding officer of the ship, and that, in any event, neither he nor Mr Churchill was justified in taking an unnecessary risk, and so he persuaded the Prime Minister to abandon his design. There are several other instances of the King's exercising his privileges of advising, warning, and encouraging his Ministers, but doing it with the utmost discretion.

There are also instances of the Prime Minister's seeking the advice of the King. For instance, in 1943 Mr Churchill was desirous of appointing Mr Eden Viceroy of India, and wrote to the King telling him how his mind was working in the matter. The King realized that this very important office needed a man of outstanding quality, but felt that the Foreign Secretaryship was of greater importance at that time, and therefore Mr Eden could not be spared. He asked the Prime Minister to bear this point of view in mind, and Mr Churchill accepted the King's advice. In his letter the King made it clear that he was merely giving advice.

A similar incident occurred when Mr Churchill asked Lord Halifax to go to the United States of America as British Ambassador. Lord Halifax was reluctant to go, because he thought that he could be of more service to the country as a member of the Cabinet. He visited the King to discuss the matter. The King encouraged him to think that the Ambassadorship was the appointment he should undertake in the national interest. It seems clear that the King exercised considerable influence in persuading Lord Halifax to go to the United States as British Ambassador, but did so with great tact and discretion.

POMP AND CIRCUMSTANCE

Most people love a good show. There are no better shows than those staged in Britain when there is a ceremonial function attended by the Queen, such as Trooping the Colour. Government is a drab business. Most people are not interested in the hard labour of administration. But their willing co-operation is necessary. They need some institution which they can understand, which they can admire, which will stir emotions of loyalty and national pride in them. That institution must be colourful, enveloped in imposing pageantry, enjoyable as well as impressive. The Crown performs this function admirably. Bagehot put it perfectly. According to him, "Royalty is a government in which the attention of the nation is concentrated on one person doing interesting actions."

The day-to-day administration of the country is outwardly a dull business, which results in the appearance of many forms and of apparently unnecessary petty regulations. The man in the street is apt to underestimate the value of the work which is done in Parliament. That is a bad thing in a country which is self-governing. People should regard government as important. The pageantry which surrounds the Queen creates the impression of the importance of the machinery of government which we want.

The country is organized on the basis of the family and of service. The Queen typifies these two ideas splendidly. The rectitude of her family life is a model for all to follow. The devotion to duty in the interest of the nation, which she and the royal family so conspicuously display, is exemplary.[1] Again, it is worth quoting Bagehot:

> We have come to regard the Crown as the head of our morality. We have come to believe that it is natural to have a virtuous sovereign and that domestic virtues are as likely to be found on thrones as they are eminent when there.

BIBLIOGRAPHY

BAGEHOT, WALTER: *The English Constitution* (World's Classics; Oxford University Press, 1928).

NICOLSON, SIR HAROLD: *King George V* (Constable, 1952).

WHEELER-BENNETT, J. W.: *King George VI* (Macmillan, 1958).

MARTIN, KINGSLEY: *The Crown and the Establishment* (Hutchinson, 1962).

PETRIE, SIR CHARLES: *The Modern British Monarchy* (Eyre and Spottiswoode, 1961).

[1] The coming-of-age, in the royal sense, of Prince Charles in 1966 made his education a matter of great public interest, and focused attention on the position of the Crown generally. The Queen's decision to enter the Prince as an undergraduate at Trinity College, Cambridge, to read for a degree, following upon his schooling at Gordonstoun and in Australia, showed a clear desire to acquaint him with the way of life and the opinions of ordinary people. This should help him to discharge his duties as a constitutional monarch more efficiently.

CHAPTER VIII

Law in Britain

The judicial system. The Rule of Law. The separation of powers—legislative, executive, judiciary. The Lord Chief Justice. The law-courts. Examining Magistrates. The County Courts. The High Court. The three Divisions. Judges' procedure. The Judicial Committee of the Privy Council. Criminal cases. Coroner's Courts. Courts martial. The legal profession. Administrative Tribunals. The Home Secretary. The law and the people.

Amid the cross-currents and shifting sands of public life, the Law is like a great rock upon which a man may set his feet and be safe, while the inevitable inequalities of private life are not so dangerous in a country where every citizen knows that in the Law Courts, at any rate, he can get justice.

LORD SANKEY, *Lord Chancellor, speaking at the Mansion House,*
on July 5, 1929

The Judiciary is the body of judges and magistrates who dispense the law in Britain. The judicial system is the way in which the dispensation of justice is organized.

The British system can be described as the Rule of Law—that is to say that anyone who is, or wishes to become, a British citizen must obey the set of laws passed by Parliament that form an integral part of the Constitution. Wherever a group of men organize themselves into a society in order that, as individuals, they can benefit from the strength which combination gives, they must draw up a set of rules. Each member must agree to comply with those rules. If a member decides later that he disagrees with one of the rules he must try to get that rule changed constitutionally, or break it and pay the penalty, or move to some other society. Any society must have rules, whether it is a cricket club, a church, a trade association, or a political system. Without some rules there would be chaos and anarchy.

THE CENTRAL PROBLEM OF THE RULE OF LAW

The essence of the Rule of Law is the drawing up of the minimum of rules—or laws—to preserve liberty, without encroaching on that liberty too much. One of the objects of the Rule of Law is to make men free. They form the society voluntarily. They agree to obey the rules of the society voluntarily. They are free men. They have freedom of speech, freedom of worship, and freedom of movement. But this liberty cannot be unlimited. For instance, if there were no laws at all the biggest and strongest men could wait until some other weaker, but more industrious and ingenious, men had built houses and furnished them and surrounded them with attractive gardens, and then take possession of these properties by force. There would be not only theft by force, but murder, arson, all kinds of cheating. No man would be able to feel secure. No man would have any incentive to build up capital for the future. There would be little or no progress.

The British Rule of Law is based on a number of fundamental principles. They are:

(a) That Parliament is sovereign provided it has been elected by a majority of the people.

(b) Only Parliament can make laws by consent of the people.

(c) Only Parliament can unmake laws by consent of the people.

(d) All men are equal before the law: there can be no privileged class.

(e) No man can be arrested without being told why.

(f) A man, if charged with an offence, must be brought to trial as soon as possible.

(g) No man can be kept in prison unless a judge is satisfied that it is in the interest of the public that he should stay in custody until he can be tried.

(h) A trial must be open.

(i) A trial must be fair and impartial, the matters being decided by an independent judge assisted by twelve "good men and true."

(j) No man can be deprived of the protection of the law because he is poor—hence the Legal Aid Act.

According to Dicey, the Rule of Law is based on three things:

(a) The absolute supremacy or predominance of regular law, as opposed to the influence of arbitrary power, and excludes the existence of arbitrariness, of prerogative, or even of wide discretionary authority on the part of the Government.... A man may be punished for a breach of law, but he can be punished for nothing else.

(b) Equality before the law, or the equal subjection of all classes to the ordinary law of the land administered by the ordinary law-courts. No man is above the law. Tribunals are being set up which will ensure that the ordinary man is not the victim of arbitrary decisions by a Government department. Some privileges have, however, had to be allowed to Members of Parliament and to judges to enable them to behave and speak without fear or favour.

(c) The laws of the Constitution, which, in some foreign countries, naturally form part of a constitutional code, are not the source but the consequences of the rights of individuals, as defined and enforced by the ordinary law-courts. This means that the remedies of the law are open to anyone in Britain.

These principles have had to be modified in tune with contemporary circumstances. Parliament has necessarily had to permit some discretionary power to the General Medical Council and the Law Society, for example, to enable these bodies to administer their professions, to ensure a high standard of conduct from their members, and to punish those members if necessary. This kind of discretion does not, however, touch the ordinary law, because it affects only people, such as doctors and solicitors, who of their own free will become doctors and solicitors, knowing the professional discipline to which they will subject themselves, a discipline which is carried out in order to protect the interest of the ordinary man.

Arbitrary power is the power exercised in a court such as the Star Chamber of Tudor and Stuart times, which was held in private, and which could and did punish men for crimes which were never disclosed, on evidence that was never published. As long as the ordinary man has the means of knowing what the law is, that, if he is tried in court, his trial will take place in public, and, if he is guilty, what the punishment will be, there is nothing arbitrary about the process. If judges were to behave in an arbitrary manner they would be removed from office by Parliament. If Members of Parliament arrogated to themselves excessive privilege they would find that the ordinary man could bring an action against them in court, when the judge would uphold his rights. Moreover, as has been said, in due course the electorate would exact its revenge by electing an entirely new Parliament, pledged by mandate to abolish any excessive privilege.

THE SEPARATION OF POWERS

In order to ensure that the Rule of Law is observed the theory of the Separation of Powers has been evolved. When Montesquieu, the French jurist and philosopher, who was one of the inspirers of the French Revolution, studied the British Constitution he decided that it was based on the Separation of Powers. According to him, it consisted of three parts:

           (a) The Legislature.
           (b) The Executive.
           (c) The Judiciary.

The Legislature passed the laws. The Executive carried them out. The Judiciary interpreted them in cases of dispute.

Moreover, still according to Montesquieu, the three parts were separate, so that each part was independent of the other two. No part could dominate and give itself privileges it denied to others. This, to him, was the crux of the Constitution, because, to a Frenchman, the main weakness of the French system was the mass of privileges enjoyed by the nobility and clergy at the expense of an oppressed peasantry. When the American Constitution was being framed the same central theme prevailed. The three powers were separated so that the President and his Cabinet cannot be in Congress, just as a member of Congress cannot be a member of the Executive, while the Judiciary is independent of both, though appointed by the President. Complete separation seems impossible to achieve.

But Montesquieu was wrong. He misunderstood the system. In the British Constitution there is not, in fact, a true Separation of Powers. The Legislature (the Houses of Commons and Lords) provides the Executive (the Cabinet). The Judiciary is more or less independent, except that its head, the Lord Chancellor, is a member of all three parts, being leader of the House of Lords and a Cabinet Minister. Nevertheless, the British method, as usual, has been a compromise in order to set up a flexible arrangement of powers, so flexible as to be capable of modification as circumstances change.

Quite soon after Montesquieu was writing George III, through the King's Friends, dominated the Commons. The King did, in fact, choose the Prime Minister, and, indeed, the Cabinet. The Executive was therefore independent of Parliament to that extent, and could make peace or war, send and receive Ambassadors, and so on, as it wished. To-day the Crown exercises certain prerogatives only because Parliament consents to this for its own convenience. The

House of Commons controls the Executive—*i.e.*, the Crown and the Civil Service—through its representatives, the Cabinet, all of whom are members of Parliament. In theory, the House of Commons can defeat any Government of whose actions it disapproves. In practice, as we have seen, the party leaders who form the Government wield great influence over the House of Commons. The balance of power is so delicate that it is difficult to describe simply. The important fact is that each part is able to exert influence on the others. Therefore no part is likely to behave in an arbitrary manner. Similarly, the judges, though independent, are in the first instance appointed by the Prime Minister and the Lord Chancellor acting together, but by convention the former always takes the advice of the latter. The judges cannot add to their number by their own choice. Nevertheless, to protect the ordinary man from possible wrong done to him by Parliament, the judges are independent, and the Constitution has ensured such independence in a number of ways.

The independence of the Judiciary has been secured in the following ways:

(a) Judges are in fact appointed by the Lord Chancellor, not by the Prime Minister or by the Queen.

(b) Judges are appointed for life, and can be removed from office only by an address to the Crown by both Houses of Parliament.

(c) Judges' salaries are paid out of the Consolidated Fund, the details of which are never discussed by the Commons.

(d) Judges are protected from action against any words they may say in court in connexion with the case they are trying.

These conditions are laid down in the Act of Settlement, 1701, and it is significant that since that year only one Irish judge has been removed from office, and that the British Judiciary has become famous for its impartiality and integrity, which are now taken for granted. The Lord Chancellor has almost without exception been appointed for his legal eminence, and he in turn has almost without exception appointed judges for purely legal reasons, and not on political grounds.

The retirement of the Lord Chief Justice threatened to raise an important constitutional issue in 1958. That issue is the principle on which the Lord Chief Justice is to be chosen. According to Sir Ivor Jennings, "The Law Officers seem to have established a sort of claim to the offices of Lord Chief Justice, Master of the Rolls, President of the Probate, Divorce, and Admiralty Division, and Lord of Appeal in Ordinary." Of course there have been 'political' appointments in the past, but the convention is gradually being established that future appointments must be based on legal qualifications only.

Lord Goddard, who was appointed in 1946, had never held a political appointment, and had risen through the normal judicial line of succession. He had no connexion with any political party, and had been completely independent. This is more than ever important to-day, when the Executive has assumed such great power, when Parliament is tempted to grant itself greater privileges. Grenville said in 1843 that "it is one of the greatest evils of the way in which political influences work in this country that we have never any security for having the ablest and fittest men promoted to the judicial office." That should not happen to-day.

The Lord Chief Justice is essentially a judge who sits in court like the ordinary judges. He, by his personal example, sets the very high standard of probity and fairness and intellectual ability required in the administration of justice.

To quote *The Times*:

> Rarely, if ever, has the Queen's Bench Division shown more efficiency in the despatch of business, yet without loss of courtesy and consideration towards those who must attend the proceedings. Never has the prestige of the Queen's Bench stood higher. Practical test has thus added its evidence that judicial capability is the first requirement.

There is no longer the inducement to practise at the Bar and earn an income of £30,000 or so a year, instead of a mere £8000 a year on the Bench, because taxation has made it impossible for a man to keep a very high income for his own use. It ought, therefore, to be comparatively easy to persuade the ablest members of the Bar to accept judicial office as the culmination of a distinguished career. But, to quote *The Times* again:

> Service as a Law Officer of the Crown is not an argument against a man being appointed Lord Chief Justice. On the contrary, the experience of the Law Officers in political and administrative matters, and still more their constant engagement in the most important cases in which the Crown is involved, are bound to be a very considerable asset to them in the rôle of First Judge. Nor would anybody seriously suggest that any holder of the proud office of Attorney-General becomes in any way prejudiced in favour of the Executive.

We are often reminded of what Mr Gladstone has said. He did, in 1873, say, when appointing Sir John Coleridge as Chief Justice, that the promotion of Law Officers "would henceforward rest on qualification and service only, not on possession of the post of Law Officer."

THE LAW-COURTS

The existence of a Rule of Law, the enactment every year by Parliament of laws, entails the establishment of courts to administer these laws, to interpret them, to decide whether a man has been guilty of breaking the law or disobeying it, to inflict punishment upon a man who is found guilty of an offence against the law. These courts start with the Petty Sessions, in which members of the public, acting as magistrates, dispense summary justice in relatively unimportant cases, and end with the Supreme Court of Appeal in Britain—the House of Lords acting in its judicial capacity. Any man who is not satisfied that he has been fairly treated in a court can appeal against the decision of the court, and go on appealing until he reaches the House of Lords. In 1958 Colonel Wintle, acting as his own advocate, fought a case as far as the House of Lords, and was successful in persuading their lordships to revoke the decisions of the lower courts. It is clear, therefore, that the British system does enable the ordinary man to get justice done if he is determined to surmount any obstacles in his path.

The Petty Sessions, or Courts of Summary Jurisdiction, are those with which the general public are most likely to come into contact if they are involved with the law. Each county, and boroughs with separate Commissions of the Peace, has a Bench of Magistrates, who are usually amateurs, but sometimes professionals. The former are Justices of the Peace, the latter Stipendiary Magistrates.

Each county maintains a panel of J.P.'s, which is kept up to strength by appointments which are made by the Lord Chancellor on the recommendation of the Lord Lieutenant, who has himself been advised by a committee, whose composition is secret, so that the members cannot be canvassed. The Lord Chancellor not only appoints J.P.'s, but he alone can remove them for misconduct. They are required to retire at the age of seventy-five.

The J.P.'s are rarely legally qualified, and they are not paid. They are chosen from eminent local worthies who wish to take part in governing the country, who have a good record of success in their professions, who have a reputation for integrity of character, who are likely to come to reasonable, impartial decisions in court. The sorts of person appointed are retired officers, clergymen, headmasters, businessmen, trade-union leaders, bank managers, and so on. In a country which takes a great pride in being genuinely self-governing it is clearly of immense importance that the ordinary man and woman of suitable qualifications should be encouraged to take part in the day-to-day administration of the country by serving on local-government councils and local Benches of Magistrates.

Such people not only render valuable service, which saves the public purse much money, but probably approach their tasks in a sympathetic spirit, and pass judgment in an eminently common-sensical fashion. It is not without significance that few men elect to be tried in a higher court; they prefer the paternal, humanitarian justice of the magistrates. And it is still considered by some persons to be a great honour to be appointed a Justice of the Peace.

The J.P.'s have been criticized on three main grounds:

(a) They are not legally qualified and cannot be expected to deal with the law competently.

(b) They know too much about local affairs and personalities and may well be prejudiced.

(c) They are swayed too much by the clerk of the court or the police.

These criticisms were so well sponsored that a Royal Commission was appointed to look into the matter. This Commission recommended that the existing system, though imperfect, was the best that could be devised, and ought, therefore, to be retained. In its opinion paid magistrates would cost too much of the taxpayers' money; it might be difficult to find that number of suitable barristers; it would discourage ordinary men and women from helping to govern themselves, and therefore be contrary to the spirit of the Constitution.

It recommended that every local Bench of J.P.'s should have a clerk, who should be a solicitor who is a full-time official and who would advise the J.P.'s on the law, but who must retire from the room when the Bench were considering their verdict. The clerk must not try to influence the Bench. He can only advise them on points of law pure and simple. These clerks are appointed by the Home Secretary. The criticisms are, as we have seen, that the Justices, because they are not legally qualified, are obliged frequently to seek the advice of the clerk of the court. The latter, if he is a man of strong personality, can influence the Justices to such a degree that he is virtually the judge. This is a possible risk, but not a serious one, bearing in mind that the kind of person who sits on the Bench is usually one of strong opinions and distinct character. J.P.'s may be acquainted with the accused, or have prejudices concerning certain local activities, but they display a sense of public spirit in declining to sit on cases in which they might find it difficult to be completely impartial. There is a danger that they will accept police evidence as indisputable, but if this is a fault it is one on the right side. It would indeed be a sad day if police evidence were corrupt.

Procedure in these courts is informal. Witnesses are allowed to tell their stories in their own way, and it is the job of the Bench, with the help of the clerk, to separate the wheat from the chaff. The idea is to allow freedom of speech and to search for justice. The magistrates are often called upon to display patience and a sense of humour when witnesses ramble about in a maze of irrelevancies, but in the end the truth is discovered. A man can be legally represented, and this is not unusual in these courts, but most cases are of a simple nature, no legal niceties are involved, and the twin objects are achieved of getting justice done swiftly and inexpensively. These two things matter a great deal to the ordinary man. He hates having to wait a long time while the case hangs over his head, like the Sword of Damocles. He is not, as a rule, rich, and he does not wish to spend money on lawyers if he can avoid doing so. The accused can, if he wishes, elect to be tried by a judge and jury, but so convinced are most people that the magistrates' courts are run wisely and generously that they are content with the justice dispensed there.

In the case of young persons under seventeen the court takes its proceedings in private, and the names of the offenders are not divulged. The police do not wear uniform, and there must be a woman J.P. on the Bench. In other words, the court is anxious to give these young persons a second chance, to reform them rather than to punish them. Similarly, when cases of domestic trouble are being heard the public is excluded, and there must be not more than three magistrates on the Bench, and these must include both sexes.

The cases which are heard in these courts are those concerning:

(a) Petty larceny.
(b) Motoring offences.
(c) Debts up to £15.
(d) Maintenance orders.
(e) Assault.
(f) Drunkenness.

Their powers of punishment are limited to:

(a) Imprisonment up to six months.
(b) Fines up to £100.

Most of the criminal cases which arise are heard in these courts. Some 600,000 cases are heard in these courts annually, whereas only a few thousand go up to higher courts.

The Justices have some other functions of an administrative

nature. The Watch Committee of borough councils or the Standing Joint Committees of county councils, which deal with police forces, are comprised partly of councillors and partly of Justices. Applications for licences to sell alcoholic liquors or to alter shopping hours are referred to the Justices for a decision. Once a year the Justices, accompanied by a doctor, visit institutions for mentally defective persons to inspect them and to make sure that no one is improperly detained there.

Once a quarter the Justices attend Quarter Sessions. These are held in selected towns. Criminal cases which have been considered too difficult for the Justices to deal with, because of the legal aspect of evidence, or the punishment for which is more than six months' jail, are heard by the Quarter Sessions, over which a barrister or solicitor of not less than ten years' standing, appointed by the Lord Chancellor, presides. The J.P.'s sit on the Bench, study the manner in which the barrister conducts the cases, gather valuable experience in this way, but take no part in the proceedings. Nearly all courts of Quarter Sessions have taken advantage of the provisions which enable them to have a Chairman and Deputy Chairman with legal qualifications appointed by the Lord Chancellor. In the case of boroughs with Courts of Quarter Sessions they have a Recorder sitting as sole judge, who is a practising barrister. Many eminent Queen's Counsel seek these appointments, perhaps because they may lead ultimately to a seat on the Bench of Judges of the High Court. The Recorders sit with the aid of a jury, and they are paid a salary out of borough funds. These courts constitute a court of appeal against a conviction by the local Bench. Frequently a person appearing before the Justices has the option of accepting the punishment, if any, of the Justices or of electing trial by Quarter Sessions, because the punishment appropriate to the case is more than six months' imprisonment.

In the County of London and certain boroughs which have specifically requested Stipendiary Magistrates these Courts of Summary Jurisdiction are presided over by paid, legally qualified magistrates. They have to be barristers of not less than seven years' standing. They are appointed by the Lord Chancellor, who can also dismiss them for misconduct. They are required to retire at seventy-two. Only one of them sits at a time, whereas the J.P.'s have to make up a Bench of two at least. They are sometimes described as Police-court Magistrates, but the courts are not run by the police, nor are the Stipendiary Magistrates connected with the police. They are the Queen's courts. The term is used for convenience only. The same sort of humanitarian common sense prevails in these courts as in those over which the Justices preside. The magistrates become sage philosophers who temper justice with mercy, and who usually succeed in giving a great deal of good advice to the people who appear before them, particularly the regular offenders. A feature of these courts is their connexion with probation officers, whose task is to reform young people who are not habitual offenders. In a large city like London, where young people can easily get into trouble, juvenile cases are tried in a separate court. The magistrates are chosen from a special panel in the London area, appointed by the Home Secretary. Outside London the Justices elect from their number. Every effort is made to save these young people from further crime. The great importance of these courts in the largest city in the Commonwealth is that they provide indisputable evidence to the public that the British system of justice is fair and humane. The publicity which the newspapers give them is probably an advantage in this respect.

Proceedings before Examining Magistrates

Under the British penal system a person accused of a criminal offence is often charged by the police, to begin with, before the local Bench of Magistrates to establish whether there is or is not a case worth taking before a Judge of the High Court. Judges are hardworked, and their time is valuable. They ought not to be asked to listen to cases unless it is known that there is a strong argument in favour of the prosecution. Conversely, a man ought not to be put to the expense of defending himself against a charge unless the police are sure that there is strong evidence against him. Sometimes it is possible to decide whether to prosecute or not without a preliminary hearing. Sometimes it is desirable to have the case heard before the Justices to test the evidence.

This method, however, has the disadvantage that the publicity given to a case might result in the jury in a higher court having preconceived opinions. The problem was referred to a committee presided over by Lord Justice Tucker. This committee unanimously recommended that proceedings should continue to be heard in public, but unless the accused person is discharged by the Justices any report of the proceedings should be restricted to particulars of his name, the charge, the decision of the court, etc., until the trial at the higher court had ended.

The committee viewed with distaste any suggestion that a case should be heard behind locked doors. The Press felt very strongly that the exclusion of the reporters was not in the best interests of the administration of justice. The recommendations are an attempt by the committee to compromise between this undesirable extreme and the existing practice.

The Press in Britain is free to make fair comment on any matter of public interest. It regards itself as the watchdog of the public, ready to pounce upon and expose any injustice. It considers that, if a case is heard in camera, evidence could be suppressed that ought to be heard, verdicts returned which might be based on inadequate evidence. The Press spends a great deal of time and money in ferreting out evidence, and there are cases on record where the persistence of the Press has resulted in the conviction of a criminal or the release of a person wrongly imprisoned. Even if there is only a shadow of doubt the accused person should be given the benefit of that doubt. The really serious danger of allowing certain proceedings to be heard in private is that this may turn out to be the thin end of the wedge. It is hard to conceive this happening in Britain, but it is possible. It did, in fact, take place in England in the Star Chamber under the Tudors. Furthermore, if the public does not know what has actually happened in court, but can only speculate, there will certainly be an undesirable current of rumour, some of it most mischievous, conjecturing what has been said and done, forming conclusions that may be right and may be wrong— probably a mixture of both. For these reasons, presumably, the Tucker Committee recommended that no cases should be heard in private.

The decision to restrict reporting in a case where the accused is to be tried in a higher court is surely wise. Reporters have been present all through the proceedings. They have not been able to report the matter in full, but they have a full record available. They will have been very active, no doubt. If and when the accused is committed for trial in a higher court they will then have the opportunity of reporting the later proceedings in conjunction with what has already happened. They lose nothing. They can divulge anything which in their opinion ought to be made public. If, on the other hand, the magistrates had acquitted the accused person reporters would be free to say what they liked about the case. If they feel that the verdict was wrong then they can say why. They can discharge what they consider to be their duty to the public.

In short, this is a delicate problem. There is much to be said for and against hearing a case in private before magistrates. In consequence, the customary British compromise is probably the best solution.

THE COUNTY COURTS

There are fifty-nine of these, each presided over by a County Court judge, who must be a barrister of not less than seven years' standing at the time of appointment by the Lord Chancellor. There are sixty-five judges. Though they are called County Courts and usually are held in county towns, they are not necessarily connected with the administrative counties. They were instituted in 1846 in order to settle minor disputes swiftly, and so save cluttering up the High Courts with cases that could be settled satisfactorily and inexpensively 'on the spot.'

The cases they deal with are:

(a) Claims up to £400.
(b) Property up to £500.
(c) Disputes over rents.
(d) Bankruptcy proceedings.
(e) Enforcement of orders to repay debts.
(f) Various matrimonial disputes.

It is noteworthy that they confine themselves to civil cases.

Since 1934 appeal from a County Court is direct to the Court of Appeal. Both solicitors and barristers have the right of audience. The judge has the help of a registrar (who must be a solicitor), who acts as an arbitrator out of court. Many disputes can be settled quickly in this way without coming into court. Very often this is the best way of dealing with them informally, privately, round a table. The judge works very hard, because there is such a mass of business before him, and he has to pass a medical examination of physical fitness before he is appointed.

A typical day's work for a judge is to hear:

(a) A petition to adopt a child.
(b) An application to pay money out of court.
(c) Several judgment summons.
(d) About a dozen landlords' claims for possession.
(e) Some civil actions.
(f) A dissolution of partnership.

This is a wide variety of cases involving a sound knowledge of the law, much patience, a large capacity for taking pains. It is a long day, and the judge is expected to deal with all these cases very thoroughly and quite impartially.

The High Court

The High Court is in London in the Strand, and is usually referred to as the Law Courts. It is divided into three divisions:

(a) Queen's Bench.
(b) Chancery.
(c) Probate, Divorce, and Admiralty.

By statute there must be not fewer than twenty-five puisne judges,
but owing to the large increase of litigation there were in fact by
1966 sixty-five judges. Even so, cases may have to wait some time
before they can be heard, especially in the Divorce Courts. The
term Puisne Judge simply means that he is not a specialist but can
hear any case, Civil or Criminal.

It is worth repeating that judges are appointed for life by the
Lord Chancellor, and they can be removed only by an address to
the Crown from both Houses of Parliament. No English judge has
been removed since 1701, so that one can reasonably infer that the
system of appointment is sound. Judges must be barristers of not
less than fifteen years' standing. Usually they have been practising
at the Bar for longer and with distinction, having become Queen's
Counsel. Although the judges are highly paid at £8000 a year, to
secure them from temptation of bribery and corruption, many of
them give up large incomes at the Bar in order to accept the great
honour of a judgeship. The Lord Chancellor takes into consideration the opinions formed by existing judges of the character and
ability of the counsel who have been appearing before them. The
Bar is a profession noted for its intimate brotherhood and independent spirit. It is not surprising, therefore, that the quality of the
Judiciary is very high indeed.

There must be thirty-seven judges in the Queen's Bench Division,[1]
nine in the Chancery Division, and eighteen to cope with the increase of work in the Probate, Divorce, and Admiralty Division.
Once a judge has been appointed to a Division he is not transferred
to another except with his own consent and that of his senior. In
this way judges can specialize and become experts in a particular
field of law—an important qualification.

Each judge has a room in the Law Courts together with a
personal clerk, who acts as his secretary, gets his books together,
marks the places he wishes to refer to, writes his letters, makes his
appointments, and so on. Judges are frequently called upon by the
Prime Minister to preside over, or take part in, Select Committees
or other forms of inquiry which the Government wish to be made,

[1] Including the Lord Chief Justice.

in which impartiality and the ability to weigh up a complicated tangle of evidence and argument are necessary. For example, Lord Radcliffe was asked to write a Constitution for Cyprus, and has conducted an inquiry into the monetary system. Lord Denning has considered certain aspects of security. Lord Justice Parker was Chairman of the Tribunal on the alleged leak concerning the bank rate. Lord Macmillan conducted a Committee on Finance and Industry. Lord Sankey made a famous Report on the coal industry.

The Work of the Three Divisions of the High Court

The Queen's Bench deals with every class of common civil action, such as:

> Fraud.
> Libel.
> False imprisonment.
> Breach of promise.
> Investigation of accounts.

The Lord Chief Justice is head of this Division. Before 1949 there could be two kinds of jury:

> (a) Special.
> (b) Common.

The former was generally composed of men of higher educational qualifications to enable them to understand complex cases. Since 1949 the distinction has been abolished. There is still a jury drawn from the City of London to consider commercial cases.

The Chancery Division deals with:

> Partnerships.
> Mortgages.
> Trusts.
> Specific performance of contracts.
> Estates of deceased persons.
> Company business.
> Bankruptcy.

The Lord Chancellor is the formal head of this Division, but seldom sits in the court, because he has too many other duties.

The Probate, Divorce, and Admiralty Division deals with:

> Wills.
> Divorces.
> Marine actions.

The Admiralty Division used to be a very busy court when prize-money was awarded to the Navy, but nowadays its affairs are much less interesting, dealing mainly with disputes about insurance and cargoes. The head of the Division is the President.

Judges' Procedure

It is the custom for the judge to sum up for the instruction of the jury, and for the jury to decide the verdict. The judge tells the jury what to bear in mind and what to ignore. This judicial summing-up is of vital importance, and arguments arise as to whether the judge was right or wrong. An appeal goes to the Court of Appeal, which is part of the Supreme Court of Judicature. Its effective head is the Master of the Rolls, assisted by nine Lord Justices of Appeal, but the Lord Chancellor, the Lord Chief Justice, and the President of Probate, Divorce, and Admiralty Divisions are also members who sometimes sit. There is no Jury; only a panel of not less than three Judges. The senior Judge gives the decision of the Court together with reasons for it; and the other members of the Court may also add their comments.

A further appeal may be made to the House of Lords, which is the Supreme Court of Appeal in Britain. As we have seen, by convention, only the legal members of the House sit when it is acting as a court. The members are the Lord Chancellor, any ex-Lord Chancellors, and the nine Lords of Appeal in Ordinary. There must be not less than three members. The judgment is a majority decision, which is given in writing with reasons; each member is entitled to state his own views. It is published in the *Journal of the House of Lords*.

The Judicial Committee of the Privy Council

This is the Supreme Court of Appeal in the Commonwealth. Most of the self-governing Dominions have abolished the right of appeal from their courts to the Judicial Committee of the Privy Council. Australia and New Zealand have retained it. When a case is heard from an overseas Dominion or Colony a Judge of a Superior Court in the State or Colony in question may be summoned to sit as an assessor. From three to five members hear an appeal. The Committee give their unanimous advice to the Crown, which is always accepted, and the decision of the Crown published. The Committee is composed of the Lord Chancellor, ex-Lord Chancellors, and Lords of Appeal in Ordinary, and Lord Justices of Appeal are also asked to sit when business is heavy. In addition to cases from abroad, the Committee deals with ecclesiastical cases and special constitutional issues which may be referred to it. For example, the House of Commons recently asked the Committee to consider a case of privilege in relation to the Privilege Act of 1770 and express an opinion on the legal point of view for the information of the House. (See Appendix.)

CRIMINAL CASES

Criminal cases are tried separately in the Central Criminal Court, popularly called the Old Bailey, in London, or in one of the seven Assizes which go on circuit periodically and are held in various provincial towns. There are seven Circuits. The judges are found from the Queen's Bench Division. The object is to bring the Queen's courts to the people, rather than put the people to the expense of coming to London. Members of the Bar decide which Circuit they propose to practise in. They join that Circuit, if it will accept them, and rarely transfer. The opening ceremony is formal and full of pageantry. The Lord Mayor or Lord Lieutenant, followed by the judge and other dignitaries, walks in solemn procession to church, and, having asked for divine guidance, then goes to court.

Appeals against convictions on sentences go to the Court of Criminal Appeal, over which the Lord Chief Justice presides usually. The Court consists of three to five judges of the Queen's Bench Division. There is a further appeal to the House of Lords.

CORONER'S COURTS

These are held in order to determine whether death has been by natural causes, misadventure, suicide, or murder. If the latter no names are mentioned. The case is one which should be referred to a higher court for hearing. Proceedings in these courts are informal, because the object is to obtain information. Coroners are either barristers, solicitors, or doctors. As a rule, they possess both a legal and a medical qualification. They are appointed and paid by Local Government authorities, but the appointments are approved by the Home Secretary.

COURTS MARTIAL

These are military courts. Any member of the Fighting Services is subject both to civil and military law. He can be tried either in a civil court or in a military court. Usually he is tried in a military court, which consists of senior and experienced officers. The charges are framed by the Judge Advocate General, and the proceedings are watched by a legally qualified officer, whose job is to see that the rules of evidence are properly observed, that the court is advised on legal points, that there is a judicial summing-up.

E

THE LEGAL PROFESSION

This consists of two parts:

(a) The Bar (*i.e.*, the four Inns of Court).

(b) Solicitors, most of whom are members of the Law Society.

Only barristers have the right of audience in the High Court. They do not communicate with the general public, and are briefed through a solicitor. The four Inns of Court are:

> The Inner Temple.
> The Middle Temple.
> Lincoln's Inn.
> Gray's Inn.

The Inns of Court date back to the time of Queen Elizabeth I and have Royal Charters of Incorporation. They are independent societies who themselves decide who shall be admitted as students and how they will qualify. The General Council of the Bar, composed of members of the four Inns of Court, deals with professional problems; and the Council of Legal Education, which is appointed by the four Inns, deals with the professional examinations. Each Inn is responsible for the professional conduct of its own members and can disbar them. The governing bodies are known as Benchers. They are composed of judges and eminent barristers. Each society is very much a fraternity, which dines together periodically, and a tradition of integrity and independence is sedulously cultivated.

Solicitors qualify by becoming articled as clerks to a practising solicitor and passing the examinations set by the Law Society. After admission as solicitor by the Master of the Rolls, it is usually necessary to take out a certificate to practise. He is the 'contact' of the law with the general public. He advises the public on legal matters. He will obtain counsel's opinion for them. He will brief counsel for them. Much of his work is in the conveyancing of property, the arrangement of mortgages, and the management of estates as trustee.

ADMINISTRATIVE TRIBUNALS

The enormous growth of departmental business in which Government departments come into contact with members of the general public and the inevitable huge increase in the number of Statutory Instruments which the Government departments publish have resulted in many disputes between citizens and departments. In the past these disputes have usually been settled either by the Minister

or by a Tribunal which he appoints. The system was not satisfactory, and the Prime Minister set up a committee, known as the
Franks Committee, to go into the matter and report. This was done
in 1958, and most of its recommendations have been accepted by
Parliament.

The roots of the trouble were that:

(a) The Minister had been judge and jury in his own defence.
(b) There had been no appeal against his decision.
(c) The citizen never knew on what grounds the decision had
    gone against him.

The matter came to a head in the now celebrated Crichel Down
case. A piece of farmland was compulsorily purchased by the
R.A.F. as a bombing-range in 1940. In 1950, as the land was no
longer needed for this purpose, it was handed over by the Air
Ministry to the Ministry of Agriculture. The original owners offered
to buy it back, but after a long correspondence the Ministry de-
clined to sell and instead installed a tenant farmer of their own
choice to run a model farm. One of the owners was a retired naval
officer, a determined man, the other, his wife, was well connected,
and between them they caused questions to be asked in Parliament,
with the result that a Court of Inquiry was set up. The Court found
that the Ministry had acted in an arbitrary manner. The Minister
accepted responsibility for the action of his civil servants and resigned. The three chief civil servants concerned were transferred to
other posts in which they were unlikely to have direct dealings with
the public. This case left an uneasy feeling that the public needed
to be protected from the Government departments.

The Franks Committee said that the work of the Tribunals ought
not to be handed over to the law-courts. The Tribunal system
should stay, but it must aim at three things:

(a) Openness.
(b) Fairness.
(c) Impartiality.

The aim could be achieved as follows:

(a) *Openness.* All Tribunals must be held in public, except in
    such cases as are of a very intimate, personal nature, or
    where a man's professional reputation is at stake.
(b) *Fairness.* The department concerned must state in writing
    the reasons for its actions, in order that the citizen can
    criticize such actions and state his own case adequately.

(c) *Impartiality*. The Tribunals, being independent of the departments, will give their decisions without fear and favour; the right of appeal must be to a special Appellate Tribunal appointed by the Lord Chancellor.

The Committee felt that the need for Tribunals was likely to be permanent. There must be day-to-day administration. This must not only attain its objects, but also pay regard to the balance between the public interest, which it promotes, and the private interest, which it disturbs.

Tribunals have the following advantages over law-courts:

(a) Cheapness.
(b) Accessibility.
(c) Freedom from technicality.
(d) Rapidity.
(e) Expert knowledge.

The Tribunals should be appointed by the Lord Chancellor. The chairmen should be lawyers, who would not only be able to sift the evidence skilfully, but also ensure complete impartiality. They would be paid expenses. The other members would be local people with an expert knowledge of the matters involved. The highest standards should be aimed at. There should be no payment. Members should be encouraged to regard it as a favour to serve on a Tribunal. They would come forward in the same spirit of service to the community as Justices of the Peace.

The procedure of Tribunals should be laid down in a statute. The aim should be a formal procedure combined with an informal atmosphere. The attitude should be sympathetic, with a clear willingness to get justice done. The decision should be given in writing, stating the reasons, so that all shall know why certain decisions have been reached. Moreover, these decisions, like judge-made law, will serve as precedents for future cases. If possible, both parties should be present, but the intentional absence of one ought not to allow a hearing to be delayed too long. Witnesses, who should give evidence on oath, should be allowed privilege of speech.

The man in the street, that shadowy figure, is usually ignorant of his legal rights, and is afraid of the law because he thinks it is expensive. Ample publicity ought therefore to be given to the existence of Citizens' Advice Bureaux and the availability of legal aid to poor persons under the Act of 1949. Steps are being taken to establish everywhere in England and Wales panels of solicitors willing and able to give advice free or at very low charges to citizens who feel they might have a legitimate grievance. Services of this kind are already being given in many areas.

Some Types of Cases for Tribunals

(a) National Service, where a dispute arises over an application for deferment, or exemption because the applicant is a conscientious objector. With the ending of National Service these Tribunals also ended.

(b) National Insurance, Industrial Injuries, National Assistance, Family Allowances, Compensation Appeals, Pensions Appeals, are very common cases in the modern Welfare State, and tend to increase in number.

(c) Land is a frequent source of dispute in connexion with rent, or acquisition, or the valuation of the land for a sale.

(d) The Rent Restrictions Act caused many appeals to Tribunals. The Rent Act, 1957, has reduced the number largely, but tenants still require to be protected from the bad landlord, and perhaps the good landlord will occasionally still need redress against the bad tenant.

(e) Public and Goods Vehicles' Licensing.

(f) National Health. This service often results in complaints by patients against doctors and dentists. These are the cases in which it is often necessary to hear the evidence in private, because a professional man's valuable reputation is at stake. If a case is proved against him that is time enough to give the result full publicity.

(g) Income-tax matters. Here, again, it may be desirable to hear the case in private, because a man's personal affairs and income are being discussed, and people will sometimes suffer an injustice rather than have such a matter made public.

THE HOME SECRETARY

In some measure the Home Secretary shares with the Lord Chancellor the responsibility for the administration of justice. He appoints magistrates' clerks. He is responsible for the efficient running of the police force, the prisons, the probation officers, the special reformatory institutions. There is little point in providing law-courts to reach decisions unless those courts are backed up by the means of enforcing their decisions.

Finally, the Home Secretary is responsible for advising the Crown in the all-important matter of pardoning offenders or reprieving persons convicted of murder. This is an immense responsibility, and there is ample testimony from former Home Secretaries, such as Lord Templewood and Lord Morrison, that it is taken very seriously. It is a subject on which a civilized nation like the British, with a liking for fair play, is deeply divided. Mr Sydney Silverman's Bill to abolish capital punishment aroused conflicting but sincere opinions in Parliament. This great responsibility has been assigned to a politician, and not a judge, because it is not a matter of law: it is a question of tempering justice with mercy. This is not to say that judges lack compassion, but they can pass sentence only according to the verdict of a jury. They are not in a position to let off a man who is found guilty, even though there may be extenuating circumstances.

THE LAW AND THE PEOPLE

Appeal to the courts to redress his wrongs is the right of every man. But in the past the average man has been deterred from litigation by its high cost. As Lord Justice Darling is said to have remarked once, "The law, like the Ritz Hotel, is open to all." The Legal Aid Act, 1949, was designed to rectify this state of affairs. Under this Act any person who needs legal advice and representation can obtain such help free provided that his income is less than £420 a year, or contributory help if his disposable income is not more than £700 a year and his capital is not more than £500. The Lord Chancellor's office made inquiry into the circumstances, and decided what expenses could legitimately be allowed.

The Law Society is making arrangements to set up panels of solicitors who are prepared to give up an hour or so a day to interviewing people free of charge and giving them advice and opinions on what their rights are and whether it is worth their while to take legal action. So many people suffer injustices meekly because they are so ignorant and afraid of the law.

Every citizen of respectability who is a householder or landowner with property above a certain value is liable to serve as a juror.[1] He is not as a rule called upon to serve more than once. If the case is a long and painful one, if the verdict is a difficult one to make, the judge will generally recommend that the jury should be exempted from further duty. It is an important part of a system of self-government that every man and woman should play some part in it, however modest.

Every man is entitled to trial by a jury of twelve of his peers or equals. He can object to any of them if there are grounds for think-

---

[1] There are a number of exceptions to this—M.P.'s, doctors, and lawyers are a few.

ing that the person concerned might be prejudiced. The judge himself must be beyond suspicion of partiality. When he is travelling any distance he is usually given a reserved compartment in a train to make sure that no member of the public can speak to him and cloud his mind.

THE OMBUDSMAN

It was suggested that an impartial Parliamentary Commissioner should be appointed to investigate matters in which a citizen claims to have suffered an injustice at the hands of a Government department, of a nature which a tribunal or an M.P. cannot examine and put right. This official recommends to Parliament what should be done to remove an injustice. The first Ombudsman (officially Parliamentary Commissioner for Administration) was appointed in April 1967.

The kind of grievance is a complaint by a shopkeeper that his application for a telephone was turned down whereas another person in the same area applying later, with a lesser need, was nevertheless successful; or the finding by an officer of the Armed Forces that he has been unjustly deprived of his command.

BIBLIOGRAPHY

ARCHER, PETER: *The Queen's Courts* (Penguin Books, 1956).

WADE, E. C. S., and PHILLIPS, G. G.: *Constitutional Law* (Longmans; fifth edition, 1955).

HANBURY, H. G.: *English Courts of Law* ("Home University Library," Oxford University Press; second edition, 1953).

VINOGRADOFF, SIR PAUL: *Common Sense in Law* ("Home University Library," Oxford University Press; third edition, 1959).

JACKSON, R. M.: *The Machinery of Justice in England* (Cambridge University Press; fourth edition, 1964).

HEUSTON, R. F. V.: *Lives of the Lord Chancellors, 1885–1940* (Oxford University Press, 1964).

The English Legal System (H.M.S.O., 1962. C.O.I. Pamphlet, No. 49).

ALLSOP, P.: *The Legal Profession* (Sweet and Maxwell, 1960).

RUBINSTEIN, R.: *John Citizen and the Law* (Penguin Books, 1963).

Administrative Tribunals and Enquiries (H.M.S.O., 1957. Cmd. 218).

Report of the Committee on Ministers' Powers (H.M.S.O., 1932. Cmd. 4060).

CHAPTER IX

The Civil Service

The need for a Civil Service. Recruitment. Organization. Method. Relationship with Ministers. Social background. Relationship with the public. Relationship with Parliament. Functions of Ministers. Summing-up.

Example is the school of mankind.

EDMUND BURKE

And if you go into the Civil Service or Politics, there is no greater or finer work. There is not much financial gain in it; there are many disappointments; but if you do your work in the right spirit, you will find the deepest satisfaction in it.

EARL BALDWIN, *in a speech delivered at The Leys School, Cambridge, on June* 26, 1936

From a long and varied experience of the British Civil Service . . . I have in general formed a high opinion of the energy, ability, resourcefulness and incorruptibility of our Civil Service.

LORD MORRISON, *in "Government and Parliament"*

The British Civil Service is held in general respect throughout the world because of its efficiency, its integrity, and its method of recruitment by talent and not by nepotism.[1]

Nevertheless, it has its critics. Some of them paint a fantastic picture of a monster with a split personality. Sometimes we are shown the Civil Service as a group of idlers, relatively highly paid, sitting in their offices from 10 A.M. to 4 P.M., impeccably dressed, drinking tea, and passing papers from department to department. This libellous portrait of an industrious community has been aggravated by what is now known as Parkinson's Law, according to which every time you appoint a civil servant he must find some one to discuss his work with, some one to approve of his action, some one to do the 'donkey' work for him, so that as the task diminishes the staff dealing with it grows.

This is bad enough, but there is the other caricature of a secret

[1] A system of favouritism under which appointments are made within an exclusive circle, the members of which usually belong to a small group of families.

society, working behind closed doors in Whitehall, engaged in oppressing a defenceless and blameless citizenry who have no means of redressing their grievances, no way of securing compensation for the injustices which their bureaucratic oppressors inflict upon them. Ever since Lord Hewart's book *The New Despotism* was published in 1929, depicting a nation which was governed by a tyrannical bureaucracy in fact, and by a sovereign Parliament in theory, the second of these lurid versions of the Civil Service at work has gained ground. It is often alleged that Parliament has no control over departmental expenditure, and that Ministers are the puppets of their permanent advisers.

The facts are that there has been an enormous growth of Government business since 1945, that Ministries have multiplied both in size and number, that the number of Statutory Instruments has increased vastly. The results are that an overworked Cabinet and Parliament find it increasingly difficult to control the spending of public money, and have been obliged to delegate legislative powers to the Government departments. Such a state of affairs is inevitable in a complex modern society in which the Government takes such a large part in framing economic policy, in running public enterprises, and in administering a gigantic scheme of social welfare. The conclusion is inescapable that, no matter how the parliamentary system is organized, some legislative and administrative powers must be delegated: the central Government cannot control the entire machine in detail.

That being the case, it follows that the Civil Service must be recruited with the utmost care, to make sure that it does its job efficiently, and also to try to ensure that it is composed of men and women who put the public interest first and appreciate the fact that they are the servants, and not the masters, of the public. Our first concern, therefore, is with the way in which the Civil Service is recruited and organized. Up to 1855 the Civil Service was a small body of men whose work consisted mainly of copying letters. The Government departments were few in number, and their work was comparatively simple, carried out at a gentle pace. Ministers were able to control the work of their departments in detail. The civil servants were appointed by Ministers through the ancient system of patronage. If a man was related to the right people he had little difficulty in obtaining a well-paid sinecure.

After the Trevelyan-Northcote reforms had been introduced to cope with an increase in work the modern Civil Service was built up. To-day it is recruited on the following principles:

(a) Entry can be made only by competitive examination.

(b) All candidates must be suitably qualified.

(c) There is no influence exercised by friends of candidates.

(d) All candidates must be of suitable character.

(e) Pay will be high enough to attract good candidates.

The actual process of recruitment is run by the Civil Service Commissioners. They insert advertisements in suitable places, notifying the public that there are vacancies and how application shall be made. They arrange for the examinations and interviews to take place and the results to be published. There is a great deal of work to be done. There are seven Commissioners, two of whom have scientific qualifications.

The examinations vary according to grade. Candidates for the highest grade, the Administrative, must reach University Honours Degree standard. Entry nowadays is obtained to this grade in three ways. There are some fifty-odd vacancies each year. Two-fifths of these are awarded on the result of the competitive examination (Method I); two-fifths of the vacancies are filled after an interview (Method II); and the remaining places are filled by graduation from the Executive grade (Method III).

The examination in Method I consists partly of a written competition and partly of an interview. The first part is designed to discover whether the candidate has a good general knowledge and can express himself clearly on paper. There is one paper on English, an essay, and a current-affairs paper, which are compulsory. There are four other papers which can be taken from a very wide variety. Usually history and languages are chosen. As there are generally something like ten times as many candidates as there are vacancies, the standard is very high, approximating to First-class Honours level. The interview is designed to find out if the candidate has the ability to meet strangers with confidence, to chat pleasantly and sensibly on a variety of subjects, and has a good presence and an attractive personality. He is questioned closely about the books he reads, the hobbies he enjoys, the games he plays. A man with a personality is sought, not a mere scholar. Very careful inquiry is made about the candidate's background, to make quite sure, as far as is possible, that he has the character and integrity to put the public interest before his personal profit, and that he can safely be entrusted with secret matters. In these days when the bogey of Communism is an outstanding consideration the candidate's political activities and his family's political beliefs are closely inquired into. The Burgess and Maclean[1] episode at the Foreign Office is a warning that cannot be ignored.

[1] These two men, while in the service of the Foreign Office, betrayed secret information to Russian agents because they had become Communists by conviction. They disappeared, and made their way to Russia.

The competition by interview (Method II) was started after 1945. Candidates must already possess either a First or a good Second-class Honours Degree. To begin with, the candidates were invited to spend a long week-end at a country house, when their behaviour in strange company, living together, was studied. Who had outstanding powers of leadership? The idea of the week-end was borrowed from the War Office Selection Boards. In due course the expense was held to be unjustified. A long interview still is held, but it now takes place in London. It is still on the same lines as the interview just mentioned, however, and has the same objects in view.

The third way in (Method III) is after many years of experience in the Service, during which the candidate has been regularly reported on favourably by his superiors for the administrative ability which he has displayed in the discharge of his duties as an Executive Officer. The zeal he has shown in carrying out dull tasks, the initiative he has evinced in tackling difficult problems, the way in which he has mingled successfully with a variety of people, all these things have been noted in the course of time. He may not possess the learning of the university graduate, but he has acquired a wide practical knowledge of Civil Service work and of men.

The examination for the Executive grade is about the standard of the Advanced Level Certificate of Education. The candidates are usually eighteen to nineteen years of age. For the Clerical grade the standard is equivalent to the Ordinary Level of the General Certificate of Education. In all cases English and the essay are important in order to ensure that successful competitors are able to express themselves clearly and concisely on paper. Typists obviously are tested for their ability to type efficiently. 'Functional' civil servants, such as messengers, are generally ex-Servicemen with a good record of 'regular' service. They are not examined, but taken on trust.

For the many scientific and professional posts there is no written examination, but all candidates must possess the appropriate professional qualifications, and pass the customary interview. For instance, a doctor desirous of filling a vacancy in the Ministry of Health must have passed all his professional examinations with credit and have had some professional experience as well. A lawyer must be either a barrister or solicitor with some practical experience. The qualifications are high and are stated in the conditions of the competition. As with the Administrative grade, the interview is important. Successful candidates must possess a pleasing personality, the ability to express themselves convincingly and clearly. No Board of Selection can be infallible, but so much care is taken to interview the candidates thoroughly from every angle that the Board seldom picks the wrong men.

To prevent a return to the old system of patronage, it is always stated very clearly that any attempt to canvass support will disqualify the candidates in question. The net of nepotism spreads its meshes very visibly and in many walks of life; it is cynically remarked that it is not what a man knows, but whom he knows, that counts. That cannot happen in a competition for entry into the Civil Service, or at all events every effort is made to prevent its happening.

Pay is an important point. However much a man is attracted by a desire to serve his country, his pay is still a primary consideration. Our society is organized in such a way that a man needs money in order to buy the necessities of life. He needs that little extra income to purchase some of the more modest comforts and luxuries that transform a mere existence into a satisfying life. When a man marries and has to bring up a family the cost of living is a very significant fact. In consequence, the able and ambitious young man is certain to compare the relative rewards which the Civil Service and industry and commerce offer. It is sometimes alleged that the prospects in business are so much brighter than those in the Civil Service that fewer and fewer of the best young men at the universities enter the Service. In fact, except for the very few top jobs in industry—the chairman of a great company, for example—the pay of the higher civil servant compares very favourably with the income he would earn in any other profession or occupation. The disparity is in any case more or less removed by progressive taxation. Furthermore, there are two other factors which count enormously in making the Civil Service an attractive profession.

The prudent man with a family is mindful of his old age, when he is too old to work but his cost of living is the same. He has to save money during his working life in order to provide for his retirement, or contribute substantially towards a pension. The civil servant has no anxieties on this score, because he is sure of a reasonable pension which is non-contributory, as well as a substantial gratuity. This form of security was a big attraction to most men, but is not so important when most firms have pension schemes.

The other great attraction is the power that the senior civil servant has. He possesses information that is denied to most people. He is in a position to meet Ministers and other 'great men.' He is able in a quiet way to influence important events. He is the power behind the throne. He not only enjoys a highly respected social status, but can look forward at the end of his career to an 'honour,' perhaps a knighthood. These considerations may not appeal to everybody, but they are a strong attraction to some men.

THE ORGANIZATION

The Civil Service is essentially a hierarchy—*i.e.*, it is arranged in ranks or tiers. It looks like a pyramid, with the lowest grade forming the broad base and the highest grade comprising the apex of the pyramid. Thus in 1958 the establishment was:

Administrative	2,540
Executive	67,300
Clerical	181,100
Typists	26,500
Messengers, etc.	35,600
Inspectors, etc.	2,620
Post Office	200,000
Professional and Grade I ⎫ Scientific and Grade II ⎬ . .	72,100
Technical	41,500
Total	629,260

The members of each grade know who are above them and who are below them, who gives them orders and to whom they give orders. There is a known order of precedence, which in a huge organization not only is necessary to efficiency, but is an immense help to the individual civil servant.

The Administrative grade think out and formulate policy. They advise the Minister. The Executive grade carry out that policy, and are allowed an increasing amount of scope in doing so. The Clerical grade, at the bottom, obviously do the purely routine duties that form so much of the paperwork of the departments. As the Ministries have increased in number and size and taken on duties of a highly technical nature, it has become necessary to recruit scientists, engineers, doctors, accountants, and so on, as well as technicians, to carry out these duties in, for example, the Ministry of Health, the Ministry of Supply, the Ministry of Labour, the Auditor-General's department.

The Treasury has become the controlling department. It is divided into two main parts. One is concerned with monetary, economic, and fiscal affairs, with a Permanent Under-Secretary in charge. The other part is concerned with the running of the Civil Service, also under a Permanent Under-Secretary, who is now the head of the Civil Service. He advises the Prime Minister on promotion to the higher appointments in the Service. Naturally,

Ministers themselves have a say in the matter, and they in turn are advised by their own permanent assistant, but the final decision rests with the Prime Minister and the head of the Treasury. This prerogative gives great power to the Treasury.

The Treasury also works out the scale of pay and pensions, bearing in mind changes in the cost of living, the state of the country, the comparative pay in industries and trades which compete for the available labour, the nature of the work done. The important consideration is to offer pay which is large enough to attract good labour, but not so large that the Civil Service gets the best labour at the expense of all other rivals. If that were allowed to happen the distribution of available labour would be unbalanced.

The Treasury is also responsible for deciding the 'establishment' of each department—*i.e.*, the number of people needed to carry out the functions of the department satisfactorily, and the grades of these people. Clearly, the Treasury must give a department an adequate establishment, but not too many people. Professor Parkinson's now famous law has brought out the tendency of departments to increase. The Treasury has to watch out for this tendency and to keep it under control. Each department has its own Organization and Method branch, which studies constantly the way in which the department works, which is continuously trying to improve the method, which has to decide whether improved methods have made some of the staff redundant, or which has to justify to the Treasury the case for an increase in staff. The Treasury itself has an Organization and Method branch which studies the way in which the whole of the Service is functioning, constantly seeking to improve its efficiency and to remove any extravagance. An inspection by an 'O. and M.' team is a salutary experience. The team will spend a week or so with its victims, observing what each individual does, how he does it, how many files are dealt with, what registration has to be done. The team knows from experience that certain yardsticks can reasonably be applied, such as, for example, that one clerk ought on average to be able to cope with so many files a year. Experience also shows that as a result of these inspections there is generally better coordination in the department, and often some diminution of its staff.

The Treasury is also responsible for studying the departmental estimates every year. From August to February the departments put up their draft estimates. Each draft is examined both by the Finance branch of the department and by the Treasury. Each item is scrutinized expertly and compared with what was done in previous years. Every effort is made to prevent extravagance and wastefulness. The departments are estimating what they will require in the following year to pay for staff; equipment like typewriters, dictaphones, stationery; and for the actual services provided, such as education, police, aeroplanes, or tanks. The Treasury is not necessarily parsimonious. On the contrary, it may nowadays suggest expenditure to stimulate production in the national economy. But its power over the purse is an enormous advantage to the Treasury.

Each department is organized in accordance with what is called its 'family tree.' At the top of the pyramid will be the Minister and Junior Minister, who provide the parliamentary control over the department. Then comes the Permanent Under-Secretary, who is supported by one or more Deputies and several Assistant Secretaries, according to the size of the department and the complexity of its work. The department is divided up into a number of branches. Each branch is subdivided into a number of sections. Over each of these sections there are the Principals and Assistant Principals. These are all Administrative Officers. Some of these appointments are given to the most senior Executive Officers, particularly those sections dealing with organization and method and staff, which require, above all, a long experience and detailed knowledge of the work of the Service and of the civil servants themselves.

THE CIVIL SERVICE METHOD

Ministers may come and Ministers may go, but the Civil Service goes on for ever. That is the essence of the Service—its permanence. This permanence means stability and continuity. It ought to mean consistency. It sometimes also results in rigidity. Indeed, one of the commonest criticisms of the Civil Service is that it is so completely bound up with red tape, with reverence for precedent, with worship of the book of regulations, that it suffers acutely from administrative inertia. There is alleged to be a distressing absence of initiative. The civil servant is accused of a chronic reluctance to act. He passes an awkward problem on to some one else, who passes it on to some one else. The problem goes round from branch to branch, when possible from department to department, until it has died a natural death, at which point of convenience the file strangely comes to the surface again and is closed with appropriate relief that there was another awkward question dodged. This picture of a hidebound, evasive bureaucracy, experts in the negative art of masterly inactivity, is, of course, an exaggeration. Admittedly, a problem takes time to be solved. It is true that an inquiry from a private citizen, a complaint, takes a long time to be dealt with decisively.

The citizen is tempted to think that the department is hoping he will lose patience and give up the chase.

A huge organization employing more than half a million people is too complicated to be allowed to function as a large number of small units each operating according to its own ideas. There must be a common thread running through the gigantic pattern. That thread is the method of working, a method that is characteristic, so that to-day it is a boast that a civil servant can move from one department to another and do his new job as well as the old one. There was a time when a civil servant stayed in the same department all his working life. To-day the policy is to move civil servants occasionally.

As far as possible everything is reduced to writing, so that the problem and the manner in which it is settled are preserved. Every department, therefore, has a central registry. As soon as a matter is raised the registry searches to see whether it is new or has already been under consideration in the department. If it is new a file is created. If it is an old story the appropriate file is found. The file is then sent to the appropriate section or branch for action. Every department has an elaborate directory stating the work that each section does, the senior official in the section, and his telephone number. The file will find its way to an Executive Officer, who will have the necessary facts and figures dug up and checked for accuracy. He will then consider the matter and either deal with it himself or pass it back to a Clerical Officer to draft a reply, or, if it is important or difficult, he will submit it to his Principal, with his recommendations, and await further instructions. The Principal will think about it for a day or two. He is considering a number of other problems at the same time. Eventually he will make a decision. He will either write a letter or memorandum or minute, or pass the file back to his subordinate with his directions. The time is taken in checking to discover whether this problem or something like it has come up before. On the principle that there is nothing really new, the department may as well use the wisdom of experience. If the action taken in the past proved to be satisfactory, then it ought to be taken again. If the circumstances are partly different to-day, nevertheless it is worth considering what happened before. It must throw some light on the matter. Otherwise, what is the value of history? Furthermore, there must be a continuity in the policy of the department. It cannot say one thing to-day and another thing to-morrow, or there will be chaos; the public will not know what the official policy is and can challenge one decision by bringing up another contradictory decision. Above all, the department must be meticulously accurate. The work is therefore never hasty. But when a matter is urgent action is usually taken with commendable speed.

Moreover, as the Civil Service is so vast the officials in the department must take care that their policy is not in conflict with that of another department. The Ministry of Health, for example, and the Ministry of Labour are both interested in the safety regulations in a factory. It would never do for them to be at variance with each other, or the administration would be discredited. Consequently a registered file will soon grow into several volumes. They are all carefully indexed and cross-referenced. Each contribution to the file is numbered in sequence. Whenever a decision is made copies of the decision are sent to every department or branch that may be interested.

A similar policy is adopted towards legislation. As we have seen, nowadays a department puts out a very large number of orders and regulations every year, known as Statutory Instruments. Occasionally it will sponsor a Bill in Parliament. Each of these administrative instruments will affect some of the people, some of them will concern most of the people, and a few will affect all the people. These repercussions must be foreseen and considered thoroughly before action is taken; otherwise unexpected and disagreeable consequences will ensue. Injustices to a small minority of people will be inflicted unintentionally, or loopholes will appear which a few ingenious and none too scrupulous individuals can exploit.

In consequence, policy is deliberated upon at great length before thought is translated into action. This is where the Administrative Officers come into their own. They must think hard; they must display imagination in order to foresee unexpected consequences. They need all the sense of humour, all the patience and tolerance, they can muster to bear with all the contradictory advice they get, all the frustrating disagreements that arise and delay the reaching of a solution. Usually a departmental working party is set up to go into a problem. This party, or it may be a committee, will hear evidence from all interested parties in the country. All the pressure groups will be invited to send their representatives to the Ministry to be questioned and to question. All the leading experts will be consulted and their advice sought. If necessary, other interested Ministries will be approached, and sometimes an inter-departmental committee will be established. A mass of evidence and opinion is collected. Above all, the Treasury must be consulted to make sure that at the last minute a financial hitch will not occur.

It is the duty of the Administrative Officers to wade through the voluminous papers, summarize the arguments for and against, set out the possible courses of action, and make a recommendation to the Minister. The latter is responsible to Parliament for the actions of his department. It is therefore up to his civil servants to consult him and keep him well informed. All this preparation takes many months, and eventually a departmental Statutory Instrument is published, or the Minister introduces a Bill in Parliament, having convinced his Cabinet colleagues that the Bill is expedient. It is difficult to understand why there are critics who see the Civil Service as an army of autocrats, engaged on an administrative spree at the expense of the defenceless citizenry. More will be said about this when the relationship between the Civil Service and the general public is considered.

As an example of the need for inter-departmental co-ordination, the case of factory inspection has been quoted. It is generally agreed that the method can be improved. The Ministry of Health think that it is primarily a medical matter, and therefore one for them. The British Medical Council agree. On the other hand, the trade unions think that the problem is essentially industrial, and ought, therefore, to be handled by the Ministry of Labour. The Cabinet will have to resolve this conflict of opinion.

The Local Government Bill, 1958, is an excellent example of the care with which a matter is thoroughly probed before a Bill is presented. The question had been under discussion for four years. A White Paper was produced in 1956, and two more in 1957, each dealing with a different aspect of the matter. All along there had been close consultation with the local authorities to get their views and, as far as possible, their agreement.

The Relationship between the Civil Service and the Minister

This is a hotly debated question. Some critics claim that the growth of departmental business has been so immense that Parliament has lost control of the administrative machine. It is said that the spending of money by departments is more or less unchecked by Parliament, which can only debate the principles of the Budgetary proposals and the Estimates. The details of the Estimates—in particular the amount of money to be spent—are ignored by Parliament because M.P.'s have neither the time nor the knowledge to go into financial detail. Ministers are alleged to come and go with such frequency that the senior civil servants are necessarily masters of the situation. Ministers are unable to argue with their permanent advisers because they lack the necessary knowledge. If this alarming picture were accurate the situation would indeed be serious, because Parliament would clearly no longer be necessary, and the country could be administered by the Civil Service, with the sovereign as a titular figurehead.

Happily the situation is not like this. Man being fallible, there will be the occasional weak Minister, but normally a Minister is a man of outstanding character and personality. He has had a long climb up the political ladder, and has had to compete against many ambitious rivals. He will have caught the eye of his party leader because of his energy, his speech-making, his ability to get on with other people. He will have made himself an expert on some subject. He will have become a public figure in the national Press, on the radio and television, and will have plenty of self-confidence. He will have served in several posts of junior rank, which will have given him experience of the administrative machine. In short, the Minister will be a strong man who will not give way easily to his civil servants. He will be much more likely to fail the other way by trying to stamp his personality on his office regardless of all opposition. In other words, there will be struggles from time to time, but the Minister must always win, because it is he who is responsible to Parliament.

The Minister will set about his task in such a way that he concentrates on the big things—just a few of them—and leaves the many smaller things to his subordinates. There are usually five or six first-class matters alive in the department to which the Minister must give his personal attention. He will, at his daily meeting with his senior assistants, lay down his general policy and reply to any questions that may be raised. If he is a good leader and gives his confidence to his subordinates he will find that the trust is mutual. They will not let him down, but back him up loyally and keep him informed of what they are doing, and take no decisions on matters which they think he will wish to deal with himself.

In a relationship of this kind much will depend on the personalities of the senior civil servants. That is why so much trouble is taken in selecting men of the 'right type.' That is why, for a century, close attention has been paid to the building up of a tradition of service, of the public interest first, of absolute neutrality. In a two-party system, in which each party is in power for a time, it would be disastrous if the Civil Service were partisan, as it was in the days of patronage. During the period of Conservative-Liberal rivalry it was not too difficult for the administrative class to be neutral, because there was no fundamental difference of view and of social background between the two parties. Moreover, the senior civil servants came from the same schools and universities, belonged to the same clubs, and possessed the same social habits as the politicians. They belonged to the same social class. They got on well together. There was no grave problem.

When the Labour Party rose to power a new situation was created. Many of the Ministers were drawn from the so-called working classes. They were trade unionists. Few of them had been either to a public school or to a university. They had thus little in common with the senior civil servants. They held political opinions that would very likely be in conflict with those of the officials. The question which was in the minds of every student of the Constitution was how the civil servants would react to the revolutionary ideas of the Labour Party? The answer was soon clear. The Civil Service maintained its traditional neutrality with impeccable behaviour. The Ministers were given advice, and no doubt they were warned and perhaps discouraged from doing some things, but once they declared their policy the civil servants carried out that policy loyally and to the best of their ability. The flood of Socialistic legislation, the central planning, the nationalization of the great industries, were all dealt with smoothly. No Labour Minister complained that he was not backed up loyally. When the Labour Party was defeated in the General Election of 1951 and was succeeded by a Conservative Government, which proceeded to carry out a very different policy, the civil servants adapted themselves at once to their new political masters.

SOCIAL BACKGROUND

Another criticism, almost a conventional point of view, of the Administrative grade is that they are out of touch with the mass of the people. They need the politicians to keep them on the right lines. This may well have been true thirty years ago, say. Until very recently this grade was recruited almost entirely from young men of the upper-middle classes, educated in the oldest, most famous, and fashionable public schools and either at Oxford or at Cambridge. They were nurtured on games and on the Classics. They knew one another, and they usually knew the M.P.'s as well. They belonged to families with a long tradition of service, and often had private means. They probably knew very little about how the majority of the working classes lived. They were not unsympathetic, but they did not understand the point of view of the general public. Their idea of government was rigidly theoretical. Accepting this picture as accurate, for the sake of argument, it is not surprising that Sir William Harcourt said that the duty of the Minister was to tell the civil servant what the public would stand, and that if civil servants were allowed to govern the country without the House of Commons they would do so admirably for a week, and then they would all be hanged from the lamp-posts.

This is, of course, a distorted picture to-day. The Administrative grade is gradually changing in social content. For some time an increasing proportion of the annual entry has been of men—and women—from the newer universities, who have been educated at grammar schools and come from working-class families. They have reached the top of the ladder through their brains. They know what the man in the street is up against and how he is thinking. Assuming that they keep in touch with their families, they can form an accurate picture of popular opinion. They may not possess as many contacts with people as the M.P. does, but they have these family connexions. They read the newspapers and listen to the radio. They know what their subordinates in the Service think. Many Service bodies, such as the Post Office, or the Ministry of Labour, or the Ministry of Social Security, are in constant touch with the public. The higher civil servant, with all this information at his disposal, bringing to bear a first-class intellect on his problems, is unlikely to misread popular opinion with marked inaccuracy.

It is worth while having a look at the entry for 1953.[1] There were fifty-two vacancies to be competed for by examination or interview. The successful candidates came from the following universities:

Oxford	.	.	.	.	26
Cambridge	.	.	.	.	15
London	.	.	.	.	5
Scottish	.	.	.	.	5
Nottingham	.	.	.	.	1

Their schools were:

Public schools	.	.	17
Grammar schools	.	.	35

Their family beginnings were:

Working class	.	.	12
Lower-middle class	.	.	17
Upper-middle class	.	.	23

[1] In 1959 all but two of the successful candidates came from Oxford or Cambridge, and the majority were from the public schools. There were 70 vacancies in 1960, filled by Method 2—a short non-academic examination, followed by a series of tests and interviews, and a final interview for selected candidates. As a result there were 39 successful candidates from Oxford, 27 from Cambridge, and 4 from the other British universities. As far as men were concerned, there were 36 successes from the established public schools and 32 from other schools. Three women candidates were selected. The candidate at the top of the list came from Johnson Grammar School, Durham, and New College, Oxford. According to the Civil Service Commissioners the predominance of 'Oxbridge' was mainly because a large majority of the candidates came from those universities.

What is more, seven of the twelve working-class candidates went up either to Oxford or to Cambridge and took Firsts.

Is this broadening of the base a good thing? If it is true that the traditional Administrative Officer was cut off from the general public, then it is a good thing that an increasing proportion of this grade should come from the 'common people.' On the other hand, if Plato's idea of the guardians was sound it may well be that the disappearance from the Civil Service of families who, generation after generation, regarded serving the country as the best career for a young man is a bad thing. These young men were brought up at home and school to believe that there was nothing more worthy than 'service.' They were taught to think that they were born to administer. They upheld the hereditary tradition. They certainly set an astonishingly high standard of integrity and unselfishness and impartiality. They were content to do good by stealth, and were repaid for their modest anonymity by the occasional 'honour.' It is of the utmost importance that the new men should also be imbued with the ideal of service. As the Welfare State takes an increasing part of our income and spends it on our behalf, as many of our great industries are nationalized, administrators of the highest calibre are required to run the activities of the nation competently. These men will come forward only if they consider it an honour to serve, and if they can expect to earn as much as they would in other comparable jobs.

THE CIVIL SERVANT AND THE GENERAL PUBLIC

As we have seen, for many years the ordinary citizen had an untrue picture of the Civil Service, which he regarded as an indolent and autocratic race of men. Mr Punch popularized the familiar scene in the post-office of a swarm of impatient and irritated customers waiting for attention, while the assistants chatted away, ignoring their wishes. The ink-wells were full of sludge; the pens had twisted nibs with which it was impossible to write. In those days the Government departments had little to do with the general public.

To-day, however, the position is entirely different. Not only has the number of civil servants increased, but several Ministries have very wide and close contact with the public. Civil servants themselves are taxpayers and citizens as far as certain Ministries are concerned. There is a general realization that the relations between the civil servants and the general public must be good, that the former owe the latter the best possible service they can give in a Welfare State.

For instance, the Post Office is in almost continuous touch with some members of the public, either through a telephone-exchange or a telegram or through the ordinary day-to-day business in a post-office. The public go to the post-office to buy stamps and postal-orders, to send parcels, to purchase Premium Bonds and National Savings Certificates, to draw pensions, to put money in or take it out of the Savings Bank. Most people visit a post-office at least once a week. The Post Office has made great efforts to publicize the many services which it does for the public, and its staff have been encouraged to look upon themselves as employees of the general public, who expect, and ought to get, good and 'civil' service from them.

The Ministry of Labour also has close contacts with the public. In every town there is at least one branch of the Ministry. The local branches exist essentially to notify unemployed persons of jobs; to help them to get those jobs; if necessary, to advise them that there is work in another town or district; perhaps even to assist them to move to the place where work is to be had. As the pattern of British industry alters the task of the Ministry in keeping labour mobile is a most important one. These branches also pay out unemployment benefit. The Ministry has also been responsible for the registration and calling up of young men for National Service. Finally, the Ministry is responsible for acting as mediator in industrial disputes. The habit is growing, when the two parties to a dispute cannot come to terms, of seeking the help of the Ministry's conciliators. In a highly industrialized community, where wages are negotiated on a national basis, the rôle of conciliator is important. The Ministries of Health, Labour, and Social Security are all constantly in touch with a considerable number of citizens. These contacts unfortunately often end in differences of opinion, in a feeling of resentment on the part of members of the public. A system of Tribunals has been in active operation for some years, but it has not functioned satisfactorily. There has been an inquiry into it, and the Government is reorganizing it. The main change in policy is to make the Tribunals independent of the Ministries, to conduct their proceedings openly, and to require the Ministries to give reasons for their actions. This matter is dealt with in detail in Chapter VIII.

This seems a convenient point at which to try to define the term 'civil servant.' He (or she) is a person employed by a Government department on the public business in a civilian capacity and paid out of taxation which Parliament has authorized by statute. The definition is of some importance at a time when the State owns so many great industries and employs about one-third of the working population. Is a coal-miner or a policeman or a gas-meter inspector or a train guard a civil servant? Is the sovereign the highest paid of all civil servants? Are the workers in ordnance factories, Admiralty dockyards, and Army depots civil servants? They are all performing a service for the public. They are controlled by one Minister or another.

It is generally agreed that coal-miners, gas and electricity workers, and railwaymen are not civil servants, because they are paid out of the income received by the corporations that employ them. It is also agreed that policemen and firemen, local-government officers, and schoolteachers are not civil servants, because only a part of their pay comes from taxation and part from the revenue raised by local authorities, and it is impossible to decide which part of a schoolteacher belongs to the authority and which part to the Ministry of Education! The Armed Forces of the Crown are obviously not civil servants, because they are military persons.

All Ministries now have Public Relations Officers, whose job is to inform the public, through the Press as a rule, what the Ministry is doing, and why it is doing it in that particular way. The strict rule of anonymity is still pursued. It is always a Foreign Office spokesman who has explained why a Diplomatic Corps representative in London must have immunity, or a War Office spokesman who tells why Private Thomas Atkins could not be brought home from Malaya in time to visit his aged and sick grandfather. The goodwill of the general public is sought within reason.

PARLIAMENT AND THE CIVIL SERVICE

The Members of the House of Commons are the elected representatives of the people. One of the duties of the House is to control the executive on behalf of the nation. It performs this duty by appointing a Government which, through the departmental Ministers, controls the work of each Ministry and department. Whether this control is effective or not has already been discussed. On the whole it is probably quite effective. What of the back-benchers in the House of Commons? Do they play a part in controlling the Civil Service?

M.P.'s keep in touch with Ministries by letters to the Minister or by questions in the House. All Members have a voluminous correspondence with their constituents, or with pressure groups outside Parliament. Any complaint or criticism of a Ministry is at once passed on to the Minister concerned. He in turn causes an inquiry to be made into the allegation. The file goes down to the officials in question, who must prepare the Minister's answer for him. These Ministerial queries are heartily disliked in the departments, partly because they may well reveal weaknesses and partly because they add to the burden of the people affected. Therefore they are gone into thoroughly, and care is taken to ensure that they do not recur. The Minister himself will not wish to give hostages to fortune; he will have to be fully convinced that the weakness, if any, is removed, or that the injustice, if any, has been put right. He will sometimes demand a revision of the department's methods. He may even rebuke some one.

The main business of Parliament is to provide money for the administration of the country and to see to it that the money is well spent. It is alleged that, in fact, Parliament has no real control over money, but two House of Commons committees keep a watchful eye on pounds, shillings, and pence. The Committee on Estimates sits for several months; it takes each vote in turn. It cannot examine everything in detail, but it takes a cross-section. That part which is selected for scrutiny is gone into very thoroughly. If a heading shows a sudden increase in cost, for example, the Committee will want to know why. As a department does not know which part of its estimates is to be examined in detail by the Committee, it must be ready to defend and justify the whole. There has been a series of rehearsals of this defence in the arguments which have already taken place between the department and the Treasury. Moreover, the departmental heads are responsible men who are themselves taxpayers. They do not waste public money wantonly. They tend, if anything, to be parsimonious. Parliamentary control over estimates is therefore reasonably good.

The Committee on Public Accounts examines departmental accounts. The weakness here is that the Committee comes into the picture some two years after the money has been spent. In that sense it is too late for the Committee to do anything. On the other hand, revelations of extravagance or incompetence, or even dishonesty, are a grave reflection upon the permanent head of the department, who is theoretically responsible for all moneys spent. The Opposition, in particular, is on the look-out for points upon which it can criticize the Government. The Committee has the help of the Auditor-General's department, who have been auditing the accounts of each department. The Committee can summon witnesses and cross-examine them. No civil servant likes being questioned by the Committee. The report of the Auditor-General is always published, and the Press seizes eagerly on any criticisms of Whitehall's wastefulness. The value of this Committee's work lies partly in the deterrent it stands for and partly in the reforms of departmental procedure it may bring about.

The Committee on Nationalized Industries is designed to see that the Ministry concerned is exercising effective control over the industry and that the latter is giving good service to the public. This Committee was set up by the Conservative Government which succeeded the Labour Government of 1945–50, who had nationalized so many great industries. The Committee issued its first report on the Coal Board after eight months' work, in the course of which it examined witnesses from the Board, the Treasury, and the Ministry of Fuel and Power. One important conclusion of the Committee was that a public corporation must provide the information in writing to the Treasury to justify a grant of public money (raised from taxation) to the Board. In other words, Parliament was busy protecting the electorate's interests.

The Committee on Statutory Instruments examines the thousands of pages of orders and regulations which Ministries publish every year. This Committee has no power to annul an instrument, but it can call the attention of the House to any injustice or serious blunder. Moreover, anything which the Committee misses will most certainly not escape the eagle eye of some pressure group outside Parliament, which will see to it that a member of the Committee, or at least an M.P., will have the complaint brought to his attention.

THE FUNCTIONS OF SOME OF THE MORE IMPORTANT MINISTRIES

All Government departments perform an essential and an important task. Three of them, however, seem to stand out in importance. They are the Foreign Office, the Treasury, and the Home Office.

The Foreign Office

We live in an international society. The world is rapidly shrinking in the sense that the immense increase in speed of communication and transport is bringing nations at the opposite ends of the earth close together in time and space. The only real hope of peace and prosperity lies in the establishment of a truly international society— what is fashionably called at the moment 'co-existence.' Many international institutions have been set up since the War to foster co-operation, such as the United Nations Organization, the International Monetary Fund, the European Economic Union. Great Britain in particular is vitally dependent on good international relations because of the Commonwealth and because she is a highly industrialized country which can support a very high standard of living only by exporting a large proportion of her products and importing at least half of her food and a large part of her raw materials, such as cotton, oil, iron ore. It is therefore of vital importance that Britain's relations with the many countries who buy her goods and sell her their products should be close and friendly. Moreover, the Government of the day must know what is going on in these countries if it is to follow an up-to-date and constructive foreign policy.

The Foreign Secretary is usually a very close colleague of the Prime Minister. Their relationship is described in detail in Chapter IV.

The primary duty of the Foreign Office is to carry out the policy of the British people, through Parliament, the majority party in Parliament, the Cabinet, and the Foreign Secretary.

The method is to negotiate with foreign Governments and international bodies. This, in a word, is 'diplomacy.' The actual work is done:

(a) In Britain at the Foreign Office with the representatives in London of foreign Governments.

(b) Abroad through the diplomatic and consular services of Her Majesty's Government accredited to the central Governments and local authorities respectively of foreign countries.

Negotiation means constant liaison with the representatives of other countries, hearing patiently what they have to say, stating the British point of view cogently yet diplomatically.

There can be no sound policy formulated unless it is based on accurate and up-to-date facts. These facts must, however, be summed up and commented on, so that the Foreign Secretary can assimilate them rapidly, understand what is happening and why, and can be advised that there are various alternative ways of dealing with the current situation, each of which has advantages and disadvantages, but one of which must be recommended as the best course to follow. Both the man on the spot and the man at home, each looking at the problem from a different angle, must give an opinion. What is apparently a purely local affair may, in fact, have many repercussions elsewhere which can be seen and forecast only by some one in the Foreign Office looking at the situation as a whole. For instance, a rising in Iraq has its repercussions in Jordan, in Kuwait, in Turkey, and so on. Some one must study the reports from these countries and compare them.

The Foreign Secretary will in the meantime be hearing what the other countries think through visits to him by their Ambassadors.

He will have a chance at these interviews to explain the British attitude.

As foreign affairs are so closely connected with economic affairs and defence, the Foreign Office must work in co-operation with the Treasury, the Board of Trade, and the Service Ministries. All our Embassies abroad have military attachés whose job is to study the Fighting Forces of the countries to which they are accredited, assess their military strength, state of morale, organization, and weapons. On the economic side the Embassies must constantly be collecting and collating masses of material about factories, prices, products, trade in general.

The essence of all this activity is secrecy. People will give information only if they are convinced that the sources from which it has been obtained will not be divulged. Indeed, as a rule the fact that the information is known is not disclosed. It is usually best to use information with the utmost discretion. A vast part of the work is humdrum, routine getting together of facts and figures. Only very occasionally is there a touch of the romantic cloak-and-dagger method.

Governments of the British Commonwealth, who trust one another, help one another by sharing information fully. For instance, Great Britain will act on behalf of any Commonwealth country which has no Embassy in a certain capital. The British Embassy in this capital will look after the Commonwealth country's interests. And this service will be reciprocated.

Members of the top grade of the Foreign Service—the equivalent of the Administrative grade in the ordinary Civil Service—must be men of the highest quality. They must be diplomatic and tactful, get on well with other people, and possess the ability to listen gracefully to a great number of boring platitudes and perhaps malicious gossip. Men of culture and wide reading, a diversity of interests, and strong constitutions are necessary. As half their work is done abroad in many lands, they must be willing to learn the history of the peoples among whom they are working, to understand those peoples, to know how they are thinking. The best way to do all this is to know the language. Furthermore, as so much of the work consists of accumulating and interpreting economic facts, they must be economists. They are consequently encouraged to learn languages and study economics after passing into the Service. At one time entry was in practice restricted to a very narrow circle, because of the requirement that a candidate must have private means. The Service was divided into two parts—the Diplomatic, from which Ambassadors were found, and the Consular, a junior branch, or poor relation. Sir Anthony Eden, a great Foreign Secretary, reformed this unsatisfactory system. He made just one Service, recruited by open competition in which languages, history, and economics were important subjects. He abolished the 'means test.' The pay and allowances nowadays are large enough (in theory, anyway) to enable a man, while serving abroad, to send his children to boarding school in England; to entertain without being out of pocket; to be able to devote his full energies to his work without the distraction of financial worries.

The Home Office

The Home Secretary has two principal tasks. They are:

(a) The maintenance of the Queen's Peace.
(b) The discharging of the Royal Prerogative of Mercy.

In detail these duties are:

(i) Police administration.
(ii) Fire Service.
(iii) Civil Defence.
(iv) Children's department.
(v) Public well-being, safety in factories, etc.
(vi) Control of aliens.
(vii) Nationality and naturalization.
(viii) Administration of justice.
(ix) Probation service.
(x) Residuary legacies.

The last of these duties covers a wide variety of ground. Whatever problems crop up for which no existing department will admit responsibility are handed over to the Home Office to tackle. This rôle of maid of all work may in some ways seem a drab one, but in fact it should be welcome, because it entails some most interesting tasks. For instance, at present the Home Office is responsible for:

(a) The redress of grievances.
(b) The conduct of elections.
(c) The sponsoring of Private Bills in Parliament.
(d) The protection of wild birds and animals.
(e) Summer time and calendar questions.
(f) Charitable collections.
(g) Taxicabs.
(h) Marriage guidance.
(i) Prison administration.

The Queen's Peace

This is a difficult problem. As Dr Johnson once said:

> The danger of unbounded liberty and the danger of bounding it have produced a problem in the science of government which human understanding seems hitherto unable to solve.

But the illogical British, in their blundering, muddling manner, have succeeded, more by good luck, perhaps, than good management, in keeping an even balance between too much and too little liberty.

The object of prohibiting certain activities is to prevent interference with more desirable and important activities. For instance, there is a law which forbids small boys to throw stones at windows. This law is not designed to deprive small boys of exciting pleasures, but to protect the peace and property of householders, who are entitled to sit securely indoors without having their windows suddenly shattered. Similarly, shops are closed, not in order to prevent people from enjoying the pleasure of shopping, but to protect shop assistants from having to work excessively long hours.

On the other hand, when Sir Winston Churchill was Home Secretary in 1911 he was asked to stop children roller-skating in the streets because one or two old people had been knocked down. He decided that it would be wrong to deprive young people of the chance to display agility and initiative, and he refused to make an order. The elderly had to take the risk of being in collision with skaters. He considered the liberty of the youthful skaters more precious than the possible risk to old people. The answer was for each party to exercise vigilance.

Fortunately for the Home Secretary, his task in allowing the widest possible liberty consistent with law and order is eased by the fact that the British are a law-abiding race. They queue up patiently in accordance with a notice. They keep off the grass in public parks. (Alas, they habitually shed litter all over the place!) They enjoy the privilege of grumbling at the iniquities of the Government, but they are rarely to be stirred into revolutionary activity. They respect the impartiality of the courts and the fairness of the police, and are willing, therefore, to submit to the law.

In carrying out his task of administering the police or the Fire Service the Home Secretary lays down the general policy, the standards of efficiency, the rates of pay, the equipment to be used. He provides part of the money through Central Government grants to local authorities. The latter find the rest of the money and do the detailed running of these services. The Home Office exercises its control partly through the purse and partly through a system of regular inspections.

The Prerogative of Mercy

The Home Secretary makes the necessary inquiries, sometimes of a long and very extensive nature. He then gives the matter his most careful consideration and consults the appropriate experts. Finally, he gives the sovereign advice, which will, conventionally, always be taken. Any man of imagination and normal compassion will hate the responsibility of deciding whether one of his fellow-men is to die by hanging or be imprisoned for life.

The Treasury

The First Lord of the Treasury is the Prime Minister.

The Second Lord is the Chancellor of the Exchequer, who is the political head of the Treasury. The department is divided into two main parts. One is concerned with the administration of the Civil Service. The other is responsible for the administration of the economic affairs of the nation. The Earl of Avon, when he was Prime Minister, realized that these two rôles were too much for one man to perform well, so he appointed two Permanent Under-Secretaries of State. The one who deals with the Civil Service is its head, and, as we have seen, advises the Prime Minister on promotions to the principal posts in the Service. This part of the Treasury deals with establishments, organization, and method.

The other part of the Treasury is concerned with the raising of public money and the spending of it. All the year round a division of the Treasury is studying the yield of each tax and building up a plan for the following year. As the Government needs to raise some £5000 millions a year, how to find this large sum is an immense problem for the Treasury, who must devise a plan of taxation. Such a plan is not a simple matter, because a good tax must be fair and equitable. As far as possible, a man must pay according to his means. It must be simple, so that it is difficult to evade and easy to collect. It must be sound economically; otherwise it may be a big disincentive to people to work harder if too large a proportion of their earnings goes away in taxes; or it may invoke the Law of Diminishing Returns. A high tax will raise the price of an article. If the price goes too high people will buy fewer of these articles, and the revenue from the tax may be less than when a lower tax was levied.

The Treasury is also concerned with going through departmental estimates with meticulous care to prevent extravagance and incompetence. But in an era of planning the Treasury is also amassing an enormous collection of statistics on the economic state of the country. This enables the Treasury to advise the Chancellor whether the Bank Rate is to be raised or lowered; whether Treasury Bills are to be bought or sold; whether industry is to be stimulated to expand or discouraged into contraction. The Treasury employs a distinguished body of professional economists to advise on all these immense problems.

The Other Departments

These are all of importance, and each plays an equal part in the team. There is no space here to describe in detail what each Ministry does.

SUMMING-UP

Parliament from time to time appoints a Commission or Select Committee to examine the state of the Civil Service. There was the MacDonnell Report (1912) and the Tomlin Report (1929–31).

An efficient system of bureaucratic administration demands:

    (a) Allocation of regular official duties.
    (b) Authority to enforce policy.
    (c) Methodical performance of duties.

In order to meet these demands the following things are necessary:

    (a) Differentiation of function.
    (b) Qualifications for office.
    (c) Hierarchical organization and discipline.
    (d) Precision and consistency.
    (e) Objectivity.
    (f) Discretion.

This means written documentation of files and other similar records. Government by committee has evolved inevitably.

The British system has now acquired the following characteristics:

    (a) Recruitment by open competition; no nepotism or patronage.
    (b) Promotion by merit.
    (c) Incorruptibility.
    (d) Political impartiality.
    (e) Complete loyalty to the Government of the day.
    (f) Anonymity.

The disadvantages of the system are (or are alleged to be):

(a) An excessive self-importance.
(b) Obsession with precedents until inflexibility is attained.
(c) Mania for regulations and formality.
(d) Preoccupation with one department to the detriment of the administration as a whole.
(e) Failure to distinguish clearly the relations between governors and governed.

That is why in a democracy it is considered essential that the Civil Service must be controlled by the elected representatives of the people—*i.e.*, Parliament.

The conclusions which emerge from this brief survey of the Civil Service and its work are:

(a) That in a modern complex society the Government of the day and Parliament are unable to deal with the detailed day-to-day administration of the country; therefore a Civil Service is essential to do this work.
(b) That it is essential for Parliament, through departmental Ministers, to control the Civil Service, and that this is done reasonably well.
(c) That, in order to ease the heavy burden on an overladen Parliament, it is necessary for a great many Statutory Instruments to be put out each year by departments, and that reasonably adequate safeguards now exist to prevent this delegated legislation being framed to the detriment of the general public.
(d) That as civil servants are brought more and more into contact with the general public they develop a better sense of proportion; they serve the people better. The broadening of the base of recruitment at the top has made the Service much more in touch with the needs and feelings of the people.

BIBLIOGRAPHY

CAMPBELL, G. A.: *The Civil Service in Britain* (Penguin Books, 1955).
The Foreign Office, The Home Office, The Colonial Office, The Treasury, and *The Ministry of Labour* ("New Whitehall" series; Allen and Unwin, 1954–64).
MONCK, B.: *How the Civil Service Works* (Phœnix House, 1952).
DUNNILL, F.: *The Civil Service: Some Human Aspects* (Allen and Unwin; fifth edition, 1957).
FURSE, RALPH: *Aucuparius* (Oxford University Press, 1964).

CHAPTER X

Local Government in England and Wales

Local government—a long tradition. Pattern of local government. The Electoral System. Main functions of local government. Central control. The Committee System. Grants and Loans. Rates. Local-government officers. The Government of Greater London, The City of London.

I am the mother of five boys.
I am a School Lady.
I am a Visiting Lady.
I am a Reading Lady.
I am a Distinguished Lady.
I am on the Local Linen Box Committee and many General Committees.
I am a Woman of Business.
You cannot tire me if you try.

This remarkable woman was Mrs Pardiggle in Charles Dickens' "Bleak House." We have all met her or some one very like her.

Local government . . . is not just a machine or a piece of organization. If one is dealing with a machine or a piece of organization, one can take each part separately and look at it separately. Local government seems to us to be much more like a living thing, an organism, in which each part or function is not self-contained or connected externally with other parts. Each part is integrally concerned with each other part. The nature and function of each part affects, and in some degree determines, the nature and function of each of the other parts. The whole is not just a conglomeration of the parts . . . Local government is with us an instance of democracy at work, and no amount of potential administrative efficiency could make up for this loss of active participation in the work by capable, public-spirited people elected by, responsible to, and in touch with those who elect them.

Report of the Royal Commission on Local Government in
Greater London 1957–1960, p. 59.

A LONG TRADITION AND HISTORY

Local government can be traced far back in England. After the Norman Conquest most of the Saxon civil institutions were abolished, but the Courts of the Hundreds were preserved, and a manorial system begun under major-bailiffs—the mayors of to-day. The ecclesiastical parish remained, under which the parish priest summoned his flock to a vestry meeting to deal with both Church and civil matters. There is now a separation between the Church and the civil administrative parish council.

The Tudors, who did establish a strong central government, had to set up local-government authorities: poor transport and communication made control from London difficult. Prominent country gentlemen were appointed Justices of the Peace, with authority to try offences locally and to preserve order. In 1601, under the Poor Relief Act, the parishes were empowered to levy rates and to appoint officers to do the executive work locally. In 1834 the Poor Law Amendment Act created groups of parishes called Poor Law Unions, each under a Board of Guardians with central authority vested in the Poor Law Commissioners.

People accustomed to dealing with their local affairs guard this independence jealously. The successful struggle by Rutland in 1963 to avoid being swallowed up by Leicestershire is an example.

PATTERN AND STRUCTURE

The Municipal Corporations Act of 1835, and another in 1882, extended the suffrage, introduced a Borough Audit, and separated the administration of justice from that of local affairs. The Local Government Act, 1888, set up the county councils and the county boroughs, which were made independent of the counties. Another Act of 1894 set up the rural and urban district councils, as well as parish councils or meetings within the rural areas. The London Government Act, 1899, introduced the metropolitan borough councils, and the distinction between London and the other counties was drawn. The Local Government Act, 1933, which is still called 'the principal Act,' codified the previous legislation, and the London Government Act, 1939, brought London into line with general policy.

The pattern at the beginning of 1967 (excluding London) was:

58 County Councils
82 County Boroughs
270 Non-county Boroughs
535 Urban Districts
472 Rural Districts
7500 Parishes approximately
3300 Parish Meetings approximately

As the concentration of industry has brought about shiftings of population and the rapid growth of new towns, the size of these areas in terms of people has altered, until in 1963 the largest parish had 27,000 inhabitants and the smallest county only 23,000. Non-county boroughs vary from 10,000 to 200,000 and rural and urban districts from 5000 to 50,000. Most parishes look after a few hundred people. These discrepancies are puzzling, and from a purely administrative angle inefficient, but the strength of tradition is formidable, and reform is therefore slow and gradual. However, there have been changes, and the central Government has laid down guides, such as 100,000 minimum for a borough and 125,000 in a borough within a conurbation, where a special problem exists. A few actual examples are interesting to note. Lancashire has 2,230,000 inhabitants, whereas Rutland is only 23,900 strong and Radnorshire a mere 18,400. The County Borough of Birmingham has a population of 1,105,000 compared with that of Canterbury, 30,000, and so on with other administrative divisions. These are, of course, extreme examples, but they reveal the need for some uniformity.

The size in terms of inhabitants with substantial financial capacity is important because an authority that is too small cannot afford to pay the salary that a first-class administrator will require, nor can it offer work to interest him. Moreover, a small council may not be able to pay the high cost of services like education. The optimum number for a self-supporting education authority is perhaps between 150,000 and 250,000.[1] This problem of size is constantly under review.

The general pattern has two tiers—the county councils on top; below, the other councils within each county, and more or less dependent upon them. The county boroughs are, by tradition and statute, independent of the counties, and are all-purpose authorities, and form an exception to this general pattern. The non-county boroughs possess similar constitutions, but are not entirely independent of the counties.

COUNTY COUNCILS

A county council, by the Local Government Act, 1933, consists of a chairman, aldermen, and councillors. The chairman is elected annually by the council from among the aldermen and councillors. He is usually remunerated in office to enable him to devote time for the work of the council, and to furnish official hospitality. He is also by virtue of his office a J.P. A vice-chairman is also appointed who may act as deputy to the chairman in all matters, except on the judicial bench.

[1] This is despite the White Paper figure of 100,000.

The councillors are elected every three years under the Representation of the People Act, 1949. The county consists of divisions,
each of which returns one councillor. The number of divisions was
fixed by the Act of 1888, but a council may appeal to the Home
Secretary for alterations under the Act of 1933.

The aldermen are elected by the councillors for six years in the
proportion of one alderman to three councillors. Half the aldermen
retire every third year, and their successors are elected at the annual
meeting ending their term of office. An alderman need not be a
councillor, but must possess the same qualifications. No one can be
both alderman and councillor simultaneously. Aldermen do not
meet separately, nor do they exercise special powers. Their existence
is now a controversial topic. They are not publicly elected, which is
thought undemocratic. Moreover, elderly councillors who do not
wish to undergo the stress of an election remain on the council in
this way, while candidates who have actually been defeated in a
division can be elected as aldermen, which is a negation of the
electors' wishes. What is more, the present system can be used to
enable a party which has gained a narrow majority of one in the
election to acquire a clear majority by electing all the aldermen from
their own ranks at the first council meeting. These are grave weaknesses.

However, the present system does enable the council to invite
persons with special qualifications to serve with distinction, nor do
most councils abuse the electoral system. Some councils by convention appoint aldermen in proportion to the party strength of the
councillors.

Meetings

County Councils must meet four times a year by statute, but they
may, and usually do, meet more often, normally once a month.
Counties are usually based on the old traditional 'shires.'

BOROUGHS

There are three kinds of borough, county, non-county, and metropolitan, the latter being dealt with in the section on London. All
boroughs are created by Royal Charter, but a county borough must
be approved by Parliamentary Statute, which is not forthcoming
unless the borough is a large one. The Act of 1888 created sixty-one
county boroughs, and in 1963 there were eighty-three. The last
county borough to be created was Doncaster in 1927, while Eal-
ing and Ilford have recently had Bills introduced which were
defeated.

The promotion of a rural or urban district to the status of non-county borough is granted by the Crown on the advice of the Privy Council following an inquiry and recommendation by the Minister of Housing and Local Government. There is no statutory minimum size for recognition as a non-county borough, but it is unlikely that a district with a population smaller than 20,000 will succeed. As a result of the Act of 1958 some non-county boroughs whose populations had become very small became part of a rural district with the functions of a parish council, but the mayor remains though the aldermen have departed. This is a curious compromise between tradition and efficiency.

There is no constitutional difference between a county and a non-county borough, and the council consists of a mayor, the aldermen, and the councillors. In some cases the Crown by letters patent has elevated the mayor to the dignity of a lord mayor. If the borough is a city (usually the result of ancient custom or an Order-in-Council, and because there is a cathedral) the people are citizens, otherwise they are burgesses.

The Mayor

The Mayor holds a very ancient office, now defined by the Act of 1933. He is elected by the council at their first meeting for a period of one year, and he may seek re-election. He need not be a council member, but must possess the qualifications. Like the chairman of a county council, he has many civic and ceremonial duties, and he is paid a salary as mayor. He is sometimes returning officer at parliamentary elections, and *ex officio* a J.P. He usually has precedence within the borough.

The Councillors and Aldermen

The councillors are elected for three years. Each year a third retire, and there is an election. They are eligible for re-election. Many boroughs are divided into wards, with three councillors or a multiple of three for each ward. The aldermen are elected by the councillors for a term of six years, and half of them retire every third year, in which there is an election.

Meetings

The council must by law meet at least four times a year, but usually they meet more often.

URBAN AND RURAL DISTRICTS

Urban and Rural District Councils are as laid down by the Act of 1933. They consist of a chairman and councillors. They do not have a mayor or aldermen. The chairman is elected for a year by the council from among themselves, or from an 'outsider' possessing the qualifications to stand for the council. He is paid a reasonable salary in recognition of the work he does. Like the chairmen of county councils and the mayors in the boroughs, he is the only paid member of a council. The others are all unpaid administrators who do the work for its moral satisfaction. He is a J.P. for the county while holding office.

Councillors are elected for three years at elections held either annually or every third year. By law, one-third of the council must retire each year, and there is an election at which they may stand again, but if the county council can be persuaded so to direct, the whole council may retire every third year in a body. Most of the rural and some of the urban councils prefer this method. The size of these councils is determined by the county council, which presumably gives it some influence.

Meetings

The law requires four meetings a year, but most councils meet more often, usually once a month or every six weeks.

PARISHES

Under the Act of 1933 rural parishes with a population of more than 300 must have a council. If the number is less than 300 but more than 200 the county council must authorize a council if the parish meeting asks for one. If the number is under 200 the county council will not direct that there shall be a council unless the parish is insistent and there is a good case. In some instances several very small parishes share one parish council.

The council consists of a chairman and between five and twenty-one members as determined by the county council. Members are elected for a term of three years, and the council must meet at least four times a year.

The parish councils may be poor, their functions unimpressive, and their constitutional importance insignificant, but they are in fact not only a traditional English local-government unit—they are lively. To the council and the parishioners their local affairs are all-important. Probably a much keener interest is taken in parish affairs than in those of bigger councils. The moral is surely that a local-government authority can be too big, and its affairs must really be local.

THE ELECTORAL SYSTEM

In general the system is based on the same fundamental principles as a parliamentary election, and follows largely the Representation of the People Act, 1949. Any person who is more than twenty-one, is a British subject (or a citizen of the Irish Republic), and is properly registered on the Roll is eligible to vote. In order to qualify for registration a person must be resident in the area or occupy as owner or tenant any rateable land or premises of an annual value of not less than £10. A person who has a residential qualification in one area and a non-residential qualification in another area is entitled to a vote in each area. This does not seem to fulfil the principle of one person, one vote, but so far there does not seem to be any serious wish to amend the privilege. The Roll has to be published once a year, and the registration officer, who is usually clerk to the council, must see to it that this is done, and the register is properly kept.

Voting

Voting is by secret ballot at polling stations under a presiding officer who is specially appointed. Voting is usually done in person, or by post or by proxy if the voter cannot attend. The voter has one vote for every seat contested in his electoral area. Thus if it is a ward with three seats he has three votes, one for each seat.

THE VOTER AND THE COUNCILLOR

The Voter

The voter ought to be interested in the membership of his council, but the proportion of the electorate who bother to vote is disappointingly small. According to figures compiled by the Registrar-General between 1955 and 1958, under half the electorate voted at elections, on average. In the counties the figure was as low as 33 per cent. in 1958, and was only 40 per cent. in the boroughs. Things were a little better in rural districts with a figure of 46 per cent. Perhaps the low poll means administration is satisfactory, but probably more and more voters think that it is the parliamentary election that is the vital one.

The story is much the same regarding uncontested seats. In 1958 no fewer than 60 per cent. of the seats on county councils and 75 per cent. of those on rural district councils were uncontested, which suggests apathy of a high order, or possibly a lack of candidates. Things were a little better in county boroughs, where only 18 per cent. of the seats were uncontested, no doubt because party organization was strong here.

The Councillor

The councillor is, or should usually be, a local 'worthy,' like the country gentleman who used to administer the parishes three hundred years ago. The leaders of the community ought to want to serve on a council and ensure that their beloved districts are efficiently administered. Unfortunately, they are deterred from standing, either because they find the work likely to be dull and unsatisfying because the central Government has taken over so much that is important, or because they cannot spare the time. The Act of 1958 tries to do something to attract councillors of the appropriate standing; and the fact that councils and their committees do not meet more than once a week or thereabouts, and then in the evening probably, ought to attract the attention of married women of attainment whose household duties stop them going into Parliament; they could perform useful local-government work.

If local government is important—and it is—then it ought to be in the hands of competent persons who possess at least some of the following qualifications:

(a) They should know the people of the area intimately, their needs and hopes and fears, and they should be familiar with the district as well.

(b) They must know how to use professional advice without treating it as sacred.

(c) They must manage to work in close harmony with the officers of the council by giving them support and making the decisions that they need without interfering with them in the execution of their duties.

(d) They must be able to act as a link between the council and the party, trying to serve both the people of the area and the party interest intelligently and fairly.

These are high qualifications. Men and women who will serve the public interest devotedly and disinterestedly are rare. They must be offered satisfying work if they are to be attracted to serve on the council. The Act of 1958 tried to do this by revising the system of grants in order to give councillors more scope.[1] It was argued that under the percentage grant a council had so much and no more to spend on a certain object, which gave the councillors no chance to get the maximum benefit from the minimum expenditure, whereas under the block grant the council are encouraged to give as good a service as before, and yet may by more efficient administration spend less in one direction in order to be able to spend more in another.   They might perhaps even succeed in reducing the rates a little, whereas the usual experience is for the rates to be raised, thus antagonizing the voters.

[1] This problem is admirably dealt with on pp. 62–64 of the *Report of the Royal Commission on Greater London*.

If men wish to influence their fellows, membership of a council surely does offer rewarding work. Two of the most extensive and vital functions performed by a council are education and housing. One council may prefer the grammar school, and another plumps for the comprehensive; there are differing opinions about co-educational schools; the eleven-plus examination is a vexed question; the design of schools, the provision of an adequate supply of books, the problems of providing further education for adults that shall be wide in range—all this presents interesting work for a councillor. An enthusiastic and well-informed education committee who are genuinely interested in the schools they administer cannot ask for more satisfying activity. The same sort of comments apply to housing. One of the most important of services is to house the people of a district in a decent standard of comfort and security. The houses must be allocated on a fair basis, knowing the demand will be greater than the supply.

PARTY POLITICS

Local government is LOCAL SELF-government—that is the essence of it. Its affairs must be purely local to be exciting. A house match at school is a great occasion, but a game against another school is even more exciting. A councillor ought to feel a proper pride in his district, and to believe that it is better looked after than are its neighbours. This is a proper sentiment of parochial pride. From this point of view men of independent mind perhaps make the best councillors because they will not allow the prejudices of party politics to sway them in a decision, say, whether to transform a secondary modern school into a grammar school. They will study the matter, talk to parents and teachers and children, they will consult professional advisers and then make up their own minds honestly. This is a difficult problem because it can be argued that too many independents could produce administrative chaos. Perhaps "local" parties concerned with "local" affairs rather than with the national parties would be the answer.

Alas, the supply of such councillors seems to be diminishing. The apathy is increasing. The standing for election, though the expenses are modest, nevertheless involves the spending of money. Some vexatious local affair will not be adequately publicized—so that a proper public opinion can be formed—unless a considerable sum of money is spent, and a great deal of work is done. A few independents are not likely to be able to muster the support and provide the organization that is required; but a big, wealthy political party can do so. There are obviously substantial advantages in encouraging the national parties to step into the local arena. They have means of

persuading eloquent speakers to come down and talk, they can produce attractive propaganda, they can educate the electorate effectively, dramatically; they may possibly stimulate the voters to shake
off their apathy; but will they do all this at too big a cost? The
emphasis on local affairs will tend to become blurred, and that on
national party politics will be heavily accented. Local-government
elections will tend to become a rehearsal for the parliamentary
election, in which the parties will try their strength, will perfect
their organization, and might even lose sight of the object of the
election, which is to put people on a council to administer a district,
with its own peculiar problems that are often of little or no interest
to outsiders. Are the beach huts let by the ambitious town of Small-
hampton-by-Sea encroaching on the respectable privacy of the
adjoining parish of Onyting-on-Rust? It is hard to see how there
can be a Labour or a Conservative point of view on this essentially
local affair. Once the council is in session, the whips set to work,
and both debates and divisions tend to become artificial. Possibly
some councillors will find this position even more stultifying than one
in which there is no party basis. Moreover, the party system can
result in sudden and upsetting changes in the balance of power. A
system of proportional representation might be the answer, because
the weaknesses of such a system in a national parliament do not
apply to local government.[1]

It has been suggested that councillors should be paid, as the
'working man' is otherwise precluded from standing. This ought
not to be necessary if committees were less frequent, or were smaller
and met out of ordinary business hours. The vital feature of the
English system is the partnership between the amateur administrator
with his wide range of interests and the professional with his exper-
tise. Paid councillors would damage this association. They might
even destroy it. On the other hand, there is probably a reasonable
case for appropriate out-of-pocket expenses to be paid to councillors in a huge conurbation like London.[2]

Suitable Publicity

Perhaps the answer is to give the meetings of the council more
space in the newspapers. A stern battle in council or committee
fought by independents, whose votes cannot be relied on implicitly,
and who will be debating from intimate local knowledge, must be
interesting.

[1] For an excellent discussion see *A Report to the Liberal Party: Local
Government, 1963*, pp. 96–106.
[2] These expenses are in fact paid.

The Main Functions of Local Government

The purpose of a council is to administer the affairs of an area, which means in practice to provide the inhabitants with those services that help to make life worth while. A council also is obliged to control some of the activities of its people. It can make by-laws and punish non-compliance. Some of the activities it controls are:

(a) Management of a park or swimming-bath.
(b) Rowdy behaviour in a street.
(c) Hours of business of shops.

A council may therefore be described as:

(a) Legislative—it passes by-laws.
(b) Administrative—it manages affairs.
(c) Executive—it carries out functions delegated to it.

The functions which a council performs depend on the status of that council. Perhaps the best plan is to take a county borough, which is an independent all-purpose authority and to list its functions and then to make comparisons with other councils by status to see in what way their functions differ.

The main interests of a county borough are:

Accommodation for the Aged
Allotments
Ambulances
Baths
Births and Deaths
Care of the Blind
Care of Children
Cemeteries
Education
Fire Precautions
Housing
Libraries
Maternity
Parks
Police
Rates
Refuse Collection
Road Maintenance
Street Cleaning
Town Planning
Transport
Water
Weights and Measures

It will be seen that though assistance to the needy is now furnished by the Ministry of Social Security, the councils still do a great deal of important welfare work—in the form of subsidized rents, for example—and they have a close link with the local office of the Ministry.

The other authorities do not carry out all these functions. In the table that follows will be found those services for which they are NOT responsible.

	County Council	Non-county Borough	Urban District	Rural District
Aged		No	No	No
Allotments				No
Ambulances		No	No	No
Baths	No			No
Births and Deaths		No	No	No
Blind		No	No	No
Building	No			
Cemeteries	No			
Children		No	No	No
Education		No	No	No
Fire Precautions		No	No	No
Maternity		No	No	No
Police		Sometimes	No	No
Rates	No			
Refuse	No			
Roads				No
Street Cleaning	No			
Town Planning		No	No	No
Transport	No	Sometimes	Sometimes	No
Water	No	Sometimes	Sometimes	Sometimes
Weights and Measures	Sometimes	No	No	No

The main differences between a county and a non-county borough are that the former is responsible for education, fire, police, town planning, and water. The latter does none of these tasks except that some non-county boroughs have a part in police administration and water provision. And, of course, the county borough does not contribute to the coffers of the county council. A big, rich non-county borough will sometimes resent its partial dependence on a county council, and will hanker after county borough status. Occasionally, as in Middlesex, according to the White Paper of 1957 and the Royal Commission on Greater London of 1960, the relations between county and non-county boroughs are deplorable, and if Middlesex had been deprived of its boroughs it would have ceased to exist. As a result of the London Government Act, 1963, the County of Middlesex has in fact disappeared.

It will be seen that the local-government authorities carry out some important and valuable services. The United Kingdom is now a welfare state, and the councils are concerned with the care of the old and the young, the blind and the sick. They provide homes and attention for them. They are no longer delegated the work of managing hospitals, but they do sometimes arrange for people to be taken to hospital by ambulance. They are concerned with public health, because they keep the streets adequately lighted and cleaned. They arrange for refuse to be cleared away and disposed of; they manage sewage and sewage farms. They inspect drains, and ensure that inoculation and vaccination are carried out. They deal with epidemics if they occur. They are responsible for housing their inhabitants. They are in many cases responsible for providing transport by bus. Some of the bigger councils run their own bus services, and when they rely upon a commercial firm to run the buses there must be consultation with the council about stops, routes, shelters, frequency of service, and so on.

It is impossible in a book of this nature to discuss these functions and powers fully; but it can safely be said that there is scarcely any social activity in a local-government area that is not in some way influenced by the council.

THE DISTRIBUTION OF POWERS

A local authority exists because it is created by an Act of Parliament. It possesses the power to carry out certain services because Parliament has delegated these powers to it in various statutes. What Parliament has delegated Parliament can always take away, because it is dissatisfied with the conduct of a local authority or because it decides that some function, such as the provision of electricity, is better performed by a public corporation under the control of the central Government. The ultimate source of power therefore resides in Parliament, and so there must be a close relationship between it and the councils. Parliament knows that it lacks the time, the local knowledge, and the technical information to perform in detail the functions which it has perforce delegated to local authorities.[1] The usual problem in any political system arises as to how far the central Government allows the local government to go without interference, and clearly the aim should be to give the councils as much scope as possible, if only to encourage the best people to serve on councils. It is a nice problem to draw this administrative line, especially if a party believes in a strong central Government which is responsible for planning the activities of the whole country.

[1] This must be considered in the light of the traditional right of local communities to govern themselves.

Recent legislation gives an interesting picture of the continual effort to solve this problem.

THE EFFECTS OF NATIONALIZATION

The two Labour Governments of 1945–51 enacted a vast amount of fundamental legislation, resulting in the nationalization of several great industries and services and inevitably taking away from some local authorities several of their most cherished functions. Moreover, where by statute powers were delegated to a council to give a service the Minister concerned was sometimes given the right of inspection, occasionally the right to make decisions that might deny the council permission to continue with a project, usually the right to recommend the reduction or withdrawal of a Government grant, thus crippling the ability of the local authority to do its job. It is presumed that even the block grant can be reduced to create this effect.

CENTRAL CONTROL

Central control is exercised in three ways:

     (1) By Parliament.
     (2) By Government departments.
     (3) By the courts.

It is repeated that all local-government power stems from parliamentary statute. Anything done by a council which has not been provided for in the statute is *ultra vires*, and the Council must promote a Private Bill to obtain the necessary sanction, such as the periodical Enabling Bill of the London County Council.

The National Assistance Act, 1948, took away from councils the function of helping the poor and needy. The Police Act, 1946, brought certain aspects of police administration under central control, and there is a growing feeling that all police forces, such as the Metropolitan Police, should come under the Home Office. The National Health Service Act, 1946, transferred the management of hospitals to the Ministry of Health. The Local Government Act, 1929, transferred the maintenance of all roads, except trunk roads, to county councils (though boroughs, as mentioned elsewhere, deal with roads in their areas). The trunk roads come under the Ministry of Transport by the Act of 1946. Similarly, the Electricity Act, 1947, and the Gas Act, 1948, transferred the supply of these two services from local authorities to central authorities and put them under the ultimate control of the Minister of Power. The Local Government Act, 1948, transferred the valuation of property for rating to the

Board of Inland Revenue. Enough has been said to show the power of Parliament.

Government departments usually lay down minimum standards of administration below which services given by councils must not fall. Inspections, the auditing of accounts by the District Auditor, the submission of building schemes to the Minister, are the principal means by which administrative control is carried out, but, naturally, Government departments are wise enough not to behave arbitrarily. They consult the local authorities and try to work with them as far as possible. The merit of this method is that it secures some uniformity of policy, and enables the collective wisdom and experience of local government to be pooled and used for the benefit of all.

The courts exercise judicial control by means of:

(*a*) An order of mandamus given by the High Court commanding a local authority to perform a certain public duty.

(*b*) An injunction by the High Court that prevents a local authority from carrying out an act outside its powers, such as a demand for payment of money for a purpose which is challenged as *ultra vires*.

(*c*) An order of *certiorari* issued by the High Court prohibiting a local authority from continuing proceedings in which it has failed to act in a proper judicial manner, such as the way in which it comes to a decision to grant or to refuse a licence.

These safeguards are probably necessary to protect the citizen from arbitrary behaviour, and to maintain the Rule of Law as well as the Sovereignty of Parliament.

The Committee System

Democratic government in practice devolves into a process of discussion before action is taken, which suggests a group of people sitting round a table in private, talking over a common problem. This is a committee, a relatively small group of people to whom a question has been referred by a larger group for consideration and report to the larger group, and sometimes for action as well. This committee system is characteristic of the British Constitution, and is the fundamental method of the local-government authorities.

Every council delegates its work to functional committees, some of which the council must form according to statute and some of which will be introduced as a matter of administrative convenience. The number of these committees will, of course, depend on the size of the area and the nature of the authority. They will be broken down into sub-committees according to the magnitude of the work.

For instance, the Education Committee of the London County Council has such a huge problem to tackle that it has sub-committees on Adult Education, Recruitment of Teachers, Building of Schools and their Maintenance, Supplies of Educational Equipment, Special Schools, and so on. There is always the risk that committees will multiply prodigiously unless this tendency is checked.

The disadvantages of too many committees are that some of them tend to be self-perpetuating, and that they tend to overlap in function.

The advantages of many committees are that firstly they can be small in order to give each councillor membership of at least one committee—and a small committee tends to be more efficient than a big one; secondly, they can offer a councillor the chance to specialize in one branch of the council's work; thirdly, a great many questions can be tackled simultaneously. A reasonably quick, decisive policy is much more impressive. The Education Committee by law must co-opt professional educationists, but councils tend to make too little use of their power to co-opt specialists to help to deal with particular problems. These people perhaps cannot find the time to sit on the council but they are willing to serve on a committee. The greater use of this power will help to compensate for the abolition of aldermen if that reform is to be introduced. Possibly these co-opted members would introduce a spirit of sturdy independence, as they would be less under the influence of the party whip or the chairman, though it might be argued that they would be invited because they are likely to be obligingly agreeable in committee.

TYPES OF COMMITTEE

The committees are (a) standing—of a permanent character; (b) special—formed to deal with a particular matter; (c) joint, when two or more councils work together. By law some councils must form certain statutory committees. The provisions are as follows:

(1) All county councils and county borough councils must have health, children's education, and welfare committees.

(2) County councils and metropolitan boroughs must have a finance committee.

(3) County borough councils must have a Watch Committee, consisting of the Mayor and not more than one-third of the council, to deal with the borough police force.

(4) County councils must have a joint committee consisting half of councillors and half of J.P.'s of the county to deal with the police force.

The Finance Committee

Most councils appoint finance committees which deal with financial policy in detail. On some councils the chairmen of the more
important committees compose the Finance Committee; on other
councils they do not belong to it on the ground that they would tend
to delay the allocation of resources between competing claims. Both
points of view obviously have advantages.[1]

The Watch Committee

This committee's proceedings do not need the council's approval.
This is the only committee which has this right. The aim is presumably to keep the administration of the police removed as far as
possible from the party politics of the council.

The Education Committee

This committee must, by statute, co-opt members who are not
councillors but who are specialists in education, provided that the
latter are in a minority on the committee. The presence in its de-
liberations of teachers, as well as of people like parents or doctors
familiar with the peculiar problems of the district, should ensure
that this committee does deal with the important questions in a
practical way.

THE WORKING OF COMMITTEES IN GENERAL

The chairman is usually a senior member of the council with both
prestige and experience. He could also be an expert on the subject.
He will probably be a member of the majority party on the council,
and that party will no doubt be in the majority on the committee.
Sometimes the convention of the council results in the deputy chairman being a member of the opposition, in which case there could
easily be a conflict of opinion. This makes it difficult to have faith
in the committee from one point of view, but as discussion is the
life-blood of the democratic process, this difference of opinion
ought not to matter unless there is a danger that a change in the
control of the council results in a radical change in policy. This is
a danger that is perhaps theoretical. The good sense and tolerance of
local-government politicians will in all probability ensure that this
kind of problem does not become unmanageable.[2]

The secretary of the committee is the Clerk of the Council,
though he will often delegate this job to a member of his staff who

[1] For an interesting discussion see A. H. Marshall's *Financial Administration in Local Government*, pp. 41–45.

[2] For a good discussion of this see H. V. Wiseman in the *Journal of Public
Administration* (summer 1963), p. 137 *et seq.*

will be helped by the appropriate officer. The latter is therefore the professional member with all the details at his fingertips, with continuity, who is well versed in the art of expounding a complicated matter and persuading his listeners. There is naturally a risk that an officer with a sense of mission will tend to dominate the committee. On the other hand, if the members are worthy of their places they ought to have the common sense and general knowledge, the character and energy, to be ready to form and defend their own opinions. Indeed, it is this cut-and-thrust of debate between the dedicated professional and the enthusiastic amateur which enables committee work to be done with such effectiveness.[1]

CENTRAL GOVERNMENT GRANTS

From 1835, when the first grants were made, they were distributed on a percentage basis. Under the Local Government Act, 1929, grants were made on a block basis. In assessing the size of the grant the Government took into account the size of the population of a district weighted by the number of children under five, a low rateable value, abnormal unemployment, and sparsity of population. The Local Government Act, 1948, brought back the percentage grant, and the Act of 1958 restored the block grant except for certain services like the police that are still given a percentage grant.

The block grant, it is argued, gives a council greater scope to make the best use of its money, and so encourages people to stand as councillors. The supporters of the percentage grant argue that this system ensures that a cheese-paring council cannot cut a service too low, and so ensures the maintenance of all services at a high level. Obviously both schools cannot be right, but it is equally plain that both methods have merits, and time alone will tell whether the 1958 change was justified. It is, however, a pity that the grants can become the shuttlecock of national party politics.

LOANS

Borrowing is done under the Act of 1933. Authorities can borrow from the Public Works Loan Board or by the issue of stock to the general public or by mortgages. The current debt is approximately £5000 million. The Ministry of Housing and Local Government usually fixes the term of the loan.

FINANCE

It is the function of local-government authorities to give services

[1] For a good discussion of this problem the reader is referred to K. C. Wheare, *Government by Committee* (Oxford University Press), pp. 36–42 and pp. 179–184.

to the people in their areas. The range and quality of their services tend to widen and rise respectively. In consequence, the expenditure of councils grows ever larger, and so must their revenue increase correspondingly in order to pay these bills. A council therefore needs a large sum of money annually to pay its way. It has three main means of raising revenue:

Rates.
Central Government Grants.
Private Trading.

PRIVATE TRADING

A council raises revenue by hiring out tennis courts and cricket pitches, by providing swimming-baths and deck-chairs, by running a bus service in some cases, and so on; but the receipts are relatively small. They were:

1952	1956	1960	1962	1965
25	36	52	55	60

(£ million)

A council also usually owns a large number of houses and property which it rents to its people, often at rents considerably below the economic rent. It has, however, had to pay large sums to build these houses with borrowed money which must partly be repaid out of the rents. Revenue from rents has been:

1952	1956	1960	1962	1965
136	240	360	450	600

(£ million)

RATES AND GRANTS

A council's two main sources of revenue are Rates and Grants. The figures are:

	1952	1956	1960	1962	1965
Rates	392	556	768	915	1200
Grants	389	544	780	926	1150

(all £ million)

RATES

A rate is a kind of local tax imposed by a council on houses and business and industrial premises within its boundaries. The rates have the merits of being simple in nature, easy to collect, and direct, but they have the demerit of being regressive. They do not try to distinguish between rich and poor. The rate is an old tax that goes back to the Poor Relief Act, 1601, which empowered the churchwardens to assess the rateable value of all immovable property in the parish. The Rating and Valuation Act, 1925, established the general rate, and the parish was replaced as a rating authority by county boroughs, non-county boroughs, urban and rural districts.

Agricultural Land

The Local Government Act, 1929, de-rated agricultural land and buildings in order to encourage the British farmers and prevent the decline of agriculture. It is estimated that this exemption costs the local authorities some £45 million annually.

Business and Industrial Premises

Under the Local Government Act, 1958, industrial premises pay a rate equal to 50 per cent. of the hypothetical annual rental at a 1939 assessment. This figure is now calculated at a contemporary assessment. Under the Rating and Valuating Act, 1957, business premises pay 50 per cent. of their annual rental.

Dwelling-houses

The Local Government Act, 1948, transferred the assessing of rateable values to the Board of Inland Revenue. A dwelling-house was assessed at its annual rental as at 1939, taking into account the number of rooms, the size of the garden, the frontage on the road, the situation, the size of the rooms, and so on. If the owner or occupiers disputes the valuation he may appeal to a local valuation court which is independent, and thereafter appeal to the Lands Tribunal, which is appointed by the Lord Chancellor under the Act of 1949.

Fixing and Paying of Rates

The rateable value of a dwelling-house is not the rate charged, but is a basis for calculation. A council will annually estimate its probable expenditure for the next year, deduct from this the estimated income from sources other than rates on dwelling-houses, and then determine the balance which will be collected as a rate on the dwelling-house and expressed as a fraction of a £. Thus if the amount needed is £5,000,000 and the rateable value is £7,500,000, then the rate is two-thirds of £7,500,000—i.e., 13s. 4d. in the £. Some councils are much richer than others, dependent on the value of industrial property in the area and the kind of dwelling-house. For instance, a wealthy residential district like Bournemouth had a rate of 12s. 4d. in the £ in 1958–59, whereas a poor mining town like Merthyr Tydfil had a rate of 26s. in the £. To some extent the central

Government tries to smooth out these differences by means of a deficiency grant. The average rate is worked out for all districts, and if a poor district is found to be below the average the deficiency will be made up by the Ministry acting as ratepayer. In 1963 new valuation lists were introduced as a result of which industry and freight transport were fully rated, and dwelling-houses revalued.

THE AUDIT

Naturally the spending of these vast sums must be controlled by means of periodical audit to ensure that there is no dishonesty, and also to ensure that no money is spent on purposes outside the Acts. The Minister appoints a District Auditor for each audit district. He is a civil servant of independent status who is expected to behave with judicial impartiality.

The accounts of all county and district councils, metropolitan boroughs, and parish councils must be audited by the District Auditor. County and non-county boroughs need not be audited by the District Auditor, except for the education, health, rating, and care of children accounts. Some boroughs have voluntarily chosen to be dealt with by the District Auditor; others, however, invoke their right to be audited by a board of three auditors, one of whom is a member of the council nominated by the mayor, while the other two are elected by the voters. They need have no professional qualifications, but must be qualified for election as councillors. The Act of 1933 does permit a borough council to resolve to be audited by the District Auditor or by a professional auditor, and most councils prefer to use the professional auditors. It can be argued that the council are more likely to take a serious interest in this work if they themselves are responsible.

As the District Auditor has the power to surcharge on unauthorized expenditure, and is impartial, there is good reason to argue that his is the best form of auditing and in the interest of uniformity all councils' accounts should be audited in the same way.

LOCAL GOVERNMENT OFFICERS

The services offered by a council need to be dealt with by full-time professional administrators, and the authorities employ about 7,500,000 officials between them. There are certain offices which a council must establish. They are, for instance, in a county council, the Clerk to the Council, Treasurer, Medical Officer, Surveyor, Chief Education Officer, and Children's Officer. Other officers are established according to the needs of the council, such as an Inspector of Weights and Measures. The Chief Constable is appointed with the approval of the Home Secretary, who will bear in mind the wishes of the council concerned.

The Clerk to the Council

The Clerk is the chief officer, and he co-ordinates the work of the departments to avoid overlapping and to ensure uniformity. He is usually a lawyer who does the legal work of the council and acts as the council's secretary. He keeps in touch with central Government departments, and he would, no doubt, be in touch with other town clerks. He can, assuming he is a man of energy and ability, become the centre of the council's activity.[1] A knowledge of the law would seem invaluable to a town clerk—particularly the law relating to local government, to make sure that he prevents the council from doing anything non-legal and sees that its proposals to the central Government are framed correctly—while he must also be a first-class administrator.[2]

THE FUTURE

All British political institutions are the result of evolutionary growth. They are by custom examined from time to time to see whether modifications are needed to keep them abreast of the times. A Royal Commission is therefore set up occasionally to consider local government as a whole, and there is a Local Government Commission in permanent session looking at particular problems.

The *East Midlands Review* of 1961 (p. 8) said that:

> To be effective, in our judgment, an authority must be able to provide for itself comprehensive services of high quality over the whole range of its functions. It is not enough that an authority is able to provide the minimum requirements imposed by Statute or regulation, it must have the capacity to go beyond those minimum requirements, to develop new aspects of services and to have in hand reserve capacity with which to meet the needs of the future. We live at a time of steady development in the social services and of technical change. An effective local authority should and would be capable of meeting any new demands made upon it and of adapting itself to the changing conditions with which it is likely to be faced.

The central Government has laid down the following considerations as important in deciding changes in local-government areas:

[1] A very good study of his duties and powers is *The Town Clerk in English Local Government*, by T. E. Headrick (Allen and Unwin, 1962).
[2] Mr Charles Barratt has discussed this well in *The Royal Institute of Public Administration Journal* for summer 1963, p. 157 *et seq*.

(*a*) Community of interest.
(*b*) Development and expected development.
(*c*) Economic and industrial characteristics.
(*d*) Financial resources measured in relation to financial need.
(*e*) Physical features including suitable boundaries, means of
      communications and accessibility to administrative
      centres and centres of business and social life.
(*f*) Population—size, distribution, and characteristics.
(*g*) Record of administration of the local authority concerned.
(*h*) Size and shape of the areas of local government.
(*i*) Wishes of the inhabitants.

These seem to make up a comprehensive summary of what causes a community itself to form a system of local government. Also there can be conflicts of interest. It is important that an area should be neither too large nor too small in order to be efficient. It must certainly have the means to provide essential services of a decent quality. Unfortunately, districts vary enormously, and commissioners have found 'the wishes of the inhabitants' a powerful factor, sometimes a real stumbling-block. For instance, many towns have grown so large and rich that they naturally wish to become county boroughs, and so independent. The counties, on the other hand, do not want to lose the financial strength that these boroughs give them. Presumably the counties are still to be looked on as the basic units, and where they have large rural areas there is, in effect, three-tier government in which the parishes supply a valuable local foundation but the parishes are not usually capable of producing much in the form of rates. The principal source of revenue must be from places of dense population and industrial concentration. But even this fact is becoming complicated by the changing structure of an affluent society. The *West Midland Special Review Area Report* (p. 19) summarizes this development admirably, thus:

> The County Boroughs ... are beginning to lose variety in the social and economic make-up of their populations. This is bad for the vigour of local government and reduces the supply of voluntary leadership of all kinds. It means that the larger authorities have difficulty in finding councillors of sufficient calibre to make the best use of the authority's potentialities, while first-class people who have moved to the outer areas either take no interest in local government or find themselves, as members of the smaller authorities, with too little scope for their abilities.

The Commission were thinking also of the needs of families with young children who want gardens for the children to play in. The higher-income families solve the problem by moving into 'the country' and making a long journey to work. They continue to make use of the town for shopping, entertainment, professional advice, and so on, but no longer have any say in the way it is run, such as the provision of parking space, so that they become disinterested.

There are also the large conurbations, apart from London, all of which pose big problems of overcrowding, traffic congestion, and a maze of minor authorities. The tangle has to be sorted out in the face of much inertia. The conurbations are: Tyneside, West York-shire, South-East Lancashire, Merseyside, and the West Midlands.

Large towns like Manchester and Birmingham are obvious problems. Should they become county councils?

At least the problem is constantly under review, and happily the wishes of the inhabitants are taken into account. The point of government is that it is concerned with the health, wealth, and happiness of people—and people with strong local pride.

THE GOVERNMENT OF GREATER LONDON

Since 1888 London has been administered by the London County Council, assisted since 1899 by the Metropolitan Borough Councils. The enormous growth of Greater London, despite efforts by the Central Government to persuade people to live and work elsewhere, made its system of government out of date. The Royal Commission of 1957–60 brought out the administrative problems created by the overlapping of many functions. The Metropolitan Police, which is under the Home Office, provides the police for London and for parts of five adjacent counties. The Metropolitan Water Board has a slightly different area. The Port of London Authority governs the waterways of the great port of London. The London Government Act, 1963, set up the Greater London Council which began to operate, instead of the London County Council, on April 1, 1965.

The counties of London and Middlesex and the county boroughs and districts in the area concerned were replaced by thirty-two boroughs, each of which has a maximum of sixty councillors and ten aldermen. The Greater London Council has a chairman, a vice-chairman, one hundred directly elected councillors, and up to sixteen aldermen.

It will be a two-tier government. The Greater London Council and the London Borough Council share the following functions: Planning, Roads, Traffic, Housing, Parks, Sewerage, Civil Defence, Building, and Entertainment, with the Greater London Council as the overall planning authority which must produce the strategic development plan. An Inner London Education Authority has been created to take over all educational services, hitherto provided by the London County Council, in twelve boroughs; while the twenty boroughs of Outer Greater London are responsible for education and youth employment service within their own boundaries.

The Greater London Council is alone responsible for the Fire Brigade and Ambulance service, land drainage, Thames flood prevention, licensing, Scientific and Supplies services, and, of particular importance, a Research and Intelligence Organization.

The Borough Councils are responsible for Personal Health, Welfare and Children's Service, Libraries, Sanitation, Noise and Smoke Abatement, Food and Drugs, Street Cleaning, Administration of Shops, Elections and registration of electors, Registration of Births, Deaths, and Marriages.

There are about eight million people in the area, and all but four of the boroughs have populations of well over 200,000. The largest are Lambeth (340,000), Wandsworth (335,000), and Croydon (328,000). The smallest are Sutton (167,000) and Kingston-upon-Thames (146,000). The rateable value of the whole area is £625 millions, the annual budget in 1965 is likely to be about £216 millions, and capital expenditure about £173 millions.

The aim is, in the words of the Royal Commission, that "the boroughs should be primary units of Local Government and should perform all functions except those which can only be performed effectively over the wider area of Greater London." Thus begins a great experiment. The special nature of this problem is well put on pages 3 and 4 of the Report of the Royal Commission, which observed that

> here is a community of unrivalled vitality. Not only has it survived the chances and changes of 2,000 years, invasion, pestilence, fire, bombing; but year by year at ever growing pace it has absorbed into itself strangers from other parts of the country and from Foreign Lands, has taught and learnt new occupations and means of livelihood, has eagerly embraced new ways of life made possible by scientific discovery and mechanical ingenuity.

THE CITY OF LONDON

Set within the County of London is the City (known as The Square Mile), which is virtually independent and is to remain independent. The survival of the City is proof of the strength of ancient tradition and local feeling, because if pure logic were used the City ought to become a London borough. As the commercial centre of the country it is enormously wealthy, its ways are quaint and ceremonious, it is full of life by day, when its population rises to about 500,000, and silent at night, when it dwindles to about 5,000.

The City Corporation has a unique constitution, with three courts:

(a) Common Hall, which consists of the Lord Mayor, the sheriffs, the aldermen, and those Liverymen of the City Companies who are Freemen of the City, numbering about seventy.

(b) The Court of Aldermen, consisting of twenty-five aldermen.

(c) The Court of Common Council, which is both a deliberative and a legislative chamber capable of changing its own constitution, and consisting of the Lord Mayor, the aldermen, and the common councilmen now reduced to 159, elected from twenty-five wards.

The Lord Mayor is nominated by the Liverymen of the City Companies, and is elected by the Court of Aldermen for one year, during which he is by virtue of his office a member of the Privy Council. He is the Chief Magistrate of the City, and is its official host at the many ceremonial functions which it holds. He receives a salary of £12,500 a year, but this is probably less than his unavoidable expenditure as Lord Mayor.

The aldermen are elected for life by the ratepayers and inhabitants of the wards, and they act as J.P.'s. The common councilmen are also elected by the ratepayers and inhabitants of the wards, but they are elected annually.

The independence of the City is a source of party friction, and there is an ever-present possibility that it will one day become part of a London borough.

BIBLIOGRAPHY

COLE, MARGARET: *Servant of the County* (Dobson, 1956).

MORRISON, HERBERT: *How London is Governed* (Barrie, 1949).

DRUMMOND, J. M.: *The Finance of Local Government* (Allen and Unwin, 1962).

HEADRICK, T. E.: *The Town Clerk in English Local Government* (Allen and Unwin, 1962).

JACKSON, W. E.: *The Structure of Local Government in England and Wales* (Penguin Books, 1960).

MARSHALL, A. H.: *Financial Administration in Local Government* (Allen and Unwin, 1960).

MAUD, SIR JOHN, AND FINER, S. E.: *Local Government in England.* Home University Library (Oxford University Press, 1953).

WARREN, J. H.: *The English Local Government System* (Allen and Unwin, 1963).

JACKSON, R. M.: *The Machinery of Local Government* (Macmillan, 1958).

BENHAM, H.: *Two Cheers for the Town Hall* (Hutchinson, 1964).

CHAPTER XI

Public Finance

Why public finance is necessary. How it is raised. A weapon of economic policy. House of Commons fiancial procedure and parliamentary control.

It is the mark of a chicken-hearted Chancellor when he shrinks from upholding economy in detail. . . . He is not worth his salt if he is not ready to save what are meant by candle-ends and cheeseparings in the cause of his country.

W. E. GLADSTONE, *speaking in Edinburgh in* 1874

No scutage nor aid shall be imposed upon our Kingdom unless by common counsel of our Kingdom.

MAGNA CARTA, 1215

No Government has ever been able to do without money. The despotic king of old taxed his people to get money either to finance his private wars or to pay for his own personal pleasures.

The modern Welfare State needs vast sums of money to pay for

(*a*) External defence.
(*b*) Internal security.
(*c*) Social services.

So far as Britain is concerned, the Cabinet Minister concerned with the raising of money and the spending of it is the Chancellor of the Exchequer. Every year in April he makes his traditional walk from No. 11 Downing Street, his official residence, to the House of Commons, carrying with him the famous and battered Dispatch Box in which are locked all the secrets he is about to unfold to an eager Parliament—and nation. He discusses his finance proposals with his Cabinet colleagues a few days before the Budget, to acquaint them with his ideas and to hear if any of them have any very strong criticisms to make. It is of vital importance that his proposals remain secret. If his intentions were to leak out anyone who had access to the information would be able to make a fortune.

Two Ministers have resigned from the Cabinet because they had been indiscreet.

As recently as the days of Mr Gladstone the Budget was comparatively unimportant, because income-tax was a new idea and was fixed for four or five years at a time. A tax of eightpence in the pound was viewed with horror, and very few people paid income-tax. To-day, however, most of the working population pay tax, and a system of heavy taxation is looked upon as a necessary evil. It has become not merely a means of raising money, but an instrument of social and economic policy.

For instance, gross inequality of income is regarded as socially wrong by all political parties. Therefore income-tax is used as a weapon to level out incomes. It has become a steeply progressive tax—*i.e.*, as a man's income increases he pays more and more tax in proportion. Another object is to prevent people from passing on enormous riches to their heirs, who have done nothing to earn the money.

The Government can also impose a high tax on goods that, in their opinion, it is socially undesirable for people to consume in large quantities. For instance, the tax on whisky and gin is very high. This has the effect of reducing consumption of these strong spirits, and consequently of greatly diminishing the amount of drunkenness in the country. Indeed, this form of taxation reduces drunkenness far more than limiting the hours at which public-houses may open. The Government seems convinced that excessive cigarette smoking can cause lung cancer; it may be that the high tax on tobacco is designed not only to raise income, but also to reduce the amount of smoking.

The Government can also discriminate in favour of those things which are regarded as necessities by making them tax-free or taxed at a very low rate. For instance, children's clothing is tax-free, whereas a fur coat or a car has a large purchase-tax added to its price. A proposal to charge a very small tax on miners' protective headgear was resisted by back-benchers on both sides of the House in 1958 as a socially unjust thing, until the Chancellor gave way.

Taxes have never been popular with the people who pay them. They are more unpopular than ever now, when people have to give up a very big proportion of their incomes in tax. These people all have votes. They may be influenced in their voting by the party which proposes to tax them least. Therefore it is always an aim of the Chancellor of the Exchequer to keep income-tax as low as possible, partly to avoid discouraging people from working hard and earning more and partly to keep his party popular with the electorate. Indeed, it is sometimes alleged, let us hope unjustifiably, that a Government which is planning an election always manages to reduce income-tax shortly before the election. In other words, the reduction is not so much the result of efficient management of our economic affairs as a bribe to the voters.

Taxation can also be a weapon of political and economic policy combined. For example, the Government feels that it is strategically desirable for the country to have a prosperous steel industry. Otherwise, if there were a war, the country would have no means of making the sinews of modern war. So the steel industry is expanded. While it is growing it must be protected from the competition of full-grown, strong foreign rivals. So a customs, or import, duty is imposed on all steel entering the country, or a subsidy is paid to makers of steel, or both. For nearly a century, indeed, when the two dominant parties were the Whigs and the Tories, the main subject of contention between them was the Free Trade and Tariff controversy.

Before 1945 the Government had no nationalized industries to manage; Parliament did not have them to discuss. The Government did have to have an economic policy, but that policy was mainly concerned with Free Trade and Protection. The City of London was allowed to dominate the commercial scene. The Bank of England decided when to put up the Bank Rate and when to reduce it. It was not *laissez faire*—very far from it—but it was a policy of interfering with industry and trade as little as possible.

To-day the situation is entirely different. The Labour Government of 1945–50 introduced a planning system which was not completely discarded by the Conservative Governments of 1951 and after. The Bank of England was nationalized in 1946. To-day its relations with the Chancellor of the Exchequer are similar to those of the Crown with the Prime Minister. The Bank's Governor can advise, warn, and encourage, but, having been consulted, he must accept and carry out loyally the Chancellor's economic policy. The Government, Labour or Conservative, has accepted the responsibility of directing our financial affairs. If the national economy is suffering from an attack of inflation the Government must reduce the quantity of money in circulation, raise the rate of interest, peg the cost of living, encourage exports. If the ailment is deflation the Government must increase the supply of money, lower the rate of interest, stimulate investment, foster a feeling of optimism that better times are coming. Most of the time of Parliament is spent in argument on economic and foreign affairs. The two are, in any event, closely connected.

The Government is the biggest employer of labour in the country. Wages and prices in the State-owned industries exercise a decisive effect on the rest of the economy. In wartime the Government can bring about inflation by employing all the nation's resources in the manufacture of the sinews of war. There is an immense boom in the heavy industries. There is an ever-increasing demand for labour, which results in a rise in wages. If there is a rise in wages in the two great national industries—coal and transport—this will probably result in a general rise in the level of prices unless the Government decides to control those prices. This problem of controlling the great nationalized industries is assuming vast proportions. It would, of course, become even more important when the Labour Party is in power, because it believes in Government selling and buying on a national scale, on international trading agreements negotiated by the Government, and not by private traders.

The Budget, therefore, has become an instrument of economic policy in that the Chancellor deliberately aims at a Budgetary surplus or deficit in order either to curb inflation or to encourage expansion.

FINANCIAL PROCEDURE OF THE HOUSE OF COMMONS

There are five main principles. They are:

(a) It is the function of Parliament to grant public money and to impose taxes.

(b) A redress of grievances must precede any grant of public money.

(c) The process must begin and be determined in the House of Commons.

(d) The process must begin in one of the committees of the whole House, go on to the House as a whole, and finally be put into an Act of Parliament.

(e) All grants and all taxes must be initiated by the Crown on the recommendation of a Minister.

The first of these principles has resulted from the long struggle between Parliament and the Crown to prevent the latter from spending money without the consent of the people. The second rule started at a time when Members asked for money to be spent on behalf of their constituents on the legal fiction of a grievance. To-day it is used as a pretext to discuss all manner of things, provided that they have some connexion with the Estimates. The fifth principle is designed to prevent individual Members from demanding money to be granted in order to appease constituents or patrons, and also to save valuable parliamentary time.

At one time taxes were raised for specific purposes. To-day all moneys raised by tax are paid into the Consolidated Fund, and all expenditure is paid for out of that Fund.

The Parliamentary Session begins in November as a rule, and the Financial Year begins on April 1. In each session, therefore, Parliament has two sets of Estimates on which to work. For instance, in 1957–58 the Supplementary Estimates for 1956–57 had to be passed, as well as the Estimates for the former year.

The Consolidated Fund Bills (1 and 2) are passed in February and March. The first Bill includes a Vote on Account for the start of the current year, Selected Service Estimates for that year, and Excess Votes, if any, for the previous year.

Supplementary Estimates are necessary when in the course of the financial year a department finds it has underestimated the cost of a service, or has not made provision for something which has arisen unexpectedly and which could not reasonably be foreseen.

Votes on Account are designed to provide money to pay for the services which the Civil Departments (such as Education) give between April and July, while Parliament is debating the Estimates as a whole. This is necessary because no money can be spent by a department until Parliament has approved. This consent takes three or four months to obtain. The departments must be paid for during this period, so an agreed sum is voted (usually £500,000,000) to cover this contingency.

The Selected Service Estimates are designed to cover the same need. Parliament agrees that the Services must be paid, so the pay part of the Estimates is passed without argument to provide funds to meet the expenses of the Services until the main part of their Estimates has been legally approved.

Excess Votes are necessary when a department has underestimated in error, and the mistake is discovered only after the contracts have been placed; the money must be paid to avoid breach of contract, so an Excess Vote must be obtained from Parliament. The money is always found, but this gives the Opposition a chance (which it never fails to take) to criticize the Government for incompetence.

A Vote of Credit is given when the Government needs money suddenly in an emergency, such as a war like the Korean War.

The Estimates are prepared by the various departments from August to February. There are three drafts, each of which is scrutinized by and argued over with the Treasury to make sure that money is not being wasted on unnecessary objects or on buying extravagantly. For instance, why buy a Rolls-Royce car for £5000 if a Daimler at £2000 will serve the purpose as well? When they are ready White Papers, if necessary, are published setting out the principles on which the Estimates are based. This applies in particular to the Fighting Services. As a rule, the Ministry of Defence publishes a White Paper on military policy. Nowadays, with strategy changing radically from year to year because of nuclear weapons, these White Papers are of great importance. Members are expected to study them, so that their criticisms are well informed.

The Military Estimates are introduced to the House by the Minister concerned, and the Civil Estimates are sponsored by the Financial Secretary to the Treasury. Each set of Estimates is the subject of a debate. As the Government is sure to win the divisions, all the Estimates will be approved. But no money can be spent until the House has passed the Finance Bills later in the session, after the Budget debate has taken place.

The Estimates are divided into five groups:

(a) Army.
(b) Navy.
(c) Air.
(d) Defence
(e) Civil and Revenue departments.

Each group is divided into classes. For instance, the Civil Estimates are divided into ten classes:

  (i) Central Government and finance.
 (ii) Commonwealth and foreign.
(iii) Home, law, justice.
 (iv) Education, broadcasting.
  (v) Local government, health, housing.
 (vi) Trade, labour, supply.
(vii) Common services.
(viii) Agriculture, food.
 (ix) Transport, power, industrial research.
  (x) Pensions, National Insurance, National Assistance.

Each of these classes is divided into votes. Class i contains twenty-three votes, including:

House of Lords.
House of Commons.
Privy Council Office.
Civil Service Commission.

Each vote is divided into sub-heads. For example, the House of Lords' vote includes the following sub-heads:

Travelling expenses.
Lord Chancellor's Department.

G

Salaries.
Chairman of Committees Department.
Clerks of Parliaments Department.

It will be seen that the Estimates comprise a formidable array of documents, which, despite every effort to simplify them, must present an extremely complicated picture. It would be impossible for the Commons to debate them in detail as far as money goes. The Commons can only discuss them in principle. This gives rise to the criticism that Parliament has no control over the spending of public money, and is therefore failing to look after the interests of the taxpayer. Up to a point this criticism is valid, but what else can be done? Any other system would involve an enormous amount of hard labour and an expenditure of time which Parliament clearly cannot afford.

However, the situation is not as bad as it seems. The Treasury does act as a watchdog. The Select Committee on Estimates examines the Estimates between March and June, asking the departments to explain the reasons for the expenditure, and trying to ensure that there has been no extravagance or folly. The Committee breaks up into sub-committees, each of which tackles a separate set of Estimates. Even so, they cannot go through them all, but have to take a cross-section. Members who have served on this Committee for some years can find their way quickly through the maze of Estimates. Each member of the Committee is an expert on some part of the Estimates, and can detect inefficient administration or unwise expenditure. For instance, ex-officers should be sound judges of military expenditure, ex-teachers experts on Education Estimates, and so on. Furthermore, the departments, knowing that their Estimates are to be scrutinized, take as good care as possible that they offer no grounds for criticism.

There is the Select Committee on Public Accounts. The chairman is by convention a senior member of the Opposition, an ex-Financial Secretary of the Treasury if possible to ensure that a thorough investigation is made of the departmental accounts, and that any incompetence or dishonesty is disclosed. The Committee has the power to cross-examine the Permanent Heads of the departments, and, if necessary, other civil servants, which they do very thoroughly. They have the assistance of the report of the Auditor-General, who has completed a separate examination of the accounts in great detail, making many comments. The handicap is that this report has taken many months to prepare, and in consequence there is a time-lag between the spending of the money and the examining of the accounts, but at least it prevents further losses from the same loophole. The Auditor-and-Comptroller-General is a civil servant who is as independent as a judge. His salary is paid out of the Consolidated Fund, and he is removable only by address of both Houses of Parliament. He has a staff of professional accountants under him. His critical remarks about the Accounts are usually given much publicity in the Press.

There are other weaknesses. As we have seen, Parliament can find time to discuss only principles, not figures. As taxes come in slowly, the Treasury does a good deal of borrowing during the year in order to pay the costs of administration. Parliament has no control over this, but the borrowing is done publicly through Treasury Bills, and it is hard to see what objection can be taken to it.

The Treasury is no longer interested merely in cutting expenditure. As the controller of monetary policy, and with so much State industrial and commercial activity, it is equally interested in spending money. There is no reason to suppose, however, that its officials are any less public-spirited than Members of Parliament. On the other hand, back-benchers are often interested in pressing for more expenditure, and less interested in economy. The huge grants-in-aid which the departments make to local authorities or to public corporations are outside parliamentary control. Here, again, there is no reason to suppose that local authorities are necessarily spendthrifts, or that the departments wish to waste public money. The senior officials concerned have a sense of responsibility. So that, with the knowledge that the Accounts will ultimately be checked, it is reasonable to assume that the system, though not perfect, is efficient.

There is, however, room for improvement.[1] The House transforms itself into a Committee of Supply when it is considering the Estimates. It goes through each Estimate in turn. It votes for each Estimate separately. Later it turns itself into a Committee of Ways and Means to appropriate money to pay for the Estimates, and goes over the same ground in detail. If the committee system were to be extended so that there were a Finance Committee, which could examine expenditure from the point of view of its effect on taxation, and then consider the effect of increased taxation on the economy of the country, Members would probably have more influence than they now have.

The House gives twenty-six days to discussion of finance. These

[1] The Government agreed in 1960 to re-examine the problem of giving back-benchers more opportunity to scrutinize the Estimates in some detail, rather than allow them to be agreed to 'on the nod' by the House of Commons.

are called Supply Days. They are normally each Thursday between February and August. The subjects to be discussed, by convention, are chosen by the Opposition. As we have seen, because of the lack of time much of the Estimates cannot be discussed. On the twenty-fifth day the Committee of Supply must report back to the House, so that the necessary resolutions can be passed on the twenty-sixth day. If this were not done, then it would be impossible for the departments to order equipment in time to get it.

Every April the Chancellor of the Exchequer makes his Budget statement, in which he reviews the past year and the prospects of the coming year. He outlines how he intends to raise the money required to pay for the Estimates. As has been said, he does much more now, as the Budget is used as an instrument of policy, a deliberate surplus or deficit being aimed at in order to check inflation or deflation. Taxation can be used to equalize incomes as well as to raise money. It can also be used to curb consumption of goods which are considered undesirable socially. A series of White Papers on the economic situation, the balance of payments, the national income and expenditure, is circulated to Members. The Budget debate lasts four days as a rule. The financial proposals are dealt with in a series of resolutions, each of which has to be passed separately by the Committee of Ways and Means. These resolutions are later incorporated into the Finance Bill.

The sequence of events is:

(a) The House as a Committee of Supply deals with the Estimates in the two Consolidated Fund Bills.

(b) The House as a Committee of Ways and Means deals with the resolutions appropriating the supply grants in the Consolidated Fund and Appropriations Bills.

(c) This same Committee deals with taxation and revenue in the Finance Bill.

(d) The House as a House passes these Bills as Acts of Parliament.

All money granted must be spent during the year. Any money not so spent must be returned to the Consolidated Fund. There is a danger that money, having been granted, will on principle be spent. Included in the Fund are the allowances made to the royal family, the payment of interest on the National Debt, the salaries of Ministers and judges, the grant to Northern Ireland, all of which are never discussed by Parliament, and are included in the Consolidated Fund (No. 1) Bill, which is passed immediately without debate. This, among other things, ensures the independence of the judges.

In 1962 the Prime Minister decided to reorganize the Treasury. It has been divided more definitely into two parts, one concerned with management of the Civil Service, and the other with economic affairs. This latter part is subdivided into three. One section is concerned with home and overseas finance together; another is the Public Sector Group dealing with all forms of public income and outlay; the third is the National Economy Group that is responsible for co-ordination, in particular to look after the private sector of industry and trade.

To sum up the financial procedure, no money can be raised or spent without the consent of Parliament; no proposals can be put forward except by the Government on the recommendation of the Crown; the House of Commons has exclusive control over money; money can be spent only on the purposes for which it has been approved; every Bill involving money must be preceded by a resolution recommended by the Crown.[1]

BIBLIOGRAPHY

HICKS, URSULA: *Public Finance* ("Cambridge Economic Handbooks"; Nisbet; second edition, 1955).

[1] In 1964 Mr Wilson made far-reaching changes. He created a new Department of Economic Affairs with special responsibility for a national incomes and prices policy and for economic planning. This department is chiefly designed to co-ordinate the work of the other departments concerned with economic matters, such as the Treasury, the Board of Trade, the Ministries of Aviation, Labour, Overseas Development, Power, Technology, and Transport. In 1965 the two sides of industry were persuaded to sign a Declaration of Intent to co-operate with the Government-of-the-day to prevent inflation. The corridors of economic power which have been created are long and full of possibilities. It is too soon to say more.

CHAPTER XII

Public Corporations

Parliamentary control. The Post Office. Ancient corporations. Development up to 1945. Nationalized industries under the Labour Government. Process of nationalization. Organization and policy.

Emphasis on the commercial aspects of Post Office business must not be allowed to subtract from its obligations to the community as a whole, though this may mean giving some services below cost.
"The Status of the Post Office," Government White Paper, 1960

A great deal of parliamentary time to-day is taken up with economic affairs. Both major political parties accept some responsibility for controlling the British economy. This is a mixed economy, part of which is private enterprise and part public enterprise—*i.e.,* State-owned. The Government of the day is responsible to Parliament for seeing that these nationalized industries are managed efficiently and give the public satisfactory service. The Government is also responsible for appointing the chairmen of the public corporations. A big problem has in consequence arisen as to the extent to which Parliament must control public corporations on behalf of the electorate.

The idea of public corporations is not new. The Post Office, the Royal Naval Dockyards, and the Royal Ordnance Factories have always been controlled by the Government. They differ from the modern nationalized industries because they are subject to the control of Parliament and the Treasury. They are presided over by Ministers, who are answerable to Parliament for their efficiency, or lack of it. Their accounts are audited by the Auditor-General's department. They cannot spend money unless the authority of Parliament is obtained. They cannot change their establishments or rates of pay without the consent of Parliament. Their estimates are each year submitted to Parliament for approval. Before their financial affairs are presented to Parliament they are scrutinized by the Treasury. They play an important part in the life of the nation.

The Post Office, for example, performs the very important functions in a modern economy, which depends so much on swift and reliable communications, of providing the delivery of letters speedily and regularly and a telegraph and a telephone service. There is a post-office (or a sub-post-office) in every small district where people live and shop and work. At these post-offices the people can, in addition to using the above services, send money by postal-order or money-order, pay in or take out money from the Post Office Savings Bank, buy Savings Stamps or Certificates or Premium Bonds. This is all part of the Government's plan to stimulate a National Savings movement. Old people can draw their retirement pensions here and mothers their family allowances. The Post Office, more than any other State institution, has a very wide and continuous contact with the general public. In a Welfare State, which in the future plans to expand its pension scheme substantially, which desires to control inflationary tendencies by encouraging saving, by persuading people to lend their money to the Government, which may even take away from the joint-stock banks the job of providing normal banking services to members of the public and handing over this task to the Post Office Savings Bank, the Post Office can become one of the most important of all the State's activities. Nevertheless, the Postmaster-General, though a Minister, is not normally a member of the Cabinet. Perhaps in fifty years' time, if this department gains in importance, he will be a Cabinet Minister.

There is another group of ancient corporations which have been granted Royal Charters and have had powers of internal government conferred upon them by Parliament. The four Inns of Court, the ancient boroughs and universities, are all public corporations. Their finances are, however, privately administered. They are not the concern of the Government of the day, or of Parliament, or of the Treasury. They do, however, possess one important characteristic in common with all other public corporations. They offer the public a service which the Government considers ought to be provided, but which it cannot administer itself. This is one example of delegated legislation.

Since 1918 the public corporations have been experimented with in a variety of forms. Direct ownership by the central Government, ownership by the local authorities, even a mixture of State and private ownership, have all been tried. The Port of London Authority was founded in 1908, followed by the British Broadcasting Corporation and the Central Electricity Board in 1926, and the London Passenger Transport Board in 1933. They are not State-owned. The public were invited to buy shares in them. The dividends were fixed, and the Government had a decisive voice in the appointment of the Boards of Management. They were all concerned with giving the public vital services. They provided an invaluable model upon which the Labour Government of 1945 worked in nationalizing certain major industries. All these industries had the characteristic of being what are called public utilities: they offered the public an important and essential service. It was held to be the duty of the Government to take them over and to make sure that the people enjoyed these services at a reasonable price, and were not exploited by monopolists. Whereas the British Broadcasting Corporation draws a large part of its funds from the Government, the nationalized industries are expected to pay their expenses out of the incomes which they earn by charging for the services which they provide. In order to avoid the criticism that excessive Ministerial control would result in inertia, the Ministers concerned were empowered to appoint the Board of Management and to give general directions of policy to the Boards, but were to abstain from interfering with the day-to-day administration of the nationalized industries. They were, however, to be kept fully informed, in order to answer questions asked in Parliament.

The Labour Government created the following:

The National Coal Board (1946).
The British Electrical Authority (1947).
The Gas Council (1948).
The Transport Commission (1947).
The Iron and Steel Corporation (1949).

They nationalized civil aviation and the Bank of England in 1946. They took over the whole of these industries, paying compensation to the owners of shares in them.

This policy brings in a new feature in our political and economic life which is a little disturbing. The two great parties are divided on this question of State ownership. The Conservatives believe in private enterprise. Since 1951 they have converted the steel industry to private ownership, with a Board to supervise it which the Government appoints. They have also partially converted public transport to private ownership, leaving the trains and the London bus service in public ownership. The Labour Government in 1964 announced that it will renationalize steel and road services. It may also nationalize other staple industries, such as shipping and aircraft-building. It must be most confusing for businessmen to be uncertain about the future. A man cannot be expected to plan a long way ahead, giving up present satisfaction for the future, if the Government changes and buys him out compulsorily. This feature of the political and economic scene has added to the tension of electioneering. Neither party can afford to let the other win an election, because their policies are in theory so fundamentally different. It would be disastrous if the economic organization of the country were to be turned upside down every five years. The parties will have to come to some kind of compromise in this respect. The Conservatives have already gone some way by allowing all the State-owned industries to be unchanged, except for road services and steel. Perhaps the success of steel under private ownership with a Government-nominated Board of Control, making the best of the two worlds, may prove to be the bridge to span the doctrinal gap between the parties.[1]

If the period 1945–50 is used as an example the process of nationalization follows a set pattern. First, the Government gives notice of intention to nationalize in a White Paper. A Bill is then introduced into the House of Commons. This Bill will necessarily be long and highly technical in character. Its principles will be bitterly debated in the Second Reading and the Report stages, because the Conservatives are so strongly opposed to nationalization. The Committee stage will be very long, with each clause being argued about fiercely. Several of the Labour Party Bills—the Steel Bill in particular—took many months of determined opposition before they were passed.

After the Bill has become law the Government is entitled to buy out the shareholders in the industry. The purchase is compulsory, but the compensation has been fair and reasonable, having been set by an independent tribunal. The industry, now one gigantic organization owned by the State, is administered by a Board, the members of which are appointed and can be dismissed by the Minister. The composition of these Boards takes a more or less common form. The chairman is usually an eminent man who has distinguished himself as an organizer. For instance, General Sir Brian Robertson, after a brilliant military career, was Chairman of the Transport Commission. Lord Citrine, after a successful career as a trade-union leader, was Chairman of the Central Electricity Authority. The other members are all men of outstanding merit. Usually there is a representative of the people who use the commodity which the industry makes or the service it provides. The trade unions have a voice. Science and administration have places. Often an academic authority on the industry is nominated. In other words, the object is to get every point of view on the Board, and to

---

[1] An important convention is that legislation is usually a compromise between the views of the parties, though it seems to be interpreted very broadly at present.

ensure that not only is efficiency arrived at, but the interest of the public will be studied.

The country is divided into a number of areas, or regions. Each area, or region, has a Board. The chairmen of these Boards will be nominated by the Minister, together with the members.

The policy which a nationalized industry will follow is laid down in very general terms by the Minister concerned. He and the chairman of the Board must be in close and constant touch with each other. He (the Minister) must be well informed about the industry. He must be able to answer questions in Parliament about its general position and policy. He is responsible to Parliament for its efficiency, to ensure that it gives service to the public. The problem is how can the Minister do this without interfering too much in its management? If he meddles too much in detail his interference will be resented by the chairman of the Board. He will not get men of the necessary quality to work for him. He must allow the Board considerable scope for initiative. It has therefore been laid down, as we have seen, that the Minister will not concern himself with day-to-day administration, and that Members of Parliament will not ask questions in the House on such administration.

That is the problem. Parliament has created these huge organizations by statute. Parliament has acted in this way on behalf of the people. Therefore Parliament is responsible to the people for seeing that the public enterprises are efficient. The Conservative Government has set up a Parliamentary Select Committee on Nationalized Industries. This committee takes one industry at a time, goes very thoroughly into its administration, and reports to the House of Commons, which can then debate this report. The Committee, for example, reported on the National Coal Board in 1958.

BIBLIOGRAPHY

JENNINGS, SIR IVOR: *Parliament* (Cambridge University Press; second edition, 1957).

MORRISON, LORD: *Government and Parliament* (Oxford University Press; second edition, 1959).

WADE, E. C. S., and PHILLIPS, G. G.: *Constitutional Law* (Longmans; fifth edition, 1955).

HANSON, A. H. (ed.): *Nationalization: A Book of Readings* (Allen and Unwin, 1963).

ROBSON, W. A.: *Nationalized Industry and Public Ownership* (Allen and Unwin, 1960).

CHAPTER XIII

Northern Ireland, Scotland, Wales, and the Channel Islands

General Introduction. Northern Ireland. Scotland. Wales. The Channel Islands.

So Scotland has her distinct judicial system and private law, but the House of Lords is her final court of appeal, and there is a common statute law on many matters for England and Scotland. This is not to say that the differences of social institutions in these countries are unimportant. They are important, and it is remarkable that they are contained within a single government. But it must be emphasized that the capacity of states to form and work a federal union depends upon some agreement to differ, but not to differ too much.

K. C. WHEARE, Federal Government

These four countries form part of the British Isles. Each of them has a measure of self-government. Each of them has a strong nationalistic spirit. In Wales there are many people who speak and write Welsh; in the Channel Islands French is spoken as much as English. If the British Parliament ever decides to lighten its burden by handing over certain powers to regional governments these countries form natural administrative regions.

Northern Ireland consists of six counties, and it returns twelve Members to the British House of Commons. The supremacy of the United Kingdom Parliament is accepted so far as laws in respect of the Crown, treaties and foreign affairs, defence, foreign trade, and coinage are concerned. Appeals from the courts are made to the House of Lords. Every year the British House of Commons votes a sum of money (£73 millions in 1958) out of the Consolidated Fund to assist Northern Ireland.

Otherwise, however, Northern Ireland is autonomous. She has her own Executive, a Governor and Cabinet, a legislature of two Houses—the Senate and the House of Commons. The Constitution creating these institutions was enacted in the Government of Ireland

Act, 1920. This was originally meant to cover the whole of Ireland, but in the end there was, of course, partition. As far as possible this Constitution is modelled on its British parent. If there is a deadlock between the Senate and the Commons the Governor may convene a joint sitting of both Houses. Any Bill passed by a majority at such a joint sitting becomes law. This comes after a Bill has passed the Commons in two successive sessions. In the case of a Financial Bill only one session is necessary. There is thus a federal kind of relationship between the British Parliament and the North of Ireland Parliament.

An example of the independence of Northern Ireland is that the National Service Act did not apply to Northern Ireland. Her citizens could not be called up, but they do join up voluntarily, and, in fact, provide the man-power for several famous regiments of the British Army.

Scotland has a common legislature with England and Wales. They are united for most purposes of central government. But Scotland has her own system of law and law-courts, her own system of education, and her own established Church.

The Sheriff Court is the most important lower court in Scotland, corresponding roughly to the County Courts in England. The Court of Session is the equivalent of the English High Court. There are fifteen judges; seven sit in the Outer House and eight in the Inner House. An appeal from the latter lies to the House of Lords. The chief Law Officers are the Lord Advocate and the Solicitor-General.

There are seventy-one Scottish Members in the British House of Commons. One of them is usually a Cabinet Minister, who is appointed Secretary of State for Scotland. He presides over the Scottish Office. He carries out for Scotland all those tasks done in England by the Home Secretary, the Minister of Agriculture, Fisheries, and Food, the Minister of Health, and the Minister of Education. He expresses Scottish opinion in the Cabinet and else-where in Parliament. The London Office of the Scottish Office is a parliamentary liaison office. The day-to-day administration is carried on in Edinburgh. All administration that can be done on a geographical basis is done by the Scottish Office. All economic functions, however, are shared with England. The same system of taxation applies. Defence is common, and National Service applies to Scotland.

Scottish affairs are discussed freely in the British Parliament, but usually by the Scottish Committee, and not by the House as a whole. All Scottish M.P.'s are members of this Committee, plus, as a rule, about ten other Members, to provide experts on every subject and, if necessary, to give the parties their relative strength in the House as a whole. The Committee stage of a Bill affecting Scotland is therefore the most important stage. The other stages are purely formal. Even those parts of the Estimates which apply to Scotland are discussed by this Committee in detail.

Local Government in Scotland was dealt with in an Act of 1929. This established county councils and district councils, which are the equivalent of the English parish. There are no Aldermen. Councillors are elected for three years. One-third retire every year. Otherwise the method is very similar to that in England.

Wales shares a common legislature with England and Scotland. There are thirty-six Welsh M.P.'s. There is now a Welsh Committee in the House of Commons, but the day-to-day administration is carried on as in England. Wales and England are, in fact, one political entity. This is a source of resentment in Wales. It is hard to say why Wales was not given a Welsh Committee before 1960. Wales was once a stronghold of Liberalism, but for the last thirty years has been predominantly Labour. Twenty-six of thirty-six Welsh M.P.'s are Labour. It was argued that if there were a Welsh Committee while a Conservative Government was in office this would clearly be a difficulty, because the Welsh Committee would not truly represent the party strength in the Commons, and there could well be two conflicting policies, one in committee and one in the House. The Committee would have to give way, or the Government would have to add enough English Conservatives to the Committee to obtain a majority there. In that event the Committee would no longer be truly Welsh. In Mr Harold Wilson's Labour Government there is a Secretary of State for Wales who has an office in Cardiff to which some day-to-day administration has been, and is being, delegated. There is a considerable measure of independence in education in Wales, which is dealt with by a separate department of the Ministry of Education. The Minister for Welsh Affairs is advised by a Council for Wales, which is representative of Welsh life and thought. It seems that a special relationship is being created.

There are extremists, romantic nationalists, both in Scotland and Wales, who ardently desire home rule for their countries. It is easy to sympathize with their aspirations, but if one is realistic it is indisputable that Scotland and Wales are economically and geographically inseparable from England. Movement of people and intermarriage have made the three races homogeneous. Even Eire is discovering that Ireland is economically tied tightly to Britain, despite the existence of the Irish Channel. If, however, in order to ease the burden on an overworked House of Commons the British system of local government is given greater power and scope, Scotland and Wales are natural local-government units. They already have their Ministers in the Cabinet, and both have Grand Committees in the Commons.

The Channel Islands are included in the British Isles, but do not strictly form part of the United Kingdom. The laws are the ancient customs of the Duchy of Normandy. The Islands are nevertheless subject to the legislative supremacy of the United Kingdom Parliament in matters such as nationality and defence. Both Jersey and Guernsey have a legislative assembly called the States, which passes such Bills as are necessary, obtaining the approval of the Sovereign-in-Council. The sovereign can legislate for the Islands by means of Orders-in-Council, which must be registered by the States. They have their own Law Courts, with an appeal to the Judicial Committee of the Privy Council.

BIBLIOGRAPHY

How Northern Ireland is Governed (H.M.S.O.).
MILNE, SIR DAVID: *The Scottish Office* (Allen and Unwin, 1958).
Handbook on Scottish Administration (H.M.S.O.).
Report of the Royal Commission on Scottish Affairs (H.M.S.O.)
Government Administration in Wales (H.M.S.O.).
The Round Table (a quarterly journal; Macmillan).

CHAPTER XIV

The British Commonwealth

Introduction. The Statute of Westminster. The 'New Look'
Commonwealth. The Crown and the Dominions. Communication
between Britain and the Dominions. Economic relations. The
general system of government. The idea of parliamentary govern-
ment. The Rule of Law. The Colonies. Canada. Australia. India.
New Zealand. The new Dominions. Summing-up.

I saw everywhere not only the mere symbol of the British
Crown; I saw also, flourishing strongly as they do here, the institutions which have developed, century after century, beneath the
signs of that Crown. . . .

Even in the loyal enthusiasm shown to the Queen and myself by
thousands of my Canadian subjects, young and old, I thought I
detected, too, the influence of those institutions. . . . Their welcome,
it seemed to me, was also an expression of their thankfulness for
those rights of free citizenship which are the heritage of every
member of our great Commonwealth of Nations.

KING GEORGE VI *said these words in a speech in the Guildhall*
on June 23, 1939, after his visit to Canada in that year

The British Commonwealth is a political association of free
nations which has evolved out of the British Empire. As parts of
the Empire were granted independence they were allowed to decide
whether they would remain within the Commonwealth or secede
from it. Most have remained.

The term 'Commonwealth' has come into use generally in recent
years, replacing the word 'Empire.' In a democratic world in which
so many African and Asiatic nations are asserting their individual
identities the word 'Empire' is obnoxious, because it suggests
Imperialism or Colonialism—*i.e.*, the domination of a coloured
people by a European race, on the assumption that the subject race
are not fit to govern themselves efficiently, and so the European
accepts this responsibility.

This is not the place to discuss the rights and wrongs of
Imperialism. It is mentioned to explain why the term 'Empire' has
been dropped in favour of 'Commonwealth.' It leads logically to

the fact that the Commonwealth to-day consists partly of a group of self-governing Dominions, the number of which is increasing, and partly of a group of Colonies, who have independent local government, but whose external affairs and defence are still the responsibility of the British Government. All these Colonies hope that one day soon they will be granted self-government.

Many attempts have been made to set out in exact terms what binds the countries of the Commonwealth together. There is no legal contract which does this. The Commonwealth is a huge political club. The members join the club because they have something important in common with the other members. If these natural advantages should ever vanish the Commonwealth would probably disintegrate. The Irish Free State (as it then was) made use of the right to resign membership in 1949. Burma decided to secede in 1947, when she was granted her independence, with effect from January 1948. India and Pakistan transformed themselves into republics, but remained members of the Commonwealth, as did the Federation of Malaya (a monarchy) in 1957 and Ghana in 1960. Thus the Commonwealth has shown itself a flexible association.[1]

The only legal interpretation of the Commonwealth is found in the Statute of Westminster, 1931, which was an attempt to set down in writing the fact that each self-governing Dominion was equal to any of its fellows, and in particular was equal to Britain. Here, again, is evidence of a passionate desire of the Dominions to express their own individualities, an irresistible wish to make it clear that Britain was no longer in the dominating position of the head of a Victorian family, who claimed to know what was best for his family—better than they did themselves. This claim was strongly challenged. On the other hand, there was considerable opposition from Australia, for example, to the proposal to set out in writing the formal relationship between the countries of the Commonwealth. The unwritten, flexible character of the British Constitution was stoutly defended. In the end the special pleading of South Africa, with her substantial non-British population, won the day, and the Statute was signed.

The ties which bind the peoples of the Commonwealth are a curious mixture. There is the oath of allegiance to the Crown contained in the Statute of Westminster, which recognizes the Crown as the formal head of the Commonwealth. There are the many common political and legal institutions. In some cases there are ties of race and religion and social customs. Even a sport like cricket

[1] South Africa, however, left the Commonwealth when she became a republic in 1961.

plays its part. It is said that the sun never sets on cricket, which is being played somewhere in the world at any time of the day any day in the year. There are feelings of gratitude towards Britain felt by recently emancipated races. Finally, there are strong economic advantages in the Commonwealth. Whether these ties will last eternally remains to be seen. Maybe by A.D. 2000 the Commonwealth will have assumed a new shape, with the Crown dividing its time between, say, Britain, Canada, and Australia, opening Parliament in each country every session.

THE STATUTE OF WESTMINSTER, 1931

The signatories to the Statute were:

> (*a*) The United Kingdom.
> (*b*) The Dominion of Canada.
> (*c*) The Commonwealth of Australia.
> (*d*) The Dominion of New Zealand.
> (*e*) The Union of South Africa.
> (*f*) The Irish Free State.
> (*g*) Newfoundland.

In the Preamble the Statute says that

inasmuch as the Crown is the symbol of the free association of the members of the British Commonwealth of Nations and as they are united by a common allegiance to the Crown, it would be in accord with the established constitutional position of all the members of the Commonwealth in relation to one another that any alteration in the law touching the succession to the Throne or the Royal Style and Titles shall hereinafter require the assent of the Parliaments of all the Dominions as of the Parliament of the United Kingdom.

That is the essence of the Statute—that all members of the Commonwealth owe a common allegiance to the Crown, and Elizabeth II is not only Queen of England, but also Queen of Canada and Queen of Australia.

Clause 2 of the Statute enacted that the Colonial Laws Validity Act, 1865, would not apply to any law made after the commencement of this Act by the Parliament of a Dominion.

Clause 3 lays it down that henceforth no law of a Dominion Parliament would be void or inoperative on the ground that it is repugnant to the law of England.

Clause 4 declares that a Dominion Parliament has full power to make laws having extra-territorial operation.

The Statute thus gave legal effect to the historic definition made at the Imperial Conference of 1926 that the United Kingdom and the Dominions were

> autonomous communities within the British Empire, equal in status, in no way subordinate one to another in any aspect of their domestic or external affairs, though united by a common allegiance to the Crown and freely associated as members of the British Commonwealth of Nations.

What had up to 1931 been convention was after that date legal and formal. The British Parliament was no longer able to amend an Act of a Dominion Parliament, and no Act of the British Parliament could apply in a Dominion unless that Dominion had requested and consented to such application. Moreover, Dominion Parliaments could now either repeal or amend legislation of the British Parliament which affected them.

In 1951 a treaty of mutual defence covering the Pacific zone was concluded between the U.S.A., Australia, and New Zealand. Australia and New Zealand thus demonstrated their power to make extra-territorial arrangements without the assent of the British Parliament. This is especially noteworthy, because the two Dominions most closely connected to Britain are Australia and New Zealand.

Another example of this sovereign independence is to be found in the United Nations Organization discussions on the 'Suez Incident.' Canada and India took a leading part in opposing Britain's policy. Indeed, it was said that the disintegration of the Commonwealth was nearly brought about by this acute difference of opinion. The significant fact is that the parts of the Commonwealth did not inevitably and slavishly follow the lead of Britain. They exercised their own minds freely. An outstanding criticism of Sir Anthony Eden's Government was its failure to consult the Dominions before action was taken against Egypt. The members of the Commonwealth felt that consultation was imperative between them before any major policy was followed. They were admitting that, while they would not all necessarily do the same thing, at least they ought to try to act together as a political entity. Therefore the Commonwealth is not a meaningless word. It is really an organic association of free peoples with common aims and ideals.

In 1936, when the King wished to marry a divorced woman, the Prime Minister of the day, Mr Baldwin, consulted the Prime Ministers of the Dominions, and, having ascertained that without exception they agreed with him that the marriage should not take place, he went back to the King and told him that he must either accept the view of his Prime Ministers, representing their peoples, or abdicate. The King abdicated. The Commonwealth was growing up and functioning as a group of political equals.

In 1939, when Britain declared war upon Nazi Germany, it was made plain that this declaration applied purely to Britain and the dependent territories. The self-governing Dominions made up their own minds whether they would also declare war upon Germany or not. In fact, each of them separately and formally did so in their respective Parliaments.

THE 'NEW LOOK' COMMONWEALTH

At the time of the Statute of Westminster the autonomous Dominions were all 'white' countries. After 1945 the picture changed. India, Pakistan, Ceylon, Ghana, and Malaya all acquired Dominion Status.[1] They are all 'coloured' countries.

The new Dominions aroused speculation as to the future. Had they added to the strength of the Commonwealth, or were they going to plant the seeds of disintegration? There was no racial tie between them and Britain. There was animosity between them and South Africa. They resented Australia's 'White Immigration' policy. They retained bitter memories of having been governed by the British for a long time.

India and Pakistan became republics partly because, for religious reasons, they could not accept as leader the Queen, who claimed to be Defender of the Christian Faith in her title. Ghana became a republic, Malaya an elective monarchy. There is the risk that new states will not always act on logical grounds, but be influenced by emotional reasons. It will be a great pity if racial antagonisms break up a great force for good in the world. A sign of this feeling of rivalry is the decision in India to drop English as the official language. There seems to be no practical object in this move, simply a nationalistic spirit asserting itself.[2]

India is setting out to assert a claim to become the champion of peace, the mediator between the aggressive nations. She has made it clear that, though a member of the Commonwealth, she will not undertake any military obligations, because she is devoted to the cause of peace. Nevertheless, the British and Indian people get on well together. They meet at cricket and tennis and hockey. Trade between the two countries continues to increase. But there is always the unspoken fear that if, at any future time, it suits India's purpose to leave the Commonwealth and undertake the leadership of, say, an Asian political group she will not hesitate to do so.

[1] A number of other countries have since followed.
[2] In 1963 it was, however, found necessary to retain English as an official language alongside Hindi at least for some years.

These ideas make students of politics ponder on the future unity of the Commonwealth. There is a school of thought which considers that Britain's future lies in a United States of Europe, the foundations of which are now being laid by the free-trade area in Europe and the European Parliamentary Congress. That West Europeans have a common religion, that there is no irreconcilable cultural or racial difference between them, that their economic interests are closely connected, that they share the need to unite to protect themselves from the engulfing tide of Communism, these are all immensely important influences towards integration. The fact that the historic enemies, France and Germany, have been able to unite successfully in a Coal and Steel Union is eloquent of what may happen in the future. Britain may have to decide whether she is to be a European or a Commonwealth nation. Whether she can be both is an intriguing question, the answer to which is far from clear. It may well be that the final solution will be the formation of a union in which Canada, Australia, and New Zealand will join with the Western European democracies. As more European immigrants, other than British, go to these Dominions, the possibility grows, gradually but steadily. This paragraph is largely an expression of personal opinion. It is hoped, however, to stimulate thought.

As we have seen, the Irish Free State seceded in 1949. In 1936 she had passed legislation removing from her Constitution all references to the Crown and Governor-General, but in a separate Act—the Executive Authority (External Relations) Act—the King was authorized to act on behalf of the Irish Free State in the appointment of diplomatic representatives and the conclusion of international agreements. In 1937 a new Constitution was enacted establishing Eire as a sovereign, independent, democratic state, with an elected President as its head. The Act concerning international agreements was retained until 1949, when it was repealed and Eire left the Commonwealth. The British Parliament passed the Ireland Act, 1949, recognizing Eire as an independent nation, but provided that Eire would not be regarded as a foreign country, nor would her citizens be regarded as aliens. Relations between the United Kingdom and Eire continue to be conducted by the Commonwealth Relations Office, and not by the Foreign Office. Citizens of Eire come to and go from the United Kingdom freely; they are eligible for National Service if they are resident in Britain for more than one year, and they are eligible for any office under the Crown, including that of Prime Minister.

Newfoundland was granted representative government in 1832 and responsible government in 1855. In 1933, because of economic troubles, the Newfoundland Constitution was suspended temporarily, and a Commission consisting of three United Kingdom and three Newfoundland representatives was established. A National Convention was elected in 1946 to recommend the future system of government, and at a referendum in 1948 the majority of voters favoured confederation with Canada. In 1949 the Canadian Parliament approved the admission of Newfoundland, and the British Parliament passed the North America Act, 1949, as a result of which Newfoundland became the tenth province of the Dominion of Canada on March 31, 1949.

THE CROWN AND THE DOMINIONS

Queen Elizabeth II is Queen of Canada as well as of England. She cannot be in two places at the same time. Her main duty is to Britain, and she must therefore spend most of her time in Britain. She is already in serious danger of being overworked. Despite the speed of modern transport—she can be in Canada in less than a day—there are so many other places with claims to her presence that she is faced with a real problem in time and space. Some sort of compromise will eventually have to be worked out. She might spend three months in Canada one year and three months in Australia another year, or perhaps one month would be enough to carry out her principal functions, to open Parliament, to hold an investiture, to show herself to the people, to remind them of their allegiance and their ties with Britain.

In the meantime the Queen delegates her responsibilities in the Dominions to the Governors-General. The Governor-General is the representative of the Crown. He is the personification of the sovereign. In the absence of the sovereign he does all the things the sovereign would do. In the sovereign's presence he discreetly fades into the background. He is aloof from party politics. He has the same prerogatives which the Crown enjoys in Britain, but which by convention he does not use, except on the advice of the Prime Minister of the Dominion. He chooses that Prime Minister in the same conventional way that the sovereign uses in Britain. It is necessary for physical reasons for the sovereign to appoint Governors-General, but there is a difficulty if the doctrine of constitutional monarchy is to be worked out fully, because the sovereign is a hereditary monarch, above party. There is no dispute about the status of the sovereign. The Governor-Generalship, on the other hand, is a temporary appointment. Some one has to be chosen. If this choice is made on political grounds by a majority party in a Dominion Parliament, and the minority party resents this choice, the sovereign could be involved in party strife. This unfortunate position arose in Australia in 1931. Moreover, the sovereign is able to remain an influence on affairs behind the scenes, completely impartial and having been trained from childhood for that particular job. If the sovereign has sat on the throne for any length of time statesmen are anxious to avail themselves of the sovereign's experience and judgment. It is exceptionally difficult for a Governor-General to establish a position of this significance.

As far as possible the Parliamentary traditions of Britain are carried on in the Dominions. When Queen Elizabeth II visited Canada in 1957 she opened the new Canadian Parliament formally and with customary pageantry. She read the Queen's Speech from the Throne in the Senate. The Commons stood at the Bar of the Second Chamber. The Speaker had to summon the Commons to attend, having to knock on the door of the Commons in the traditional manner, the Commons having locked themselves in to prevent royal interference. The ceremony was a tremendous success, and Canada is most anxious that the Queen should spend some time in Canada every year. A house will be given by the Canadian nation to serve as the residence of the Queen—her Canadian home.

This function of the Crown has its dangers. How can the Crown keep out of a dispute in which two Commonwealth countries are involved? The 'Suez Incident' illustrated this danger. Canada disagreed with Britain to the point of voting against her in the United Nations. Suppose that matters had reached a position in which U.N.O. had decided to impose sanctions on Britain and France. This might well have involved Canadian troops taking part in operations against British troops. The Queen would have been put into a most invidious position. She could not have been neutral. She would have had to take sides. Had she sided with Britain, as one assumes she would have done, Canada would have had to repudiate the Queen, and perhaps become a republic.

On the other hand, the Crown can be a very valuable link between Britain and the Dominions. The sovereign is in touch with all the Dominion Governments, and in personal touch with all the Prime Ministers. It is possible for the sovereign to convey tactfully to one Prime Minister the point of view of another Prime Minister. It is possible to advise a hot-headed Prime Minister against doing something hasty, and to counsel him to wait until the opportunity has been taken for the sovereign to speak in confidence to the other party and to patch up the quarrel.

The sovereign has the opportunity to act as an Ambassador for Britain whenever visiting a Dominion, and is looked on as the embodiment of everything that the Commonwealth likes to think is typically British. The pomp and circumstance, the colour and pageantry, which surround the sovereign are reminders of the glory and the might of the Commonwealth, and the sovereign can discreetly convey to a disgruntled ear the British point of view. The glamour and the excitement that permeate royal occasions exert a strong influence on all those present. The visit of the sovereign to a Dominion can stir up sentiments of loyalty, and feelings of comradeship with Britain, with whom the Dominion shares the sovereign.

COMMUNICATION BETWEEN BRITAIN AND THE DOMINIONS

Britain's relations with foreign countries are conducted through the Foreign Office, whereas her relations with the nations of the Commonwealth are dealt with by the Commonwealth Relations Office. Normal correspondence is channelled through this office. Occasionally, if a matter of unusual importance has arisen, the two Prime Ministers concerned will approach each other direct.

Foreign countries send an Ambassador or a representative of some sort to London, who deals with the Foreign Office. The Dominions, on the other hand, are represented in London by High Commissioners. And in return Britain sends her High Commissioners to Commonwealth capitals. All ordinary official correspondence is conducted through the High Commissioners, who act as Ambassadors of their countries.

Dominions send Ambassadors to certain foreign capitals where they have special interests. Australia has an Ambassador in New York, but not in Copenhagen. India has an Ambassador in Cairo, but not in Lisbon. Britain, on the other hand, has Ambassadors in all foreign capitals, unless for political reasons the representative has been withdrawn. The Dominions usually have attachés at the British Embassies, and their business is done through the British Embassies.

There have been conferences regularly between Great Britain and the Dominions. These used to be called Imperial Conferences. As a rule the Prime Ministers attended, and they met in London. They are now called Commonwealth Conferences, and they are more important than ever. The venue is London. The members of the conference are received at the Palace by the sovereign, and go to Downing Street as well. Photographs are always published of the sovereign surrounded by the principal confidential advisers, and of the British Prime Minister entertaining his Dominions colleagues. The Dominions are, however, beginning to feel that the meeting should be held in rotation in the Dominions' capitals—one year in

Canberra, another in Ottawa, and so on. This practice will probably be established eventually.

These conferences are of immense importance, because they are held in private. Those present can speak freely and fearlessly, as they do at Cabinet meetings. India and Pakistan, for instance, can exchange their conflicting points of view. It is an opportunity to ventilate grievances, instead of nursing them in silence until they become bitter and deep. Discussion across the table often enables constructive solutions to be found for perplexing problems. Out of all the discussion and the argument a common policy on economic and political matters can be agreed. It was at these Imperial Conferences—in particular those of 1926 and 1930—that the Statute of Westminster was evolved. Moreover, regular meetings amicably conducted enable Ministers of the different countries to be reminded vividly of the fact that they belong to an organized community. They are acutely aware that this community will be powerful if united, weak if separated. They become sensitive to the great material advantages they derive from economic co-operation.

Governments are concerned, of course, not only with peace, but with war as well. During the World War of 1914–18 Mr Lloyd George's Imperial War Cabinet had regular consultation with the Dominions. After the War was over the Dominions were granted a large measure of independence in extra-territorial affairs in recognition of the great part they had played in winning the War. They were allowed to sign the Treaty of Versailles and to belong to the League of Nations. The Dominions concerned were Australia, Canada, New Zealand, South Africa. What is significant is that India, though not in 1920 a Dominion, was nevertheless admitted to this select group. An Imperial Conference was held in 1921 which resolved that there should take place

> continuous consultation, to which the Prime Ministers attach no less importance than the Imperial War Conference of 1917. . . . The Prime Ministers should aim at meeting annually. . . . The existing practice of direct communication between the Prime Ministers should be maintained.

The Dominions had in mind fateful decisions that might involve Britain in war. Before 1914, if Britain went to war, the whole Empire was at war automatically. The Dominions naturally wished to have a say in making such decisions. That is why, as we have seen, there was much resentment at Britain's decision to enter Egypt in 1956 without consulting the Dominions. The latter were apprehensive lest what began as a small local affair would develop into a major conflict in which the Dominions, whether they liked it or not, would be involved in due course. As sovereign states they should be consulted.

For some time the Crown appointed Governors-General on the advice of the British Prime Minister. The Imperial Conference of 1930 resolved that henceforth the appointments would be made by the Crown and the Dominion concerned, which would make its views clear through the responsible Ministers in Parliament. There would be informal consultation first, followed by a formal request from the Dominion to the Crown to appoint a certain person as Governor-General. Whether by accident or design, Dominions have in the past usually chosen a Britisher with a distinguished career behind him as Governor-General. Perhaps the idea is that such a man would be neutral in Dominion party politics. He would be more likely to live up to the ideals of constitutional monarchy than a native of the Dominion. For example, Australia appointed Field-Marshal Slim as Governor-General, while Field-Marshal Alexander was a highly popular and successful Governor-General of Canada. When he retired the Canadians appointed a Canadian, Mr Vincent Massey, then High Commissioner in London, and in 1959 a French-Canadian, Major-General Georges Vanier, was appointed to succeed Mr Massey. It is possible that in future the Governor-General will always be a citizen of the Dominion concerned.

ECONOMIC RELATIONS WITHIN THE COMMONWEALTH

One of the main objects of modern government is to organize the economic affairs of the community in such a way as to keep the standard of living at a decent level, and if possible to raise it. The fundamental basis of economic prosperity is the division of labour, which means that each country in an international community concentrates on producing those things which it can make or grow or dig out of the ground more efficiently than the other countries. The only raw material which Britain possesses in abundant quantity is coal, but Britain is a highly organized and skilled manufacturer of heavy goods like trains and ships. Commonwealth countries like Australia and New Zealand are producers of primary commodities, such as wheat and meat and wool, while India is a huge country with an immense and increasing population of 400 million people, but relatively underdeveloped economically. Canada potentially is a rich country, not only of vast open spaces, in which wheat is grown in great quantity, but wealthy in mineral deposits. In other words, the Commonwealth countries possess almost everything that a modern society needs in order to maintain a high standard of living, if they organize themselves suitably. They are scattered far apart all over the globe. They possess a wide variety of climate. The essential thing is that they guarantee to one another a market for what they produce. An assured market is one of the chief factors in securing economic progress. That is what the Commonwealth has tried to do by reducing to the minimum restrictions on the import of goods from Commonwealth countries. Relatively, Commonwealth countries are Britain's best customers, and as far as possible Britain reciprocates.

The Commonwealth has organized itself into what is called the Sterling Area. Under this arrangement Britain in London acts as banker to the rest of the Commonwealth, except Canada. The members pay into London any foreign currency, dollars in particular, which they earn. Britain banks this money, provides the members with the currency they need, and with skilled advice. Moreover, British financiers invest heavily in Commonwealth countries, providing them with funds with which to build up capital resources like railways and power-stations.

THE GENERAL SYSTEM OF GOVERNMENT IN THE COMMONWEALTH

Broadly speaking, the Commonwealth has adopted parliamentary government based on the model of the United Kingdom Parliament. It is worth quoting in this connexion from a speech which Mr W. L. Mackenzie King made in the Canadian House of Commons in 1926:

> What is the real link of Empire, the most enduring of the forces which unite as one British institution in all quarters of the globe? What is the secret of loyalty to the British Crown and to the British flag? What, if it is not the liberty and the freedom ensured under British parliamentary institutions and all that is bound up in what we know and reverence as the British Constitution?
>
> It is a strange, mystical sort of thing, this British Constitution that we love. It is partly unwritten; it is partly written : it finds its beginnings in the love of the past; it comes into being in the form of customs and traditions; it is founded on the Common Law; it is made up of precedents, of Magna Cartas, of Petitions and Bills of Rights; it is to be found partly in statutes and partly in the usages and practices of Parliament itself. No one has ever seen it; no one has ever adequately described it; yet its presence is felt wherever liberty or right are endangered, for it is the creation of the struggle of centuries against oppression and wrong, and embodies the very soul of freedom itself.

Although the British Constitution is the model, there is one fundamental difference between the prototype and the new Constitutions. The British system in essence is unwritten. The Dominion Constitutions are all written.

In the Colonies the system is one of representative government[1] in that each Colony enjoys independence in administering its local affairs by an Elected Council. The members of these Councils are partly elected by the communities living in the Colony and composing its electorate, and are partly permanent officials belonging to the British Colonial Service. The Councils can be overruled by the Governors, who are appointed by the British Government. Responsible government[1] will be attained only when a Colony is granted full self-government and elects a Parliament which is responsible to the people who elect it and whose actions cannot be overruled by a British Governor. In 1948 the British Government of the day stated that:

> The central purpose of British Colonial policy is simple. It is to guide the colonial territories to responsible self-government within the Commonwealth in conditions that ensure to the people concerned both a fair standard of living and freedom of oppression from any quarter.

To this end a Constitution has been given to each Colony based on that given to Ceylon in 1833, which takes the form of a Legislative Council, consisting partly of official members from the Colonial Civil Service and partly of unofficial members representing the local population. Out of this Council an Executive Council (or Cabinet) is elected to assist the Governor to govern. As a Colony has achieved full autonomy the Council has been converted into an elected Legislative Assembly.

THE IDEA OF PARLIAMENTARY GOVERNMENT

The Commonwealth is a fascinating institution because the ties which bind its component parts together are subtle and obscure. They are often the topic of discussion when constitutional problems are being studied. Why in a world of rapid, far-reaching change does the Commonwealth endure? How did it survive the strains of the Suez Affair in 1956–57? Will it manage to overcome the difficulties inherent in a multi-racial society? One undoubted unifying force is the institution of parliamentary government. Even when the Constitution is suspended, as in Pakistan, and a military junta

---

[1] Representative government is a system under which the Government represents the people, but is responsible to some one else, whereas under responsible government, the Government represents and is responsible to the people.

established, the President announces that the action is temporary and a normal system will be restored as soon as administrators who are efficient and honest are available. In the meantime the dictatorship is relatively benevolent. Or when the Opposition are suppressed, as in Ghana, it is claimed that this drastic action had to be taken in order to prevent revolution and to give the country stability and time in which to develop its peculiar form of parliamentary government. It must be remembered that the British system cannot be transplanted completely in African or Asiatic soil, and operated by people whose passions are more easily roused, who are still emerging from the habits of a rural, peasant society, and who are perhaps being asked to participate in the politics of an urbanized, industrialized, relatively affluent community. This is a time for patience and understanding.

Despite these difficulties, the influence of the British system is immensely potent and is for the good in that the habit of discussion is being established and continued. As long as men sit round a table and talk, they are likely to compose their differences peaceably. As long as men are ready to appreciate that other men also have a point of view and should be allowed to state it, there is a chance that the greatest happiness of the greatest number will be attained, which is surely the ultimate aim of government. The more the countries of the Commonwealth talk to each other, the more likely they are to evolve a common system of parliamentary government, because sensible men will learn from the experiences of other people, and will be wise enough to amend their own Constitutions. For instance, the meetings of the Prime Ministers, which have become annual, are planting the roots of interdependence and consultation. Nor are these the only forms of contact. It is becoming usual for the Finance Ministers or the Defence Ministers to meet more often, for military officers to be exchanged, for scientific information to be exchanged, for Members of Parliament to hold conventions and to pay All-Party visits to various countries in the Commonwealth, for teachers to be exchanged, and for increasing numbers of students to be educated in the older, wealthier countries, until the principles of tolerance and fair play, of free speech, and the encouragement of an energetic political opposition, are understood and accepted throughout the Commonwealth. The formation of a Secretariat with its Headquarters in London and staffed by civil servants from all the countries is an interesting, pregnant event. The information which this institution will be collating continuously and disseminating to all Commonwealth members will end the ignorance of each other which breeds prejudice, and diffuse the knowledge of each other which will engender mutual respect.

The way in which the Prime Ministers' Conference has developed into smaller groups, each of which looks at a difficult problem in private, and then in the full meeting presents a solution which might be acceptable to all, is typical of the pragmatic English method. The problem of Southern Rhodesia, for instance, in 1964 was tactfully handled and characteristically an irrevocable decision was postponed, giving more time and another opportunity for the parties concerned to think and talk and talk and think, until, given goodwill on all sides, the answer might well be found.

THE RULE OF LAW IN THE COMMONWEALTH

Wherever the British have established an administration, the Rule of Law has inevitably been created, and it has taken the form of the Common Law, which most thinkers distinguish from Roman Law, for example, as a system which is best understood by English-speaking lawyers because the principles are expressed in the English language, and the shades and nuances of those principles can be truly appreciated only by a man who not only speaks English, but also thinks in English. Many Commonwealth lawyers continue to come to England to study the Common Law and be called to the Bar in an English Inn of Court. Although the right of appeal to the Judicial Committee of the Privy Council has been abolished by most independent Commonwealth countries, because of the subtle suggestion that somehow or other this practice perpetuated the supremacy of the British lawyer, rather than the English system of law, it is now being seriously mooted that a Supreme Court of the Commonwealth be set up with a Bench of Judges composed of eminent jurists from each of the countries. Presumably if there is a dispute between a Canadian and an Indian company the matter will be heard by perhaps an Australian and a Nigerian judge, who will adjudicate it impartially and wisely, and all countries will agree to abide by the decisions of this Court. If such a Court is established in the near future it must surely strengthen the bonds between the older countries and the emergent states because individuals and corporations and governments will get into the habit of redressing their grievances in this Court, instead of nursing resentment and even contemplating the use of force or of economic sanctions. Once this habit of accepting the ruling of this Court is deep-rooted, then the Court will exercise a profound influence upon the whole institution.

THE COLONIES

The Colonies are dependent on the British Government. They are administered by the British Colonial Office. There are four main types of Colony. They are:

(*a*) Colonies.

(*b*) Protectorates.

(*c*) Protected States.

(*d*) Trust Territories.

A Colony is a territory which by settlement, conquest, cession, or annexation has become a part of Her Majesty's Dominions, and over which the Queen, as Queen of the United Kingdom, has absolute sovereignty. Bermuda and the Bahamas were examples of settlement, Mauritius and British Guiana of conquest, Fiji and Hong Kong of cession, and Aden of annexation. The citizens of a Colony are "citizens of the United Kingdom and the Colonies."

A Protectorate is a territory over which the Crown has acquired jurisdiction by arrangement with the local inhabitants. The Protectorates were mainly in Africa. Examples are Gambia and Bechuanaland. Great Britain's protection was offered in return for the right to trade and to evangelize and to deal with external relations. The inhabitants are "British Protected Persons."

A Protected State is one which is externally protected by Great Britain, but which administers its own internal affairs, such as Tonga.

A Trust Territory is one which was taken over by Great Britain as a Mandate after the World War of 1914–18. They were formerly German Colonies. Later Britain was made responsible for their good administration. Examples were Tanganyika and parts of the Cameroons.

All Colonies have three chief characteristics:

(*a*) Each Colony is a separate unit, and not an extension of the United Kingdom.

(*b*) Each Colony is dependent on the United Kingdom, and is not an independent sovereign state.

(*c*) The link with the United Kingdom is a most flexible one.

The Colonial Office is therefore responsible for:

(i) Justifying the system of government in the Colonies to Parliament, the Commonwealth, the United Nations

Organization, etc., and protecting the interests of the Colonies.

(ii) Conveying and justifying to the Colonies the policy of the British Government.

If the Colonies, which are generally underdeveloped, require funds with which to maintain a decent standard of living the money is found by the British Government, which is also responsible for meeting any other legitimate needs which cannot be met by the Colonies themselves. Among other things, the British Government provides the Colonies with external defence.

The Governor is at the centre of the system. He is appointed by the British Government and represents the Crown. He exercises all the constitutional functions of the Crown, except the granting of Honours and assenting to legislation. He consults his Council, but is not bound to take their advice. He informs the Colonial Secretary of the state of his Colony, and is consulted by the Colonial Secretary, who will never lightly disregard the views of 'the man on the spot.'

The decision to promote a Colony to full self-government is a difficult one to take. To give way too soon could be disastrous for the Colony itself. If it lacks the men capable of administering it there will be inefficiency and corruption. The people, having enjoyed efficient government under the British, will be plunged into anarchy and misery and poverty. Each case must be considered separately on its merits and as objectively as possible. There is always strong pressure within the Colony from a small vocal minority who say, "We would rather govern ourselves badly than be governed well by an alien race." There are well-meaning sentimentalists in Britain who are ready to turn a sympathetic ear to such a plea and to ignore the practical difficulties.

The difficulties seem to be:

(a) The presence of several races in one community, especially when the races are white and coloured.

(b) Religious differences.

(c) Differing languages.

(d) Economic weaknesses.

(e) Too brief an experience of Western democratic institutions.

(f) Too small an educated population with too large an illiterate and easily influenced majority.

THE GOVERNMENT OF CANADA

Canada was the first Colony to be granted full responsible self-government. At the start of the nineteenth century Canada had representative government. There was a Governor appointed by the Crown and responsible to the Parliament of the United Kingdom. He was helped by advisers whom he appointed. The Legislature consisted of two Houses, one nominated and one elected. Differences of opinion were bound to occur between the Governor and the Legislature on the one hand and between the two Houses of the Legislature. There was no means of composing these differences, so that there were many deadlocks. This unsatisfactory state of affairs culminated in a rebellion in 1837. Lord Durham was sent to Canada to inquire into the causes of the discontents. His report of 1839 set off the evolution of self-government in the Empire. He recommended that Upper and Lower Canada should be united under one administration with control over their own internal affairs. The Executive would in future be chosen from, and be responsible to, the Local Assembly. The powers of the Governor would be those of the Crown in Britain. The Constitution, foreign relations, trade with Britain and other countries, would be controlled by the United Kingdom Parliament. In 1847 Lord Elgin became Governor-General of Canada with orders to bring in the new system of responsible government.

In 1867 the British North America Act was passed by the United Kingdom Parliament, establishing the Dominion of Canada, consisting of the provinces of Ontario, Quebec, Nova Scotia, and New Brunswick, and allowing for the admission of other provinces as and when the Dominion grew. Manitoba entered the Dominion in 1870, British Columbia in 1871, Prince Edward Island in 1873, Alberta and Saskatchewan in 1905. Finally, Newfoundland renounced her independence in 1949 and became the tenth province of the Dominion.

The British North America Act of 1949 did something else of great importance. In accordance with a request by the Canadian Parliament, the Dominion was granted legislative authority to amend the Canadian Constitution, except in respect of matters assigned to provincial legislatures exclusively, existing rights and privileges in education, and the use of both the English and French language.

The present Canadian Constitution, therefore, is written, unlike its British prototype. It is based on the British North America Acts of 1867 and 1949. It is a federal Constitution—*i.e.*, there is a central Government dealing with certain matters on behalf of the Dominion, and ten Provincial Governments, each dealing with its own affairs in accordance with the terms of the Constitution.

The idea of federation was taken from Canada's great neighbour, the United States. Canada is a huge country geographically. Its people are scattered widely. Each province has developed separately. Each province has a characteristic economy. Each has a personality of its own. Quebec is very largely peopled by Canadians of French descent, who are Roman Catholics by religion, who are proud of their French ancestry, who are determined to preserve their language and their customs. Nova Scotia, on the other hand, is predominantly a Scottish community, Presbyterian by religion, and equally anxious to preserve its Scottish background and tradition. Ontario and Quebec are comparatively densely populated and highly industrialized. Most of Canada's wealth is concentrated here. Manitoba, Saskatchewan, and Alberta, on the other hand, produce most of Canada's vast wheat yield, and the first two are also famous for their cattle-raising. New Brunswick, Newfoundland, and British Columbia contain most of Canada's immense forests, yielding timber. During the last fifty years Canada has changed from a predominantly agricultural country to an industrial-cum-agricultural economy. Canada's vast natural mineral resources are now being exploited, full use being made of the tremendous water-power which Nature has provided for the production of cheap electricity.

To-day the Dominion has a population of over 18,000,000, nearly half of British descent, and nearly one-third of French descent, almost all the remainder coming from other European races. 43 per cent. of the people are Roman Catholics, 20 per cent. belong to the United Church of Canada, and 13 per cent. are Anglicans. Ontario has a population of over 6,000,000 and Quebec of over 5,000,000. These very individualistic territories appreciated that, unless they combined politically and economically, they would be weak and must be either dependent on Britain or swamped by the U.S.A. So they resolved to federate, but each province retained certain rights and privileges in order to preserve its separate identity.

The Federal Government consists of the Crown (the sovereign being represented by a Governor-General) and two Houses of Parliament. The House of Commons is a popularly elected legislative assembly of 265 Members and a Second Chamber, called the Senate, of 102 Members.

H+

The ten provinces are represented in the House of Commons as follows:

Ontario	85 Members
Quebec	75 ,,
Nova Scotia . . .	12 ,,
New Brunswick . . .	10 ,,
Manitoba	14 ,,
British Columbia . . .	22 ,,
Prince Edward Island . .	4 ,,
Saskatchewan . . .	17 ,,
Alberta	17 ,,
Newfoundland . . .	7 ,,

In addition there is one Member for the Yukon Territory and one for the North-west Territories, neither of which has yet attained the status of a province. Representation is in proportion to the population of a province. It will be at once apparent that Ontario and Quebec dominate the scene. The life of Parliament is a five-year maximum, as in Britain.

Because of the way in which Ontario and Quebec dominate the House of Commons, the smaller states are afraid that the Federal Government might act in ways favourable to Ontario and Quebec and unfavourable to the rest. Therefore the Senate of 102 Members is not made up in accordance with provincial populations, but is composed in such a manner as to counterbalance the House of Commons. State representation is as follows:

Ontario and Quebec . . .	24 Members each
The Maritime Provinces . .	24 Members
(Nova Scotia 10, New Brunswick 10, and Prince Edward Island 4)	
Newfoundland	6 Members
Manitoba	6 ,,
Saskatchewan	6 ,,
Alberta	6 ,,
British Columbia	6 ,,

The smaller provinces have accordingly a majority in the Senate. Senators are appointed for life by the Governor-General on the advice of the Cabinet.

The Constitution has had to be written in order to specify legally what the Federal Government will do and what the Provincial Governments will do. These provisions are set out in Sections 91 and 92 of the British North America Act.

The Federal Government has exclusive jurisdiction in:

(a) Public debt and property.
(b) Regulation of trade and commerce.
(c) Raising of money by taxation.
(d) Borrowing of money on public credit.
(e) Postal services.
(f) Census.
(g) National Defence.
(h) Navigation and shipping.
(i) Fishing.
(j) Currency and coinage.
(k) Banking and note-issue.
(l) Monetary regulation in general.
(m) Indian affairs.
(n) Nationalization and aliens.
(o) Criminal law.
(p) Marriage and divorce.

The Provincial Governments have exclusive jurisdiction in:

(a) Amendment of the Constitution of the province.
(b) Direct taxation within the province.
(c) Management and sale of land within the province.
(d) Hospitals, etc., in the province.
(e) Municipal institutions in the province.
(f) Licences for shops, taverns, etc.
(g) Incorporation of companies with provincial objects.
(h) Administration of justice in the province.
(i) Education, except for the safeguarding of minority rights.
(j) Generally, all purely local affairs.

The Crown in Canada

The British North America Act provides that the Executive Government and authority of and over Canada is vested in the sovereign. The functions of the Crown are substantially the same as those of the sovereign in relation to the Government of the United Kingdom. They are carried out by the Governor-General on the sovereign's behalf in accordance with established principles of responsible government. The practical executive functions are exercised by the Cabinet as in Britain.

The title of Queen Elizabeth so far as Canada is concerned is:

Elizabeth the Second, by the Grace of God, of the United Kingdom, Canada, and Her other Realms and Territories Queen, Head of the Commonwealth, Defender of the Faith.

The Governor-General is appointed for a term of five years by the sovereign on the advice of the Canadian Cabinet. On the advice of the Cabinet he summons, prorogues, and dissolves Parliament, assents to Bills, and exercises other executive functions.

The Cabinet in Canada

The Governor-General appoints as Prime Minister the leader of the political party or group of parties that has a majority in the House of Commons. The Prime Minister chooses the members of his Cabinet. As in Britain, the Cabinet formulates policy, sponsors most legislation, and governs by means of its control over the majority in the Commons. The doctrine of collective responsibility operates. The Provincial Cabinets are chosen and work on the same lines.

There are differences from the British system. The size of a Canadian Cabinet is not defined anywhere. It usually consists of from seventeen to twenty-five members. The Cabinet is not a select committee of the Government. Because the Commons is small in size it is not always possible for the Prime Minister to find all the men he wants from the Commons. So he chooses one Minister from the Senate and others from Provincial Legislatures. It is customary to allocate a certain number of Cabinet posts to French-speaking Members. The Prime Minister has to bear in mind provincial interests, so his Cabinet will generally contain four or five Members from Ontario and Quebec and one from each of the smaller provinces. This convention means that the road to Cabinet office is not necessarily through Parliament. It also means that there are Ministers with a local standing who do not possess the national ear.

The House of Commons in Canada

As far as possible the traditions and the procedures, the conventions and ceremonies, of the United Kingdom Parliament are emulated. There are, however, differences as the Canadian Parliament has evolved, and is, in fact, still evolving. The Chamber is so shaped that the parties do not face each other. Each Member has an assigned place and desk. There are pages to carry out the errands of Members. Votes are taken by roll-call, not by division. All formal statements are made in both languages, English and French. The Speaker is not as impartial as he is in Westminster. By convention, alternate debate speakers are French-speaking Members, and the office of Speaker is regarded as a stepping-stone to Cabinet office.

The Speaker, therefore, needs to maintain his party connexions, and in consequence his rulings in the House are often sharply challenged. Members are expected to show their local affinities, and much of the debate in the House is of a parochial rather than a national character.

Main Similarities and Differences between the British and Canadian Constitutions

Similarities

- (*a*) Both countries owe allegiance to the same sovereign.
- (*b*) Both set up parliamentary government with two Houses, one of which is popularly elected and dominates the political scene.
- (*c*) Both have Cabinet government with collective responsibility.
- (*d*) The general procedure in Parliament is almost identical.
- (*e*) The powers of the Crown are substantially the same.
- (*f*) There is almost universal suffrage.
- (*g*) Parliament is supreme.
- (*h*) The Judiciary is independent.

Differences

- (*a*) The British Constitution is mainly unwritten and unitary. The Canadian Constitution is mainly written and federal.
- (*b*) The Speaker in the House of Commons in Canada is not entirely impartial.
- (*c*) The Senate is a nominated, not a hereditary, assembly.
- (*d*) Two languages are spoken in Parliament.
- (*e*) The Cabinet must have a provincial flavour about it, and Ministers are not necessarily members of the House of Commons.
- (*f*) There is a Governor-General to act on behalf of the Crown in the absence of the sovereign.
- (*g*) Canada is a heterogeneous community in which religion and race, provincial spirit and personality, exercise important influences.

THE GOVERNMENT OF AUSTRALIA

In some measure the history of responsible government in Australia is similar to that of Canada. Australia is a large country with a comparatively small population of some ten million people concentrated mainly in the south-west of the continent and living chiefly in three big cities. Australia, like Canada, is a 'new' country, with no tradition of a ruling class. Each state developed on its own, acquiring a personality and an identity. Each state was intensely proud of itself, and, while desirous of federating in order to enjoy the political and economic benefits of federal union, none of them was willing to surrender its identity. Consequently, the act of federation produced a system of federal central Government and several State Governments, with a written Constitution which laid down what each Government would do and, by inference, would not do.

The State Parliaments of New South Wales, Victoria, South Australia, Tasmania, and Queensland were set up as responsible Governments in the 1850's, and that of Western Australia in 1890. The Commonwealth Parliament came into being in 1901 as a result of the Commonwealth of Australia Constitution Act, 1900, passed by the United Kingdom Parliament.

This Act established a Federal Government and six State Governments. The Crown is represented in the Commonwealth as a whole by a Governor-General, and in each State by a Governor. There is in each case a Parliament, a Cabinet of Ministers forming the Executive Government and chosen from the majority party in Parliament, an independent Judiciary, and local governments deriving their authority from Parliament. The structure of the Australian Constitution is therefore based on that of the United Kingdom, but the distribution of power between the Federal and the State Governments, and the major principles governing their mutual relations, have been borrowed from the Constitution of the U.S.A.

Parliament in Australia

The Australian Parliament consists of two Houses—the House of Representatives and the Senate. The former has 122 Members, made up as follows:[1]

New South Wales	.	.	46 Members
Victoria	.	.	33 ,,
Queensland	.	.	18 ,,
South Australia	.	.	11 ,,
Western Australia	.	.	9 ,,
Tasmania	.	.	5 ,,

[1] The figures are from the *Commonwealth Law Book*, 1959.

There are in addition two Members who represent the Northern Territories and take part in debate, but are not allowed to vote. The House is popularly elected by a more or less universal adult suffrage for a maximum duration of three years. Apart from the fact that the life of a Parliament is two years shorter than that of the United Kingdom, there are two other important differences. One is that the voting system is preferential; the other is that voting is compulsory.

The Senate consists of sixty Members. Each of the six states has ten Members. They are elected by a system of proportional representation. One half of the Senate retires every three years. It is important to note that the states have equal representation in the Senate, whereas they are represented in the Lower House in accordance with population. The political scene is dominated by two states, and the other four fear that their interests will suffer when they conflict with the interests of the two large states. Accordingly, the Constitution provides safeguards against arbitrary action by the Federal Government. Whether the Senate actually serves the purpose for which it was originally set up is debatable. Senators were expected to speak for the interest of the states that they represented, but for some forty years they have been elected on a party basis. They have thus become largely redundant when the party majority in the Senate corresponds with that in the House of Representatives, and obstructive when the party majorities in the two Houses differ. The Senate acts as a revising Chamber, but cannot reject Money Bills. In the event of constant disagreement between the two Houses the Constitution provides for a simultaneous double dissolution.

The House of Representatives is elected by a system of preferential voting. If a candidate gains an absolute majority over all other candidates in the constituency he is elected. If not, then second preferences are counted from the votes of the candidate at the bottom of the list. The process of elimination continues until one candidate is credited with an absolute majority. Australia has worked on this system because it has a history of Governments in power who enjoyed the support of a minority of the electorate.

Voting in Commonwealth elections has been compulsory since 1925. Voters are scattered far and wide in Australia. Before the modern improvements in communications and transport it was difficult to reach them and enlist their interest and for them to reach polling-stations. Many of them did not bother to vote. Just over half the electorate voted, and it could justifiably be said that no Government represented the majority of the people. Parties were convinced that if they could get all the voters to vote they would win the election. They knew that to transport voters long distances to polling-stations cost more than they could afford to pay. So compulsory voting was introduced. Returning officers make a list of all voters who fail to vote. In due course they are asked why they failed to vote. If they give a satisfactory reason no action is taken. If they fail to give an acceptable reason they are fined up to £2.

One Senator said that "elections are becoming very costly in Australia, and there is a big section which feels that it is incumbent upon the candidates or the parties supporting them to carry them to the polling-booths." Another Senator said that "the main object is to compel those who enjoy all the privileges of living in Australia and all the advantages of Australian law to take a keener interest in the welfare of their country. If the people exhibit no interest in the selection of their representatives it must necessarily follow that there must be considerable deterioration in the nature of the laws governing the social and economic development of this country."

Opponents of compulsory voting objected to herding uninterested and uninformed electors to the polls as an attempt to manufacture public opinion, instead of allowing it to evolve on natural lines. They also complained that any savings were offset by expenditure in dealing with failures to vote. It can be argued that compulsory voting has resulted in failure by the parties to educate the electorate. It is also suggested that as people grow up who have never known anything but a system of compulsory voting they will look upon the vote as an onerous duty, instead of a privilege. Perhaps it could eventually be that compulsory voting would lead to voting in a definite way, ending in a one-party system and therefore a dictatorship flourishing under the guise of democracy.

The Speaker in the Australian House of Representatives is elected under a party label. He nurses his constituency like any ordinary member, attends party meetings, is opposed at an election, and is replaced if there is a change of government. It is quite usual for him to take part in a debate when the House is in committee. He is sometimes called upon to vote in an important division. This 'partiality' of the Australian Speaker is in striking contrast to British practice and tradition. It is, in fact, typical of the acute party spirit which animates the Australian Parliament. No tradition of 'polite' behaviour has been set by a hereditary ruling class. The 'self-made' Australian is blunt and vigorous. He usually has had a personal interest to promote in a new, expanding country. As the Australian Parliament ages and its members mellow with experience perhaps parliamentary behaviour will approach more nearly to British convention.

Committees in the Australian House of Representatives are not used as they are in Westminster. If the House wishes to speak in committee it does so as a whole, because the House is not much larger than a Standing Committee of the British Commons. This does not seem to be a very convincing argument. The House has 122 Members. Committees could be made up of, say, twenty-five Members, and could deal with certain matters, such as the revision of a Bill, much more effectively than the House as a whole. It is becoming a convention that the Government refuses to accept amendments from the Opposition when the House as a whole is sitting. This is undesirable because it tends to an absolute division within the House, and almost to the suppression of the voice of the Opposition.

Australia was the first of the countries of the British Commonwealth to pay Members of Parliament. Commonwealth M.P.'s receive £2200 per annum, and State M.P.'s usually about £1975 per annum. The Australian M.P. has for a long time been looked on as a 'professional' engaged in politics as a full-time job. His electoral district is usually much larger in area than that of a British constituency, and he is expected to be a good local member. His constituents look on him as a 'fixer'—i.e., a man who can get them jobs, who can persuade the Government to take local interests into consideration. Naturally, he has no time to build up any other career, and his old age has been guaranteed by a Commonwealth pension, earned after eight years in Parliament. The Member has to be constantly at the beck and call of his supporters, and lobbying by pressure groups outside Parliament is much more significant than in Britain.

The Cabinet system is in operation as in Britain—i.e., the Governor-General appoints as Prime Minister the leader of the majority party in the House of Representatives, who in turn chooses his colleagues. There is no distinction between 'the Government' and 'the Cabinet,' because the former is not large enough to justify the formation of a small Select Committee. Fewer Ministers are required to carry on the Government's business, and the Cabinet usually numbers nineteen to twenty. The supremacy and collective responsibility of the Cabinet, though nominally accepted, are in practice affected by the need to form a coalition so often in order to form a Government. And so far as the Labour Party is concerned, the Cabinet is affected by the Caucus. This is a practice whereby the party meets to elect Cabinet Ministers (assuming it has a majority in the House). A Prime Minister can be forced to accept Ministers against his better judgment, and he cannot dismiss Ministers without the consent of his parliamentary party. This seriously limits his powers. Perhaps this method is more democratic, but it must make for less decisive leadership, and is in strong contrast to British conventional practice. Even that the system is more democratic may well be a fallacy, because legislation can be forced through by a minority of the House if, at a private Caucus meeting, the proposal to introduce such legislation is carried by a bare majority. Mr Menzies said in 1945 that "Parliament might just as well not exist at present, because legislation is first submitted to the Caucus, and if its approval is given, then the subsequent debate in Parliament becomes a mere formality." W. M. Hughes, who said in 1911, "The repression of the individual will does not concern us, because no one is bound to come into the movement or forced to remain in it," changed his mind in 1917, when he said that "the official Labour Party is no longer master of its own actions. If a member dares to murmur or to speak as he thinks he lives with the sword of excommunication suspended over his head."

Australia was first to introduce the secret ballot in 1863. Britain followed suit in 1872. Not only had parties found it hard to get voters to travel long distances in order to vote, but when they arrived at the polling-booth they could be 'persuaded' to vote in a certain way. Readers of Dickens will remember the account of the Eatanswill election, in which voters were liberally treated with alcoholic refreshment in order to render them incapable of voting 'the wrong way,' or to persuade them to vote 'the right way.' This exciting method of conducting an election was even more vigorously carried on in Australia, so the secret ballot was introduced to enable voters to vote as they wished without disclosing to anybody what they had done or suffering any injury or injustice if they displeased some enthusiastic pressure group.

The Constitution is written because a system of Federal Government must lay down what the central Government will do and what the State Governments will do. The Constitution Act provides that, unless a power has been exclusively vested in the Commonwealth Parliament or withdrawn from a State Parliament, it will continue as before the establishment of the Commonwealth. Thus the states retained their individual personalities. The Constitution cannot be amended unless the amendment has been passed in each House of Parliament by an absolute majority and has been approved by a

majority of the electorate in a referendum. It must also be approved
by a majority of the electors in each of a majority of the states. If
there is a disagreement between the two Houses the Governor-
General may submit the matter in dispute to a referendum. No
alteration diminishing the proportionate representation of any state
in either House of Parliament, or the minimum number of representatives of a state in the House of Representatives, or altering
the limits of a state, can become law unless a majority of the
electors in the state concerned approve the proposed amendment.
This is the essence of the Federal system of government, the relationship between the Federal and the State Legislatures. The
referendum is another Australian contribution to the Commonwealth.

The powers exclusively vested in the Commonwealth Government are those relating to:

(a) Defence.
(b) External affairs.
(c) Coinage.
(d) Customs.

The following powers are concurrently vested in the Federal and
the State Governments, with the proviso that when the Federal law
is inconsistent with a state law the Federal law will prevail:

(a) Social services.
(b) Immigration.
(c) Industrial conciliation and arbitration in disputes covering
    more than one state.
(d) Census.
(e) Postal services, etc.
(f) Marriage and divorce.
(g) Banking and insurance.

Section 51 of the Constitution Act requires the Federal Government to provide just terms for the acquisition of property from
states or individuals.

Section 92 provides that trade, commerce, and intercourse between the states shall be absolutely free.

Section 116 forbids the Commonwealth to make any law for
establishing any religion or for imposing any religious observance
or for prohibiting the free exercise of any religion, and no religious
test shall be required as a qualification for any office or public trust
under the Commonwealth.

Main Similarities and Differences between the Australian and British Constitutions

Similarities

(*a*) The Australian system is modelled on the British.

(*b*) Both countries owe allegiance to the Crown.

(*c*) The powers of the Crown are substantially the same.

(*d*) There is almost universal suffrage.

(*e*) The Judiciary is independent.

(*f*) There are two Houses of Parliament, one of which is popularly elected and dominates the political scene.

(*g*) There is a system of Cabinet government with collective responsibility.

Differences

(*a*) The Australian system is Federal, and the Constitution is written. The British system is unitary, and the Constitution is unwritten.

(*b*) The Speaker in the House of Representatives is a party man, not impartial.

(*c*) The Senate is elected, not a hereditary assembly.

(*d*) Voting is preferential for the Lower House and by proportional representation for the Upper House. The British system is the single non-transferable vote.

(*e*) Voting is compulsory in Australia.

(*f*) The referendum is used if an amendment to the Constitution is proposed. No such requirement arises in Britain.

(*g*) The Australian Lower House has a three-year life; the British House of Commons has a five-year life.

(*h*) The Australian Prime Minister's powers are limited by the party Caucus, whereas in Britain the Prime Minister enjoys almost unfettered powers.

THE GOVERNMENT OF INDIA

The Constitution of India is particularly interesting because it is relatively new. It should therefore represent the combined wisdom and experience of Britain and the older Dominions. India was granted autonomy in 1947, and the new Constitution did not start life till 1950. It is an attempt to plant the seeds of Western European democracy in an Asiatic country which had at one time lived under a system of despotic government marked by almost continuous civil war. It embodies parts of the Irish Free State, Canadian, and American Constitutions, while being based mainly on the British Constitution. It has created a suffrage of some 300 million people, many of whom are illiterate peasants. Finally, it is interesting because it introduces some new principles of social and economic justice in a political framework.

In 1857, after the Indian Mutiny had been suppressed, the Government of the sub-continent was taken over by the United Kingdom Parliament. India was administered by a British Civil Service. It was divided up into a number of provinces, each of which had a British Governor or Lieutenant-Governor. The head of the Government was the Viceroy, who was responsible to the Secretary of State for India, a member of the British Cabinet. The Queen was Empress of India. But long before all this happened members of the British administration employed by the British East India Company had said in writing that Britain could not permanently govern India; ultimately the Indians must be allowed to administer their own affairs. The real duty of the British Administration was to lay a foundation of good government, to train the Indians in the arts of administration, until the time was ripe for a transfer of power. In 1917 the British Government declared that as soon as possible India would be granted Dominion status in recognition of her War effort. After the War was over India, though not yet a Dominion, was allowed to be represented at the Versailles Peace Conference, to sign the Treaty, and to be a member of the League of Nations. In 1935 the Government of India Bill was passed by the United Kingdom Parliament, granting a considerable measure of self-government, especially in local affairs, and with the object of laying the foundations upon which complete self-government could be exercised when the time was ripe. There was, of course, a sharp difference of opinion as to whether that time had or had not yet come. In 1947, after India had played a worthy part in the Second World War, autonomy was at last granted. The India Act of that year partitioned the sub-continent into two Dominions: one was called India and the other Pakistan. This was the solution arrived at in order to reconcile the deep religious cleavage between Hindu and Moslem. India was predominantly a Hindu State and Pakistan a Moslem State.

India in 1950 immediately set a new problem for the Commonwealth by deciding to become a republic and yet wishing to remain a member of the Commonwealth. India was an Asiatic country. Its people were not Europeans. They were mostly not Christians.

They were unwilling to recognize the King because he claimed to be a Defender of the Faith—the Christian faith. They felt reluctant to admit any allegiance to a monarch of alien race, because this could possibly be argued as a symbol of British superiority, whereas India was acutely anxious to establish her complete equality with Britain and the White Dominions. On the other hand, India was reluctant to secede from a political association which conferred many economic advantages upon its members. The matter was considered at an Imperial Conference at which it was agreed to accede to India's wishes, a decision that illustrates the flexibility of the Commonwealth.

The announcement made by the Commonwealth Prime Ministers in 1949 is a historic statement. It said that:

> The Government of India have informed the other Governments of the Commonwealth of the intention of the Indian people that, under the new Constitution which is about to be adopted, India shall become a sovereign independent Republic. The Government of India have, however, declared and affirmed India's desire to continue her full membership of the Commonwealth of Nations and her acceptance of the King as the symbol of the free association of its independent member nations and as such the Head of the Commonwealth. The Government of the other countries of the Commonwealth, the basis of whose membership of the Commonwealth is not hereby changed, accept and recognize India's continuing membership in accordance with the terms of this declaration.

The Government of India Act, 1935

This Act is a good example of the wisdom of the gradual evolution of self-government. The granting of premature autonomy can be disastrous. A nation has to learn how to exercise the art of governing itself. The electorate must learn to appreciate the great privilege of having the vote and the importance of exercising that vote with intelligence. A body of men must be formed with the education and the integrity to govern in the public interest. A public opinion which recognizes the necessity of treating minorities with justice must be created. These conditions cannot come into being in a day. They take many years to evolve. Under the Act of 1935 all provincial affairs, including finance, law, and order, were put into the hands of Indian Ministers, who were to be members of and responsible to provincial legislatures. External affairs and defence remained in the hands of the Viceroy. Indianization of the administration services was accelerated. The Act came into force in 1937.

The Constitution of India

The Constitution came into being in January 1950. India had decided to be a Federation. It was therefore necessary to write a formal Constitution. This historic document comprises an important Preamble, 395 Articles, and 9 Schedules.

The Preamble states that the people of India have solemnly resolved

    (a) to constitute the country into a sovereign democratic republic;
    (b) to secure to all its citizens social, economic, and political justice, liberty of thought, expression, belief, faith and worship, equality of status and of opportunity;
    (c) to promote among them all fraternity assuring the dignity of the individual and the unity of the nation.

The basic principles of the new Constitution follow the British model. There are two Houses of Parliament, popularly elected. There is Cabinet government with a Prime Minister, with the doctrine of collective responsibility. The President exercises powers substantially the same as those of the Crown in Britain. The procedures and the conventions of the United Kingdom Parliament have been adopted.

The Constitution did, however, depart from the British model in choosing a Federal system, rather than the British unitary system of a single central Government. Indeed, a unitary system already in existence in India was abolished. Inevitably the Division of Powers had to be laid down in writing formally. Any residual powers—*i.e.*, powers not specified—rest with the central Government and not with the states. In this respect the Canadian system has been followed rather than the Australian.

The Federal Government has ninety-seven subjects listed as its concern. Among them are:

> Foreign affairs.
> Defence.
> The Fighting Services.
> Trade and commerce.
> War and peace.
> Emigration and immigration.
> Shipping.
> Posts and telegraph.
> Union railways.
> Currency, etc.
> Census.
> Industrial development.

Sixty-six subjects are listed as falling within the scope of the states. Among them are:

Local government.
Administration of justice.
Police and prisons.
Public health.
Education.
Agriculture and forests.
Trade and commerce within the states.
Land revenue.
Poor relief.

There are forty-seven concurrent subjects. They include:

Criminal law and procedure.
Marriage and divorce.
The Press.
Trade unions.
Labour welfare.
Industrial disputes.
Economic and social planning.

Borrowing from the U.S.A. Constitution, the Indian Constitution states these fundamental rights:

Equality before the law.
Personal liberty.
Freedom of speech.
Freedom of religion.
Freedom of assembly.
Freedom of occupation.
Freedom of movement and residence.
Freedom to acquire or dispose of property.
Freedom from discrimination on grounds of race, religion, caste, or sex.

'Untouchability' was abolished, and its practice in any form forbidden.

All these fundamental rights can be enforced by resort to the law-courts. The Constitution in addition lays down certain "directive principles of State policy." These are really a set of moral precepts. They are not enforceable at law, but they are stated to be fundamental in the governance of the country, and "it shall be the duty of the State to apply these principles in making laws." Here the Constitution has borrowed an idea from the Irish Free State.

These principles include the following:

(a) The right to an adequate means of livelihood.

(b) The distribution and control of material resources so as to subserve the common good.

(c) The operation of the economic system so that it does not result in the concentration of wealth and means of production in a few hands to the common detriment.

(d) Equal pay for equal work for both men and women.

(e) The right to work.

(f) The right to education.

(g) The right to public assistance in case of unemployment, old age, sickness, and disablement.

(h) Just and humane conditions of work, including a living wage and the necessary leisure.

There is nothing new in these fundamental rights or directive principles. The aim of the British Governments is to guarantee these freedoms and to attain these objects. But, whereas the British Constitution deliberately abstains from setting down its principles of operating in formal documents, the Indian Constitution has done so.

The Executive in India

Unlike in Canada and Australia, where the sovereign is the executive head of the Government, in India this function devolves on the President of the Union. He is elected by an Electoral College consisting of the elected members of both Houses of Parliament and the elected members of the Legislative Assemblies of the States of the Union. He is elected for a period of five years, and can stand for re-election. There is a Vice-President, who is *ex officio* Chairman of the Council of States (the Second Chamber in Parliament). The functions of the President are the same as those of the Crown in the United Kingdom. He appoints the Prime Minister by choosing the leader of the majority party in the House of the People. He is an elder statesman who is expected to behave purely in the public interest and to refrain from participation in party controversy.

Parliament in India

Parliament consists of two Houses:

(a) The House of the People (the Lower House, corresponding to the British House of Commons).

(b) The Council of States (the Upper House, corresponding to the House of Lords).

It is interesting to note, in view of the agitation in Britain to reform the House of Lords and the desire of some people to abolish it, that the writers of the new Indian Constitution have deliberately decided to have a Second Chamber, thereby implying that there is a need to revise and to delay hasty controversial legislation.

The House of the People must not consist of more than 500 members, and of this number, all except eight are elected by direct vote on the basis of adult suffrage. Each member should represent not fewer than 500,000 and not more than 750,000 people. The President nominates eight Members, six of whom are to represent Jammu and Kashmir, one represents the Andaman Islands, and one represents the tribal areas of Assam.[1] If the Anglo-Indian community is not adequately represented in the normal way the President can nominate two members to represent them.

For the time being it has been decided that the procedure of the House will be based as closely as possible on that of the British House of Commons. In due course, as the House of the People functions, this procedure will be modified and adapted to its special needs. For instance, the use and composition of committees will be determined in the light of experience. That is the sensible way to behave—to learn from experience, to move along slowly.

The Speaker, it is hoped, will eventually be the personification of impartiality, like the United Kingdom Speaker. The problem in the Indian Parliament has been the absence of a strong, well-organized Opposition, capable and desirous of criticizing the Government, and arguing fiercely at times in the House. In order to attain independence, Indian opinion was organized into what was called the Congress Party; this party believed in parliamentary government. If it can be compared to a British party, it is something like the Liberals under Asquith, being liberal-minded and believing that the Lower House should have the power. All but three members of the House belonged to the party. Virtually, therefore, India has had a one-party system. Opposition to the Government has come from individuals. It is still difficult to see when a strong Opposition party will appear, but the signs are that Communism is growing in strength. Meanwhile the Government has been at great pains to refrain from riding roughshod over the opinions of the House.

The Cabinet in India

The President has acted like the British sovereign in appointing as Prime Minister the leader of the party with a majority in the

---

[1] There are now, besides the elected members, 20 members to represent the Union Territories, chosen as Parliament provides.

House of the People, which is looked on as the important operative part of Parliament. The Prime Minister submits to the President the names of the Ministers he would like, and they are appointed by the President in accordance with convention. The Ministers form a Council, which is the counterpart of the British Government. As the Council is a large one, a small Select Committee of the senior Ministers has developed along the lines of the British Cabinet. The conventional pattern has been followed of secrecy and collective responsibility, formulating policy and sponsoring legislation, having the monopoly of raising and spending public money.

Elections in India

The election of Parliament has been an interesting problem because of the size of the electorate and the fact that so much of it at present is illiterate. A special Commissioner for Elections has been appointed, with a permanent staff whose duty it is to see that electoral rolls are kept and that the elections are run in a proper manner. In what is a dominantly peasant community living in small villages and in the main illiterate, the preparation of the electoral rolls and keeping them up to date is a herculean task. The job of ensuring that these people vote correctly is almost as formidable.

The House of the People deals with Money Bills and financial measures alone. Here, again, the British model has been faithfully copied. If there is a dispute between the two Houses the matter is resolved in a joint session. As the Lower House is twice as large in numbers as the Upper House, it must be presumed that the former will always get its way, which is in tune with the spirit of the Constitution.

The Council of States in India

The Upper House consists of 250 members. Twelve of them are nominated by the President for their special knowledge or cultural standing—in other words, they represent art, science, literature, medicine, etc. The remaining 238 members are elected through the elected members of the State Legislatures. The Council of States is a permanent body (like the British House of Lords) which cannot be subject to dissolution on the order of the President, but, unlike the British House of Lords, the Indian Second Chamber changes every second year, when one-third of its members retire. The Chairman of the House is the Vice-President. Its main functions are to revise and to delay hasty legislation.

THE GOVERNMENT OF NEW ZEALAND

The development of self-government has followed the usual pattern. The important point about the New Zealand Constitution is that in 1950 Parliament decided to abolish the Upper House, called the Legislative Council, so that New Zealand is the only country in the Commonwealth with a single-chamber system. This Chamber is the House of Representatives, who have been popularly elected. Once the House has assembled its procedure is based as closely as possible on that of the United Kingdom House of Commons. It is elected for three years.

The grounds for the abolition of the Upper Chamber were that New Zealand's Government is not Federal but Unitary. There is no need, therefore, to have a Chamber the main object of whose existence is to protect the interests of the states or provinces composing the Federation. According to the New Zealand view, the function of the Second Chamber of revising the work of the First Chamber is done by the electorate, who will change the Government at a general election if they find that it has failed to carry out its promises. The proceedings of Parliament are broadcast regularly.

THE NEW DOMINIONS

Pakistan, Ceylon, Ghana, and Malaya were all Dominions, but in each case so many changes are taking place and so many changes are contemplated that it is difficult in a textbook to comment usefully. For instance, Pakistan was granted independence in 1947, became a republic within the Commonwealth in 1956, and the Constitution was suspended in 1958 in consequence of a seizure of power by the Army in order to put an end to corruption and incompetence. A new Constitution was announced in 1962. In Ceylon there have been communal riots. Ghana became an independent state within the Commonwealth in March 1957, and Malaya also in August of that year. In 1963 Malaya, together with Singapore, British North Borneo and Sarawak, became associated in the Malaysian Federation. In 1964 several new states were created, such as Kenya, Sierra Leone, Uganda, and Tanzania (formerly Tanganyika and Zanzibar).

SUMMING-UP

The Commonwealth is in essence a free association of nations. It is the outcome of a great political experiment by the British. They acquired a vast Empire in a variety of ways. They have granted independence to many of the countries composing the Empire, and have declared their intention of conferring autonomy in due course on those territories which are still dependent. In every case where self-government has been granted a system of parliamentary government has been established based on the United Kingdom Parliament. All the member nations (except Britain) have written Constitutions, and most of them have federal systems. The Colonies are pulsating with activity politically. Most of them are looking forward to self-government in the near future. The British Commonwealth, therefore, is a dynamic and democratic organization. It is a great force in the cause of peace and freedom in the world to-day. It is important to bear in mind that the Commonwealth is constantly changing and must in consequence be studied continuously. A great deal of change will probably take place during the next twenty-five years.

BIBLIOGRAPHY

DAWSON, R. M.: *The Government of Canada* (Oxford University Press; second edition, 1954).

NICHOLAS, H. S.: *The Australian Constitution* (Sweet and Maxwell, 1949).

JOSHI, G. N.: *The Constitution of India* (Macmillan; third edition, 1955).

WHEARE, K. C.: *The Statute of Westminster and Dominion Status* (Oxford University Press; fifth edition, 1953).

KEITH, A. B.: *Speeches and Documents on the British Dominions, 1918–31* (Oxford University Press, 1932).

MILLER, J. D. B.: *The Commonwealth in the World* (Duckworth, 1958).

WALKER, P. GORDON: *The Commonwealth* (Secker and Warburg, 1961).

BRADLEY, K. (Ed.): *The Living Commonwealth* (Hutchinson, 1961).

INGRAMS, H.: *Hong Kong* (Corona Library, H.M.S.O., 1952).

LEWIS, R.: *Sierra Leone: A Modern Portrait* (Corona Library, H.M.S.O., 1954).

ABRAHAMS, P.: *Jamaica* (Corona Library, H.M.S.O.).

HEUSSLER, R.: *Yesterday's Rulers: The Making of the British Colonial Service* (Oxford University Press, 1963).

WISEMAN, H. V.: *Britain and the Commonwealth* (Allen and Unwin, 1965).

MACKINTOSH, J. P.: *Nigerian Government and Politics* (Allen and Unwin, 1966).

Constitutional Development in the Commonwealth: Member Countries, Part I; *U.K. Dependencies,* Part II (Central Office of Information Reference Pamphlets; H.M.S.O.).

C.O.I. Pamphlets, The Making of a Nation (H.M.S.O.). No. 38, "Nigeria," No. 45, "Sierra Leone," No. 54, "Uganda," No. 59, "Kenya."

CHAPTER XV

The Future

The one talent which is worth all other talents put together in human affairs is the talent of judging right upon imperfect materials, the talent, if you please, of guessing right.

SIR JAMES FITZJAMES STEPHEN

Reform is in the air to-day. Some people want to reform the House of Commons; others to reform the House of Lords, or abolish it. Some would like to see the end of the hereditary principle. The Civil Service is said to dominate Parliament. The Treasury is alleged to have lost control of Government spending. The two major parties are in a state of stagnation; therefore a third party is needed in Westminster to inject a new spirit. Are the trade unions going to intervene in politics to gain economic and industrial ends? There have been race riots in peaceful Britain. Does this antagonism spell the end of the Commonwealth? Will Britain join the European Economic Community? If so, how will this affect British Sovereignty? Only in the future shall we find the answers to these questions.

These are some of the questions that are troubling students of the contemporary political scene. They are problems which cannot be shelved. The only way in which they can be solved is by trying to anticipate them, to find out the reasons which have brought them to life, and then to attempt to provide the answers to them. 'Reform' is perhaps too drastic a word. The essence of British political history is that parliamentary government has developed gradually. Hard words have often been said, and hard blows have sometimes been struck. But usually the traditional British compromise, reached after discussion, has been adopted towards any apparently intractable problem. These are the ways to go ahead. First, to discuss, to argue, to talk, at great length if necessary, but never to act hastily. Second, to avoid extreme measures, to find the happy medium between. Third, to play fair, to give all parties the chance to speak, to influence affairs. The paragraphs which follow are necessarily expressions of opinion. They are put forward in the hope of stimulating thought.

Proportional representation is unlikely to be introduced in Britain. On the other hand, the alternative vote may be tried. Two Speaker's Conferences in the past have recommended it. It will probably have the advantage of introducing a third party into the House of Commons which is not strong enough to upset the balance between the two dominant parties, and will not therefore interfere with the strong, stable system of government which is one of the greatest merits of the British Constitution. Not only will the third party foster new ideas (one hopes), but its very presence will pose a threat to its bigger rivals that, unless one of them really does make a genuine effort to govern the country constructively in step with modern ideas and events, the nation will turn to the third party (presumably the Liberals) and give it the chance to prove its ideas in practice.

As to planning of Britain's economy, some form of central control has come to stay. The Conservatives did not repudiate the nationalization of the Bank of England or of the public-utility industries. On the contrary, by active use of the Capital Investments Committee, by appointment of the Cohen Council on Prices and Productivity, by Budgetary control of the monetary system, by appointment of the Radcliffe Committee to consider the banking and financial organization of the country, by a strong credit policy governed by Bank Rate, by legislation to set up and stimulate new industries in depressed areas, the Conservative Party confirmed its acceptance of some measure of State control and guidance of the national economy. The only difference between the parties is now the extent of central Government control, the degree to which private ownership and the profit motive is to be given scope. In short, the British economy of the future will be a planned economy.

This close attention to economic matters is connected with the current problem concerning Treasury control over departmental estimates and parliamentary control over the Treasury. The Sixth Report of the Select Committee on Estimates (July 1958) has said in its conclusion that "what is called Treasury control is better described as a complex of administrative practice that has grown up like a tree over the centuries, natural rather than planned, empiric rather than theoretical." The Committee wondered whether the existing method is out of date, having been evolved when Government spending was a small fraction of what it is to-day. The Committee found, nevertheless, that the system worked reasonably well. They recommended, however, that a small independent committee, with access to Cabinet papers, should be appointed to report further in the matter. The problem arises from the fact that not only has the amount of money which the State spends increased enormously, having a significant influence upon the economic prosperity of the nation, but the money is being spent on new projects, like atomic power-stations, which are so scientific and technical in character that it must be very difficult indeed for the ordinary administrative civil servant, however able, to understand the technical problems involved, and thus be able to say whether the estimates in question are reasonable or not. The obvious answer is that the Treasury must recruit a small staff of permanent experts to examine these new projects all the year round.

What is to be the future relationship between Parliament and powerful pressure groups like the Trades Union Congress? The dispute over the pay of busmen threatened at one time to develop into a general strike. Fortunately the trade-union leaders as a body were sufficiently sensible and responsible not to challenge the Government of the day. There is some similarity between this problem and that of the permanent Conservative majority in the House of Lords. The trade-union movement is so intimately connected with the Labour Party that it is sometimes hard to see where one begins and the other ends. If the nation is faced with alternating Conservative and Labour Governments, then the Trades Union Congress must work impartially with both political parties. It must put its point of view on economic and political matters to the Government, and try to have its opinions accepted by purely constitutional means, but there must be no class war, because that would be disastrous to the nation's prosperity. The same sort of co-operative spirit of mutual trust is wanted here as is so urgently needed internationally. A Royal Commission has been appointed to examine the state of the Trade Unions in 1965.

The troubles which beset the world as a whole spring from the conflict of political and economic ideologies. The Communists distrust the capitalists, and *vice versa*. Even within the community of democratic States there is a strong spirit of economic nationalism. The fear of war forces nations to adopt economic policies as a matter of strategic policy, whereas it is indisputable that full international division of labour, and therefore free trade, is the only way in which the world can feed its alarmingly swiftly increasing population. In other words, some sort of international society is the ultimate goal. The United Nations Organization, the International Monetary Fund, the European Free Trade Area, these are all steps in the right direction, because they mean international co-operation and understanding. The value of discussion has never been better illustrated than in the disputes in 1958 in Jordan and the Lebanon. Pessimists feared that the arrival in these two small States of

British and American troops would provoke Russian retaliation. Happily, the trouble was referred to U.N.O. There was much talk, but no war.

The Summit Meeting has become an important problem. In a world dominated by the U.S.A. and the U.S.S.R. (with the Communist Republic of China growing rapidly in strength and creating an entirely new situation), bristling with international questions which could have very grave consequences if they are not solved, the view of most people is that the only way in which results can be obtained is by meetings of the heads of Governments. If this policy is carried out the Prime Minister of Britain must grow in status and strength. The electorate must bear in mind at a General Election who is to represent them at such meetings. They will therefore pay particular regard to the probable Prime Minister if one or the other party wins. The election could well be decided by this factor. Is it a good or a bad development? Will it tend to make heads of Governments dictatorial? Clearly, here is a possibility requiring serious thought in the future.[1]

In conclusion, the essential importance of a study of the British Constitution is that in a democratic society in which almost the whole of the adult population has the right to vote that right cannot be intelligently exercised unless every voter has at least an elementary knowledge of the Constitution. The best place in which the potential elector can make the acquaintance of the system of government under which he and she lives is at school. Not only is it important to know what happens in Parliament and why, but it is interesting because the Constitution is a living thing, which, happily, is not dying, but growing and changing. Each elector has a chance to take part in this process of growth and change. Indeed, each elector ought to take part, however humble that part may be.

BIBLIOGRAPHY

BRASHER, N. H.: *Studies in British Government* (Macmillan, 1965).

---

[1] The trend was commented on thus: "The new cabinet may be more energetic and more capable than the old and this may give renewed confidence to the Conservative Parliament, but the changes, drastic as they were, have not transformed the Government in the sight of ordinary electors. The country has moved near enough to a presidential form of government to mean that only a change of Prime Minister will persuade people that they are looking at a new ministry." (*The Times*, November 24, 1962.)

I

Appendices

A. The Queen in the Commonwealth

It is important to distinguish between the rôle of the Queen as the constitutional sovereign of countries like Canada, Australia, and New Zealand, where her function is similar to what it is in the United Kingdom (except that many of her duties are carried out on her behalf by a Governor-General, who is recommended to her by the Prime Minister concerned) and her position in those countries like India and Nigeria which are republics where she is not regarded as Queen, but where she has a symbolic significance as Head of the Commonwealth.

This raises the question whether this symbolism has any longer any practical value. The answer seems to depend on whether the Commonwealth as an organization is important to its member states. What does the Commonwealth stand for? As we have seen on pp. 213–221, it gives an economic advantage to its members, who can export goods to the United Kingdom, there is a usefulness in defence where the United Kingdom can still help other members, its voice in world affairs is louder and stronger when it acts as a united political organization of 700 million people, of whom Canada and India are noted already for their mediation. The United Kingdom gives substantial economic, financial, and material aid to less-well-off Commonwealth countries like Ghana. The Queen is the personification of this belief in common law, in good faith, in parliamentary government, in negotiation rather than war. All human associations seem to need such a symbol. Commonwealth countries have on many occasions expressed a strong wish to preserve this link between them. The Queen enables people to show friendship towards each other by demonstrating their loyalty and affection to the monarchy. The vague constitutional structure of the Commonwealth thus becomes visible and tangible in the person of the Queen.

B. The British Way of Life

Is this the main link which binds the states of the Commonwealth together? Indeed, what is the British Way of Life? Is this one of those phrases that trip off our tongues, but which we cannot define? Is the Queen part of it? I think she is because she is the incarnation of the Pax Britannica, the Queen's Peace, the guarantee that the Rule of Law prevails, that men may go about their business in safety, that they may expect a fair trial in court from an independent judge. It is a pattern of social and political customs and behaviour. The Prime Minister and the Cabinet, the Speaker and the White Paper, the Leader of the Opposition and the compromise, an impartial permanent Civil Service, police who keep their truncheons inside their trousers, and do not carry firearms, the orators at Speakers' Corner in Hyde Park in London who harangue a sceptical, ribald audience on all sorts of topics (including the abominable British) are all important figures in the British political pageant, and are examples of the British Way of Life.

C. THE FUTURE OF PARLIAMENTARY GOVERNMENT IN THE COMMONWEALTH

On pp. 219–21 we discussed the influence of the British Constitution upon democratic government in the new independent states of the Commonwealth. Since then much has happened to make one wonder whether parliamentary government on the Westminster model will be abandoned, and if so, what form of constitution will emerge, and will the new form—or forms—be flexible enough to enable the Commonwealth to survive? In Nigeria there have been two *coups*, both accompanied by violence. Nigeria was granted independence in 1960 as a Federation of three Regions. (A fourth Region, the Mid-Western, was set up in 1963.) There are significant differences of language, religion, and race between the people of the Regions, as well as a history of tribal wars. There are three major racial groups—the Hausa-Fulani in the North, the Ibo in the East, and the Yoruba in the West. In January 1966 discontent erupted in a revolution, in the course of which the Prime Minister of the Federation, the Premiers of the North and West Regions, and the Federal Finance Minister were all killed and a military government under General Ironsi, an Ibo, took over the administration. In July 1966 there was a second revolution in which there was a massacre of Ibos in the north and west and General Ironsi, among others, was kidnapped and disappeared. A new military government took over under Lieutenant-Colonel Gowon. That government is still in power, and in January 1967 Colonel Gowon officially confirmed that General Ironsi had been killed the previous July. His remains had been found: these were buried, and a day of national mourning ordered. A conference of the four Regions was set up to try to agree on a new constitution in which the independence of each Region would be carefully safeguarded. The main stumbling-blocks are mistrust of each other, and the problem of splitting the country up into twelve or more Regions. Meanwhile in Ghana, in February 1966, the opportunity of President Nkrumah's absence in China was taken to depose him, outlaw him, suspend the constitution, and set up a military government under General Ankrah. In Ghana the idea of a one-party state has been adopted, and this seems to suit the African mind, largely on the grounds that a 'new' state cannot afford two sets of politicians, and that the only way to develop is along socialist lines. In Nigeria the parties are based on tribalism and regionalism, and not on political opinions. The cult of a leader is popular, which again can have its dangers. The long reign of Nehru in India created its own problems. The great British experiment of planting the Westminster Parliamentary roots in tropical climates has grown some exotic flowers. These countries will have to find a solution themselves. The British Constitution is, let us remember, the result of nine hundred years of evolution.

The Commonwealth has much strength within it. The Prime Ministers' Conference brought together the leaders of India and Pakistan and enabled them to discuss Kashmir in an atmosphere of goodwill among friends who wanted the matter settled amicably. Even if no positive solution was achieved, progress was made. When Malaysia was threatened by Indonesia, the United Kingdom, Australia, and New Zealand came to the rescue with military and other aid. When India was attacked by China Britain gave generous help in munitions and weapons. When there were military mutinies in some of the new African states they appealed for assistance to Britain, who sent troops at once and withdrew them immediately the trouble was ended.

There are, however, difficulties. The question of Rhodesia seems almost incapable of solution. Britain is naturally anxious to settle the matter peaceably, and is unwilling to be precipitate. The Africans, on the other hand, are impatient. They suspect Britain of taking sides with the white Rhodesians. Some of them are unable to understand Britain's embarrassing situation. If Britain does join the European Economic Community, will she abandon the Commonwealth, or put it in second place? These are some of the possibilities that make one wonder if the Commonwealth is going to survive, or if it is worth preserving. Is it an important institution in a world with so many other political or economic combinations? There is NATO and SEATO, and the Organization of African States, in which Commonwealth states are associated with non-

Commonwealth states. In the Tashkent Conference Russia mediated between India and Pakistan, while the United Nations Organization seems to do everything that the Commonwealth does. The International Monetary Fund and the World Bank can offer more economic aid than can the Commonwealth. So what value is the Commonwealth? It stands for democratic government, for the peaceful settlement of disputes, economic co-operation, for the preservation of the Rule of Law. These are things of priceless importance. Any institution which promotes and protects them is worthy of survival. The Commonwealth still has, moreover, in spite of attempts to overthrow it, a common language—English.

D. THE OPPOSITION

The work of Her Majesty's Opposition is mentioned in various parts of this book. An attempt is made here to set down the functions of the Opposition in one place for the benefit of the student. Let us begin by quoting Lord Campion, once Clerk of the House of Commons:

> The "Official Opposition" is a standing proof of the British genius for inventing political machinery. It has been adopted in all the Dominion Parliaments; the lack of it is the chief weakness of most of the Continental systems. It derives, of course, from the two-Party system; but in its developed form it represents a happy fusion of the parliamentary spirit of toleration with the democratic tendency to exact party organization. The system involves the discouragement of individual initiative almost as much on the Opposition back benches as on those of the Government party, for party organization seems more adapted to frontal attack in mass formation than to individual sniping. While admitting the loss to parliamentary life resulting from the sacrifice of the independent private Member, it cannot be denied that under modern conditions the concerted action of the Opposition is the best means of controlling a Government— by criticizing defects in administration loudly enough for the public to take notice.[1]

The duty of the Opposition is in essence to oppose. Its function is that by means of its performance in Parliament in debate it shall persuade the electorate that it is an alternative Government. The Opposition fulfils its function by criticizing public Bills, both on the Second Reading and in committee. It will ask that an important Bill be debated in detail by a Committee of the whole House. It has the right to choose which parts of the departmental Estimates

[1] From *Parliament: a Survey* (Allen and Unwin, 1952), p. 30.

shall be considered when the Committee of Supply is dealing with the Estimates. It asks Questions in the House of Commons which are designed to keep Ministers alert. It provides the Chairman of the Committee on Public Accounts. It criticizes the errors of commission and omission in the Government's legislative proposals when the Queen's Speech is debated. The Leader of the Opposition, which is a specific post carrying a salary, forms a Shadow Cabinet, each member of which is the official party spokesman on one aspect of Government activity. The Shadow Minister of Health, for instance, will ask Questions in the House concerning the state of the hospitals or the pay of doctors, and so on; while the Shadow Minister of Defence will ask the real Minister why he is reducing the garrison of Malta or has decided to abandon the naval carrier. If the Prime Minister speaks on television in a party political broadcast the Leader of the Opposition may reply. Opposition back-benchers will form informal committees which will study matters like foreign affairs or housing. They will ask Questions in the House as to what the Government is going to do about Gibraltar, or why the housing programme is falling behind its target. They will write letters to the newspapers, make speeches in their constituencies at week-ends, and carry the attack to the Government wherever and whenever possible. The public will assess the efficiency of the Opposition as an alternative Government by the vigour and determination with which it harries the Government, by the impression it gives that it knows the answer to the nation's problems, and only requires the opportunity to show its worth. The Opposition will have a candidate in almost every constituency which has returned a Government member, even a safe seat, and this candidate must pursue his rival with great energy to try to unseat him at the next election. A conscientious candidate who has plenty of time to listen patiently to the woes and grumbles, the ideas and opinions, of the voters will go a long way to winning a seat in the House. The Party will publish its policy. The public are given the chance to compare the two parties.

If the Opposition fails to carry out its functions effectively the country is in practice being governed by one party alone. Some states believe in a one-party system, but we prefer the two-party (or three-party) system, because we think that if there is no opposition to the Government we are in serious danger of being ruled by a dictator, or by a party which is so sure of itself that Ministers grow slack and lazy and rest on their laurels. In this sense it is argued that the Opposition exercises the right of Free Speech by insisting on having its say in all Parliamentary discussions, either in the House of Commons or elsewhere.

E. THE PRIVY COUNCIL

Until Walpole introduced a form of Cabinet in the eighteenth century the Sovereign in Privy Council was the executive power in England. The Council has steadily diminished in importance, and most of its powers have been taken over by the Cabinet, while its work is largely done by Government departments. Its modern function is principally to publish formally policy which has been decided elsewhere. It has approximately 300 members, who are either Cabinet Ministers or former Cabinet Ministers or are persons who have been eminent in public affairs in the United Kingdom or any other country of the Commonwealth. They are appointed by the Sovereign for life on the recommendation of the Prime Minister, and are accorded by convention the style Right Honourable.

The Sovereign usually presides at meetings. Four Councillors are usually asked to attend, but three constitute a quorum. The Council never assembles as a whole except on the death of the Sovereign or when the Sovereign announces an intention to marry. Subject to the Sovereign's approval, the Privy Council publishes Orders-in-Council. These Orders arise either out of the Royal Prerogative, such as instructions to Colonial Governors, or as a result of Acts of Parliament, such as the delegation of powers to the Treasury. Although these Orders are made in the Queen's name, the responsibility for them rests with the Cabinet. The Council advises the Sovereign on the issue of royal proclamations such as those which dissolve or summon Parliament.

It works through committees which are advisory in character. The Sovereign cannot attend their meetings. They deal with legislative matters from the Channel Islands and the Isle of Man; the administration of the Universities of Oxford and Cambridge and the Scottish Universities; and the granting of royal charters to municipal corporations. There is a Privy Council Office which is controlled by the Lord President of the Council, who is usually a Cabinet Minister.

The Judicial Committee of the Privy Council is the Final Court of Appeal from the courts of dependent territories and certain independent members of the Commonwealth, as well as for ecclesiastical matters, from the Channel Islands and the Isle of Man, and from prize courts concerned with property captured in wartime. Appeals are heard by a Board of the Committee selected from the Lord Chancellor, ex-Lords Chancellor, and Lords of Appeal in Ordinary, as well as other Councillors who have held high judicial office in any Commonwealth State. The Committee advises the Queen, who acts on its reports and issues Orders-in-Council giving effect to them. The Board usually consists of four or five members, and only the opinion of the majority of the Board is expressed. The constitutional nature of the Committee was well put by Lord Haldane in *Hull* v. *McKenna and others* (1926) I.R.402 thus:

> We are not Ministers in any sense; we are a Committee of Privy Councillors who are acting in the capacity of judges, but the peculiarity of the situation is this: it is a long-standing constitutional anomaly that we are really a committee of the Privy Council giving advice to His Majesty; but in a judicial spirit. We have nothing to do with policies or party considerations; we are really judges but in form and name we are the Committee of the Privy Council. The Sovereign gives the judgment himself, and always acts on the report we make. Our report is made public before it is sent up to the Sovereign in Council. It is delivered here in a printed form. It is a report as to what is proper to be done on the principles of justice; and it is acted on by the Sovereign in full Privy Council; so that you see, in substance, what takes place is a strictly judicial proceeding.

As States of the Commonwealth have attained political independence they have exercised the right to discontinue appeals to the Judicial Committee. Only New Zealand, Ceylon, the Caribbean States, and the six Australian states now have the right of appeal without special leave. The High Court of Australia may appeal by special leave.

The Judicial Committee has a great past. It has been a strong unifying influence within the Commonwealth, especially in considering and interpreting the intricacies of new federal constitutions with complete impartiality. It has also been a powerful factor in planting deeply the roots of the English Common Law and in establishing common legal principles. It has been probably one of the strongest links which bind the Commonwealth countries together. As, however, its aura of jurisdiction shrinks and it becomes a constitutional anachronism, a curious relic of a bygone Empire, its usefulness is being questioned, and perhaps in the not too distant future it will be abolished. If that ever happens it will leave behind a rich historical legacy.

F. By-elections and Opinion Polls

The Parliament Act 1911 laid down that the life of a Parliament would be five years, this being a period long enough for the Government to carry out a legislative programme and to put through a policy effectively, but not so long that the voters were prevented from showing whether they approved or disapproved of the Government, and whether they did or did not wish to give the Opposition an opportunity to govern. If the electorate are deprived of this chance for too long they are being disenfranchized, and dangerous discontent will be fomented. When a Government has a small majority, as had Mr Attlee in 1951 and Mr Wilson in 1965, it becomes important to find out how far the Government can go in controversial matters without outraging public opinion, even to assess whether it is worth while dissolving Parliament and trying to resolve the deadlock by means of an early General Election. A party which has been in office for a long time may appear to be running short of ideas and new men. The public become bored with such a Government, and hanker after change. The Government wants to discover where it stands with the voters; it has the tactical right to decide the best time for an election, but it has to collect information upon which such a decision is made.

The by-election has become a political device by which the Government—and the Opposition—sound public opinion. Some M.P.'s resign for more or less unavoidable reasons; an M.P. may inherit or receive a title which he does not wish to disclaim, or he may be offered an office of profit under the Crown which he would be foolish to refuse, or other causes may persuade him to depart. On the other hand, the party leaders may want an M.P. to resign because they wish to sound public opinion or to make way for someone whom the leader wants in the Commons. Mr Wilson persuaded two Members to go in order to make way for Mr Cousins at Nuneaton and Mr Gordon Walker at Leyton in 1965. Lord Home, on resigning his peerage, was selected to contest a by-election as Sir Alec Douglas-Home, and thus re-entered the House of Commons. In such cases the by-election is a flexible tool, a conventional political device, which enables a party leader to recruit a distinguished supporter or to get rid of an embarrassing passenger. But the main purpose of a by-election, or at any rate the chief usefulness of one, is to assess public opinion. If the seats concerned are marginal there could be a change of party representation. Even in a safe seat the voters can demonstrate their views by abstaining from voting. They will not go so far generally as voting for the other side, but they can show their displeasure with the party line by staying at home. A fall in the vote is significant if it is substantial. The leader will be warned that he is pursuing unpopular policies. On the other hand, it may be argued that a by-election is an unreliable guide because voters are apathetic, not all bother to vote, and those who do might vote for the other side in a fit of pique because it will make no difference to the balance of power in the House of Commons, assuming the Government possesses a big majority.

Those who do not vote may abstain because they see no reason to turn out in a contest which to them is meaningless. A Conservative or Socialist who is lukewarm at a by-election may be enthusiastic in a General Election; his voting behaviour in one is no guarantee of what he will do in the other. But if the parties whip up interest, send down some of their best men to speak, put up a good candidate, and the Press and the television find the by-election worth publicizing, then the voters may be induced to take an interest and to vote in large numbers. To sum up, a by-election can be a useful pointer, but must not be given too much weight.

Is the poll a better guide? There are several well-known, reputable public opinion polls, which are in continuous operation and which as they gain in experience are becoming more and more expert in assessing public opinion. So much depends on asking the right questions. The popularity of a Prime Minister or a Leader of the Opposition is tested regularly. 'Are you satisfied with the Government?' 'How would you vote if there were a General Election tomorrow?'—these are typical questions which the polls put to a random cross-section of voters. If these polls are held regularly they can show how public opinion is shifting. We used to be rather sceptical about their accuracy, but in the elections of 1964 and 1966 they were remarkably successful. As we get more and more accustomed to being asked questions, and do not resent them, but try to answer them truthfully and sensibly, the polls will become more and more dependable.

It is contended that the poll can be an unfair influence. If a poll in a national newspaper states that the Liberals in a certain constituency have no chance at all waverers who might have voted Liberal may chose some other party because they want their votes to be effective, or some people will vote as the majority are apparently going to vote. On the grounds that this is not rational behaviour, but a sort of mass hysteria, people following each other like sheep, the influence of the polls can be considered to be bad, but it is by no means sure that they do have this effect. It all depends on the seriousness with which the average man reads his newspaper and studies what it says about the latest opinion-poll finding. It is probably a fact that few people vote for some simple reason like doing what everybody else does. Most voters are firmly committed to one of the big parties, and will vote regardless of opinion polls or the Press or the television. Some, however, do think about the election and want to find the best policy on, say, fuel—should we subsidize coal or tax oil? What the polls do quite definitely is to keep the parties informed of the state of public opinion, and influence them to vary their own policies. Public opinion is so amorphous, so fickle, so complex, on any important matter that anything which helps to define it is desirable.

G. The Paymaster-General

The Paymaster-General has few departmental duties to perform. His office may be used by the Prime Minister as a means of appointing a Cabinet Minister and giving him a special task to carry out. It is an example of the flexible nature of both the unwritten Constitution and the Cabinet. For instance, Mr Macmillan used his Paymaster-General for a time as the Minister responsible for looking after Britain's interests in the negotiations which led up to the formation of the European Economic Community, while Mr Wilson has used the office for the Minister responsible for security. Questions are often asked in the House of Commons by the Opposition concerning the duties performed by the Paymaster-General, but the replies have hardly been very informative. It must be presumed that the Paymaster-General carries out such duties as the Prime Minister assigns to him, and that they are of a highly confidential nature. He is usually, therefore, a member of the Cabinet and a member of the House of Commons.

His office acts as a banker for Government departments other than the Boards of Inland Revenue and Customs and Excise, and the Post Office. Money granted by Parliament is transferred daily as required from the Exchequer account in the Bank of England to the account of the Paymaster-General, so that departmental payments may be made by orders drawn on this account. These orders do the work of a cheque. They are presented to the commercial banks, who meet them and recoup themselves through the Paymaster-General's account at the Bank of England. The department also pays the pensions of many public servants, such as civil servants, teachers, members of the National Health Service like doctors, and officers of the Armed Forces. It must be emphasized that the Paymaster-General does not personally have any duties concerning the work of his department. His function there is purely formal. His conventional work is purely political, and is done as a member of the Government.

H. The National Economic Development Council

This body was first mentioned in July 1961 in the House of Commons by the Chancellor of the Exchequer (Mr Selwyn Lloyd). Today it has become a committee consisting of the Secretary of State for Economic Affairs, three other Ministers, who are the President of the Board of Trade, the Minister of Labour, and the

Minister of Technology; six representatives of the trade unions; six representatives of management in industry; the chairmen of two nationalized industries; two independents, one of whom is a Professor of Economics; and the Chairman of the National Board for Prices and Incomes. The Chancellor of the Exchequer used to be the Chairman, but is now not even a member. The Council works through a number of committees, each of which is concerned with a different aspect of industry such as Building, Chemicals, Distributive Trades, Civil Engineering, Electronics, Electrical Engineering, Machine Tools, Mechanical Engineering, Rubber, Wool Textiles.

I. THE NATIONAL BOARD FOR PRICES AND INCOMES

This was established in 1965 under the chairmanship of Mr Aubrey Jones, who is an economist and was a Member of Parliament in opposition to the Government of the day. It is noteworthy that he was nevertheless invited to become Chairman, a paid office under the Crown, and he therefore left the Commons. The Board is in two divisions, one concerned with Price Review, the other with Incomes Review. Its main concern is to prevent prices rising unnecessarily by insisting that any industry which wishes to raise its prices must prove that this is inevitable, and that the industry is using its factors of production with maximum efficiency; and, on the other hand, it must persuade all those industries or firms or unions who propose increases of wages to relate these to increases in productivity, since otherwise rising wages will merely have an inflationary effect, and there will be no real increase of income. It is trying to do a difficult job, because we as a nation have first to become used to this official concern with what we naturally regard as our private affairs. This will take time.

J. PLANNING BY THE CENTRAL GOVERNMENT

On p. 190 we referred to the fact that in what we call the Welfare State the Government is concerned with planning in order that the economy will be prosperous, our national product of goods and services will increase as our wages rise, that there will be full employment, that the purchasing power of our money will be stable. Inevitably we have developed institutions to deal with these matters, and the purpose of this section is to describe them.

The Cabinet Office has developed. Its staff are technically part of the Treasury, but in fact they are independent. It is responsible for the security of all Cabinet documents, and its secretary has become a confidential adviser to the Prime Minister. Mr Wilson (as we have seen elsewhere) introduced a temporary adviser, Dr Balogh, an academic economist from Balliol College, Oxford. The Cabinet Office has a statistical section which collects from all Government departments statistics relating to the national economy, and then analyses and prepares them for consideration by the Cabinet in their formulation of national economic policy.

The Department of Economic Affairs was created in 1965 out of the Treasury, but is quite independent. It consists of four departmental groups. The first is the Economic Planning Group, which is concerned with predicting the short-, medium-, and long-term growth of the economy. The second is the Industrial Policy Group, which is concerned with the efficiency and growth of individual industries. The third is the Economic Co-ordination Group, which is concerned with co-ordinating the work of the Government departments, with prices and incomes, and with the relationship between public expenditure on the one hand and the wise use of national resources on the other. The fourth is the Regional Policy Group, which is concerned with the planning of regional growth, and so with industry, employment, and transport in each of the regions into which the country has been divided, producing plans for each region. Naturally it must work very closely with the Treasury and several other departments linked with the national economy—the Board of Trade, the Ministry of Labour, the Ministry of Technology, the Ministry of Power, the Ministry of Transport, the Ministry of Housing and Local Government, the Ministry of Public Building and Works, and the Ministry of Agriculture.

Town Planning and Housing is one of the obvious spheres in which Government planning is exercised. The United Kingdom is one of the most densely populated countries in the world, and land is relatively scarce. The need to use it to the best advantage has resulted in the creation of a Ministry of Housing and Local Government, and the delegation to local authorities of important functions, both in housing and in town planning. The first Bill on land planning was passed in 1909. Then came the Town and Country Planning Act of 1932, the New Towns Act of 1946, and a series of other Acts, culminating in the Town and Country Planning (Scotland) Act 1947, the Town and Country Planning Act of 1962 for England and Wales, and, finally, in 1965, the plan to introduce a Land Commission, with powers to acquire, manage, and dispose of land for development.

The Acts of 1947 required the county and county borough councils in England and Wales and the county and large burgh councils in Scotland to submit to the Minister of Housing and Local Government and the Secretary of State for Scotland respectively plans to develop their areas. These plans consisted of maps showing the communications and existing use of the land, and proposing how development could take place over a period of twenty years. Every fifth year the local authorities had to report how the plan was progressing, and to suggest amendments and extensions. No local authority could carry out a large scheme of development without encroaching on the interests of individuals or groups, therefore the plans have to be given ample publicity so that the public may make objections which the Minister can hear, consider, and decide on, such inquiries being in public. Green belts have been created, and no building may take place on them. Acts of 1960 and 1963 provided for industry to be located away from congested urban areas. No factories may, however, be erected without the permission of the local authority concerned. The tremendous problem in London and Birmingham was dealt with by the Office and Industrial Development Act, 1965. Where New Towns are to be developed the Minister must consult and work with the local authorities concerned. The Minister, having chosen a site and approved a master plan, then appoints a Development Corporation who have powers to acquire land, if necessary by compulsory purchase, to provide houses, flats, schools, shops, industrial premises, estate roads, and all other essential buildings. The corporation is lent the capital funds needed, and is given sixty years in which to repay out of rents. When the 'New Town' is more or less completed the corporation is dissolved and the local authority (which has merely been consulted so far) takes over entirely. Some examples of new towns are Crawley, Hemel Hempstead, Welwyn, and Hatfield. Funds of up to £550 million were officially approved for this development.

The increase in the population coupled with rising standards of living have created a growing demand for new houses and flats, and at the same time the slums which are a legacy of the nineteenth century must be cleared away and new dwellings erected. The main responsibility for housing rests with the Minister. He must apportion land between the needs of agriculture, industry, and transport, as well as housing. Several regional surveys have been made to cover twenty years of development. The local authorities, however, have the task of actually providing the houses. This function is performed by county borough, borough, urban, and rural district councils, and in London by the Greater London Council and its thirty-two borough councils, and the City of London Common Council. In Scotland all town and burgh councils have a housing function.

There are over 15 million dwellings in England and Wales, and

nearly 2 million in Scotland. One house in four in England belongs
to a local authority, and one in two in Scotland. Private enterprise
at present is putting up rather more than half the houses, and local
authority the rest. In recent years councils have also lent substantial sums on mortgage to persons wishing to buy a house, especially those already renting a house and anxious to purchase it, but
who find the deposit difficult to find. Some councils will lend 100
per cent. of the price to the citizen under the House Purchase and
Housing Act of 1959. Sometimes the Council will guarantee part
of the loan made by a building society for houses costing up to
£2500.

Councils raise the funds they require either in the open market,
offering corporation stock, or they borrow from the Public Works
Loan Board, which is financed by the Exchequer and acts as lender
of last resort to councils who cannot borrow in the open market.
The sanction of the Minister must be obtained. The Greater London
Council promotes a Private Bill annually applying for Parliamentary sanction to raise money for capital expenditure. The Ministry
grants subsidies to councils which can amount to £24 a year for
each house built in the case of a poor council. Grants are payable
to provide a bath, wash-basin, water-closet and hot-water supply
in a house built before 1945 which, unbelievably, lacks these essential amenities. The housing subsidy in recent years has been about
£100 a year on average.

K. The Police

Any state, unfortunately, needs a police force, because man is
not perfect: some people cannot resist the temptation to cheat or
to steal, the traffic has to be regulated, law and order has to be
maintained, there must be no breaches of the peace, the individual
must not be allowed to promote his self-interest at the expense of
other people in the community. That, indeed, is the central problem
in a political state—how much liberty can be given to the individual before he encroaches upon the liberty of other people? If
someone wants to make a speech in which he is going to be controversial, and refer to problems on which public feeling seems
high, there is likely to be a breach of the peace because his opponents will want to break up his meeting. In that case the police
must forbid him to speak, and thus lay themselves open to the
charge that they are interfering with freedom of speech. In England
and Wales in 1965 there were 117 regular police forces, and 31 in
Scotland, numbering about 80,000 men and women. Of these about
18,000 were in the Metropolitan Police, who are responsible for

Greater London; whereas one police force in Scotland numbered only 20. The Government's policy is to reduce the number of forces and to increase in size those that remain. The problem is, how far must they go to secure maximum efficiency? Do we need a national police force, or are several regional forces better? The police, like all our public institutions, are examined critically every now and then. A Royal Commission reported in 1962, and the Home Secretary in 1967 is considering reorganization, and has announced his intention of cutting down the forces in England and Wales to 49. He will be faced with opposition from local authorities who are proud of their forces, and do not wish them to be amalgamated with some other force. This is a common problem of the Government. The large unit may be more efficient than the small unit, but if you upset people and make them discontented and unhappy, is the greater efficiency bought at too high a price? After all, government is concerned with the welfare of people; it is in essence a human problem.

At present in England and Wales the Home Secretary is responsible for the general administration of all police, and for the Metropolitan Police in particular. London is the capital, and is often the scene of great public occasions such as a Coronation or the visit of a foreign Head of State, when very important questions of security arise and the Government must accept responsibility for making sure that nothing goes wrong. They cannot delegate such a function to any local authority.

The City of London has by tradition its own force, which is administered by the Court of Common Council of the City, which appoints a standing committee to do the day-to-day work entailed.

The remaining forces are maintained by counties, either separately or jointly, and by county borough councils. The former are administered by a joint police committee and the latter by a watch committee. These are merely names. Both are in fact council committees, and both now consist of councillors and justices of the peace in a proportion of two to one. Where two or more counties jointly administer a force, each county is represented in proportion to its size as a council. The cost of these forces is borne half by the Home Office and half by the council (or councils) concerned. The Chief Constable of a force is appointed by the council subject to the approval of the Home Secretary, and is retired if inefficient, also provided the Home Secretary agrees. The councils provide the buildings and the equipment, and they must satisfy themselves that Chief Constables deal effectively with complaints of the public about police officers. They fix their own establishments, subject to the Home Secretary's agreement. The Queen appoints the Chief

Commissioner of the Metropolitan Police on the Home Secretary's recommendation. The Secretary of State for Scotland carries out similar duties to the Home Secretary in relation to police forces in Scotland.

The Home Secretary has considerable powers over the police. He may call for a Chief Constable to be retired or may ask for a report from one as to the police in his area. He issues regulations regarding uniform, pay, pensions, conditions of service, covering all police, in order to ensure uniformity. He discusses their regulations before one is published or amended with the Police Council, on which all interested parties are represented. He has under him a Chief Inspector and eight other Inspectors of Constabulary, whose task is to inspect police forces annually, keep touch with them all the time, and report to him on their efficiency. If he is not satisfied with the state of a force he can withhold the grant. He can also order the amalgamation of forces after an inquiry has been held which recommends such action. The Secretary of State for Scotland has a similar function.

M.P.'s can ask questions in the House about the Metropolitan Police, but not about other forces. Many M.P.'s would like this state of affairs changed. Others consider that there should be a national police, because there would be economy in administration and equipment, greater co-operation and control, better use of the best officers, and all parts of the force could call upon a central organization for information about criminals and their methods, and for examination by scientists of fingerprints, hair, ballistics, powder, blood—the wide variety of clues upon which scientific investigation is brought to bear. But despite these obvious advantages, there is much opposition.

The councils themselves resent any suggestion of losing control of a force on which they may pride themselves. They dislike the prospect of giving up interesting work to the Government. It is maintained that the local policeman, born and bred in the district, who knows the people and is known by them, will get much more help from the public than strangers will. It is said that a national force would be too big, and that in fact the headquarters would lose touch with the man on the beat. It is also suggested that the Home Secretary would acquire dangerous powers which if misused could create a police state, in which a secret police would eventually creep in, and opposition to the Government would be crushed. It is true that dictators like Mussolini and Hitler worked on the same principle—that power rested with the ruler who controlled the police—but it does seem unlikely that a British Prime Minister could wish to assume such powers, or that his colleagues in the

Cabinet would allow him to do so. This, however, may be an optimistic view of the national character. All we can say at present is that we are likely to have fewer and larger police forces, but not a single national force.

L. The Jury

It is probably commonly supposed that trial by judge and jury is normal in England, but in fact it is relatively rare. The great majority of criminal cases, which are of a minor nature, are heard and decided in the Court of Summary Jurisdiction (or Petty Sessions[1]), either by a Stipendiary Magistrate or by a Bench of Justices of the Peace: there is no jury. A serious criminal case which goes up to the Quarter Sessions or the Assizes is heard by judge (or Recorder) and jury. A few cases in Civil Law are also heard by judge and jury. In the County Courts, where the judge usually sits alone, there is sometimes a jury of eight if both parties desire it. In the High Court there is often a jury in cases of defamation, false imprisonment, unlawful arrest, seduction, or breach of promise to marry, when the person charged claims this right. The jury is twelve members of the public over twenty-one and under sixty who are householders, but members of certain professions are exempted from this duty of the citizen. In certain cases a Coroner's Court may have a jury of from seven to eleven jurors to decide how, when, and where a deceased person died, or ownership of treasure in a case of 'treasure trove'.

The usefulness of the jury is at present in question on the grounds that it is a less reliable means of determining guilt or innocence than trial by a judge or bench of judges. The arguments against the value of the jury are as follows:

1. Many jurors are not sufficiently intelligent or educated to understand the long and complex arguments in court, with the result that they tend to overestimate the importance of the more dramatic moments and to remember best the last stages of the case, and to be unduly influenced by the judge when he sums up.
2. Many jurors are partisan and apt to be hostile towards the police; often one juror is bullied by the others into agreeing with the view of the majority, while others are obstinate and stand out stubbornly, perhaps because they have been improperly influenced by the accused, with the result that a miscarriage of justice takes place.

[1] Or a legally qualified Chairman.

3. Some of the people who would make the most efficient jurors, like priests and doctors, lawyers and military officers, are exempt from this duty.

4. There are very few cases of appeals against the decisions by Magistrates and Justices of the Peace, so the average man must be satisfied with the dispensation of justice without a jury.

5. The fear, justified at the time of Magna Carta, that the judge was the creature of the Executive and a jury of the accused person's peers was a protection against oppression and an assurance of liberty is now out of date; modern Britain is a democracy and the Executive is appointed from Parliament, while the Judiciary is independent.

6. The public dislike this duty, they try to avoid it, they find it interferes with their normal work, and there is a danger that they will try to get the chore over and done with as soon as possible.

On the other hand it is argued that:

1. Jurors are usually sensible, patient people who are interested in the dispensation of justice and who do not want an innocent man punished or a guilty man to escape; they have a far better understanding of the feelings and circumstances of the accused than the judge has, and they are therefore much more likely to understand his motives, to estimate his credibility, and to come to a right decision.

2. The judge, being probably of conservative mind with a strong bias in favour of the existing order of things, could well be partial unintentionally; or because he has formed a wrong conclusion may misdirect the jury, whose common sense and experience of life may serve to discern what is right.

3. There are still social prejudices that could affect a judicial decision, whereas a jury of twelve chosen at random is likely to arrive at a collectively impartial verdict.

4. Service as a juryman is part of democracy, in which as many people as possible are called upon to help in the administration of the State.

5. There is not enough evidence to establish that judges are less fallible than juries.

6. It is the right of an Englishman charged by the State with a criminal offence to demand trial by jury, and it would be a most dangerous precedent to abolish this ancient institution.

Finally, there is the likely introduction of a majority instead of a unanimous verdict. This principle is almost certain to become law, but is not generally acceptable. What is the size of the majority to be—ten to two, nine to three, or what? Will a majority decision lessen the likelihood of a guilty person escaping punishment and prevent the perversion of a particular juror because this will not affect the verdict decisively? Would an educational qualification improve the quality of the jury without being too undemocratic in a socialistic state? These are at present imponderable questions which have been debated publicly in the newspapers and on television by distinguished lawyers and politicians, without general agreement. Time will tell.

The jury in Scotland has returned a majority verdict for a long time, whereas in England we are just thinking about it. The accused, however, cannot be found guilty unless there are at least two witnesses giving evidence against him, each of whom corroborates the other. In this way it is unlikely that the accused is likely to be convicted unfairly. Also, if Scotland has not found the majority verdict by the jury a weakness there seems no good reason why it should be unsatisfactory in England.

M. THE LAW OFFICERS OF THE CROWN

The Law Officers of the Crown are:

The Attorney-General
The Solicitor-General

They must be barristers of high standing and Members of Parliament. They are conventionally members of the majority Party in the House of Commons, and are Ministers in the Government of the day, but neither is usually in the Cabinet. Their rights and duties are the same, but the Attorney-General ranks as the senior. They are the Government's legal advisers, and both have important duties in the administration of the Law Courts. The Attorney-General is the Crown's representative in the courts. Any legal proceedings to enforce the rights of the public or on behalf of charity are carried on in his name. Before certain serious criminal offences are brought to court his consent to legal proceedings must be obtained. The Director of Public Prosecutions and Queen's Proctor both take directions from him. The latter is concerned with the divorce laws.

In 1957, when it was alleged that there had been an improper leakage of Bank Rate, and the Prime Minister ordered a Tribunal to take place in public, the Attorney-General conducted the inquiry and cross-examined relentlessly members of his own Party, including the Chancellor of the Exchequer and two other Ministers. In 1966 the Attorney-General personally intervened in the public discussion concerning the disaster in the Welsh mining village of Aberfan; and he also accompanied the Prime Minister (and advised him on the constitutional issues involved) at the meeting with Mr Smith, the Rhodesian Prime Minister, on H.M.S. *Tiger*.

Like the Lord Chancellor, both the Law Officers must resign if the Government resigns. In the past these offices have frequently been a stepping-stone to high judicial office, either as Lord Chancellor or as Lord Chief Justice, but more and more it is becoming a convention to avoid promotion to a judgeship in order that there can be no question of political influence and partiality on the Bench. The independence of the Judiciary must be protected.

In Scotland the Law Officers of the Crown are the Lord Advocate and the Solicitor-General for Scotland. They are the Government's advisers on purely Scottish questions, and would represent the Crown in litigation in Scotland. The Lord Advocate decides whether to prosecute on indictment in the High Court, and directs the case for the prosecution. He is head of the Lord Advocate's Department. The Parliamentary Draftsmen for Scotland work in the Lord Advocate's Department and draft all Government Bills if they affect the law in Scotland.

N. THE NATIONAL HEALTH SERVICE

The National Health Service Act, 1946, came into force on July 5, 1948. Under this Act all employed persons in the United Kingdom must pay national insurance, and are entitled to free medical services. Most of the doctors and dentists in the country are registered under the Act, and are employed by the State on a basis agreed between the medical profession and the Minister of Health. The rates of pay have recently been the subject of dispute, and have been referred to independent arbitration. About 23,000 doctors, 10,000 dentists, 7000 ophthalmic and dispensing opticians, 16,000 retail pharmacists, and 250,000 nurses work under the National Health Service. The average doctor has about 2500 patients on this panel, with a permissible maximum of 3500. The governing body of the medical profession is the General Medical

Council, set up in 1858, and its professional affairs are administered by the British Medical Association. There are similar bodies concerned with other persons in the service, such as the General Nursing Council and the Royal College of Nursing; the Pharmaceutical Society of Great Britain; and the General Optical Council. These bodies are responsible for the qualifications required to practise, the granting of certificates, the conducting of examinations, and the administration of discipline, even to the point of striking a doctor off the register in an extreme case of misbehaviour. Research is carried on under the Medical Research Council in conjunction with the universities and the hospitals and private organizations like the British Empire Cancer Campaign and the Nuffield Foundation.

The Minister of Health is aided by an advisory Central Health Services Council which he himself appoints from suitable persons. Under his direction local authorities provide certain services; these are Executive Councils aided by professional committees; Regional Hospital Boards; Boards of Governors; and Special Hospitals.

County and Borough Councils are responsible for maternity and child welfare, midwifery, health visiting and home nursing, domestic help in sickness, prevention of illness, vaccination and immunization, ambulances, and health centres. The Executive Councils, advised by doctors and dentists and pharmacists, administer the general professional services provided in 134 areas, each of which has its council. They are concerned with the efficiency of these services in their areas and with the interests of the professional people giving these services and the supply of drugs and appliances.

England and Wales are divided up into fifteen regions, each of which has a Hospital Board appointed by the Minister of Health. Under them are Hospital Management Committees which are composed to represent the community as a whole, containing doctors, members of local authorities, trade-union representatives, and others from the important social groups in the area. Between them they administer 350 groups of hospitals, each of which must have specialist services and is associated with a teaching hospital or university school of medicine. These Committees are concerned with the equipment and staffing of the hospitals, trying to ensure that the latest apparatus is available, that there is an adequate staff of doctors and nurses, dentists and so on—in short, they must manage the hospitals efficiently in order that they perform their functions satisfactorily. The Minister also appoints the boards of governors of teaching hospitals. The regional board, the medical faculty in the University, and the staff of the hospital have the right to nominate members. All these appointments to boards and committees are honorary, performed as an act of public service.

The Health Service costs about 5 per cent. of the national income (£1400 million roughly), most of which is paid for out of taxation, some out of rates, and some out of national insurance contributions. Many of the hospitals are old buildings, sadly in need of modernizing. In 1964 the Government planned to spend about £1000 million on new building over a period of ten years.[1] This service is of immense social and economic importance. It is obvious that a Welfare State must take care of the sick and try to heal their ills and alleviate their pain. It is perhaps not so obvious that if our productivity of goods and services is to rise we need a working population that is healthy and strong, which does not have to be absent from work often through illness, and which is able to put in a good day's work.

O. EDUCATION

The Secretary of State for Education and Science is responsible, with the Ministry of Education, for the efficient administration of all aspects of education in England and Wales, and of all universities in the United Kingdom. The Secretary of State for Wales supervises the national educational policy in Wales, while the Secretary of State for Scotland and the Minister for Education in Northern Ireland have a similar function for all aspects of education in their own areas, except that their function is purely advisory as far as the universities are concerned. In 1964–65 public expenditure on education was about 5 per cent. of the national income, nearly £1400 million, and it keeps on rising. If the recommendations of the Plowden Committee are carried out, if the pay of teachers goes up, if the school-leaving age is increased to sixteen—scheduled for 1970—the total costs of education will be much greater. The first attempt to provide public elementary education for all goes back to 1870 and in the case of secondary education in England to 1902. The Education Act of 1944 governs the existing system of compulsory education of all from the age of five to that of fifteen. In 1966 there were over nine million children and young people in schools, training or technical colleges, and universities, taking full-time courses of study—one-sixth of the total population of the United Kingdom. The great majority of the schools and the technical and training colleges are publicly maintained under the control of local authorities; while the universities, though autonomous, are aided by public funds through the University Grants Committee, and almost all their students are maintained by grants.

[1] In the 1967–68 Estimates the provision made for hospital services rose from £712 million to £815 million. This included pay awards, Selective Employment Tax, and increased expansion.

The Ministry of Education keeps in touch with schools by inspections which show whether the school is efficient. The Schools Council, set up in 1964, advises on curricula and examination syllabuses. There are eight university examining boards in England, who provide General Certificates of Education, both at Advanced and Ordinary Level, working closely with the schools and using teachers in the main as examiners. The Certificate of Secondary Education was introduced in 1965, for children who have been at school for five years, but will not be taking G.C.E.

Generally the local authorities are responsible to the Minister for providing sufficient schools to accommodate all the children within their boundaries, and to ensure that these schools meet the conditions of the 1944 Act in standards of buildings, equipment, and books, playing-fields, meals, and, of course, qualified teachers. They also have their own local inspectors of schools who are there to help schools rather than criticize. They are obliged (as we saw elsewhere) to have Education Committees, and to co-opt persons experienced in education. The authorities are responsible for paying the teachers in England and Wales and for agreeing the scale of pay through the Burnham Committee, on which the Minister and teachers are represented. They also appoint Boards of Governors for each school, in whole or in part. The power of the authorities is at present being tested by the proposal to make all secondary schools comprehensive and in the end to abolish the purely grammar school. This policy, which is social fundamentally, is controversial, and is bitterly contested. The struggle highlights the rights of parents to choose the kind of school to which they wish their children to go. The existence of the public schools, which are virtually private schools that are maintained by bequests and high fees, is also challenged, and their future hangs in the balance. The virtues of variety as opposed to uniformity, of the personal right of a parent to pay fees for a particular kind of education, are involved, and the eventual outcome will be interesting. This author is not gifted with the power of prophecy. In short, though the Minister has the decisive influence as he puts up most of the money, while the local authorities provide the rest of the money and control largely the selection of children to particular schools, not all local authorities are in agreement with each other. This is a fascinating example of democracy at work. In 1964 there were 330,000 full-time and 30,000 part-time teachers in publicly maintained schools, plus some 50,000 in universities and colleges—nearly 4 per cent. of the working population.

In England and Wales there are about 500 colleges giving technical and commercial education under the local authorities providing courses for over 200,000 full-time and nearly 2 million part-time students—a tremendous social service. Many of them take the Ordinary Diploma or the Higher National Diploma or Higher National Certificate.

Both B.B.C. and I.T.V. provide educational programmes.

The Government plans by 1973 to provide over 200,000 university places and 120,000 teachers' training college places. The plan is to increase the number of universities to 45. The Government provides 70 per cent. of the current income of universities and 90 per cent. of their capital requirements. It is not likely to contribute public money on this large scale without having an important say in how the universities are run. The Franks Committee set up by Oxford to inquire into the structure of the University is evidence of awareness of the need to satisfy the public that this money is being wisely spent. The suggestions so often made of favouritism towards undergraduates from independent schools is the sort of criticism that the universities must answer.

The British system of education plays a significant part in Commonwealth affairs since there were 64,000 overseas students in Britain in 1965, many of them on scholarships, who will eventually return to their own countries imbued with British ideas and ideals, a respect (one hopes) for British people and institutions, and the intention to preserve the Commonwealth. Many English teachers go overseas for periods through the British Council, and an increasing number of young people go on Voluntary Service Overseas, largely to teach, in between leaving school and going up to the university.[1]

The appointment of bodies like the Robbins Committee to inquire into educational problems and the wide public interest shown in their reports is evidence of the fact that education has become a vital part of the work done by the Government.

[1] The author can speak from personal experience of the great work which these young people are doing in countries like Ghana and Nigeria.

General Bibliography

AMERY, L. S.: *Thoughts on the Constitution* (Oxford University Press; second edition, 1953).

ARCHER, PETER: *The Queen's Courts* (Penguin Books, 1956).

BAGEHOT, WALTER: *The English Constitution* ("World's Classics"; Oxford University Press, 1928).

BAILEY, SYDNEY D.: *The Future of the House of Lords* (Hansard Society, 1954).

CAMPBELL, G. A.: *The Civil Service in Britain* (Penguin Books, 1955).

CARTER, BYRUM E.: *The Office of Prime Minister* (Faber, 1956).

DAWSON, ROBERT M.: *The Government of Canada* (Oxford University Press; second edition, 1954).

DICEY, A. V.: *Introduction to the Study of the Law of the Constitution* (Macmillan; tenth edition, 1959).

JEFFRIES, SIR CHARLES J.: *The Colonial Office* ("New Whitehall" series; Allen and Unwin, 1955).

JENNINGS, SIR IVOR: *Parliament* (Cambridge University Press; second edition, 1957).

—— *The British Constitution* (Cambridge University Press; third edition, 1950).

—— *Cabinet Government* (Cambridge University Press; third edition, 1959).

JOSHI, G. N.: *The Constitution of India* (Macmillan; third edition, 1955).

KEITH, ARTHUR B.: *Speeches and Documents on the British Dominions, 1918–31* ("World's Classics"; Oxford University Press, 1932).

MACKENZIE, ROBERT T.: *British Political Parties* (Heinemann, 1955).

MORRISON, LORD: *Government and Parliament* (Oxford University Press; second edition, 1959).

NEWSAM, SIR FRANK A.: *The Home Office* ("New Whitehall" series; Allen and Unwin, 1954).

NICHOLAS, H. S.: *The Australian Constitution* (Sweet and Maxwell, 1949).

NICOLSON, SIR HAROLD: *King George V* (Constable, 1952).

ROBSON, WILLIAM A.: *The Development of Local Government* (Allen and Unwin; third edition, 1954).

STRANG, WILLIAM: *The Foreign Office* ("New Whitehall" series; Allen and Unwin, 1955).

TAYLOR, ERIC: *The House of Commons at Work* (Penguin Books, 1951).

WADE, EMLYN C. S., and PHILLIPS, G. GODFREY: *Constitutional Law* (Longmans; fifth edition, 1955).

WARREN, JOHN H.: *The English Local Government System* (Allen and Unwin; fifth edition, 1957).

WHEARE, KENNETH C.: *The Statute of Westminster and Dominion Status* (Oxford University Press; fifth edition, 1953).

WHEELER-BENNETT, JOHN W.: *King George VI* (Macmillan, 1958).

Index